WE ARE OUR LANGUAGE

WE ARE OUR LANGUAGE

AN ETHNOGRAPHY OF LANGUAGE REVITALIZATION IN A NORTHERN ATHABASKAN COMMUNITY

BARBRA A. MEEK

FIRST PEOPLES
New Directions in Indigenous Studies

the university of arizona press   tucson

Dedicated to the wise people who have helped me on this journey,
especially Aggie, Jerry, Leda, Mary, and Rose.

THE UNIVERSITY OF ARIZONA PRESS

© 2010 The Arizona Board of Regents
All rights reserved
First issued as a paperback edition 2011

www.uapress.arizona.edu

Library of Congress Cataloging-in-Publication Data
Meek, Barbra A., 1967–
We are our language : an ethnography of language revitalization in a
Northern Athabascan community / Barbra A. Meek.
p. cm. — (First peoples, new directions in indigenous studies)
Includes bibliographical references and index.
ISBN 978-0-8165-2717-5 (cloth : alk. paper)
ISBN 978-0-8165-1453-3 (pbk. : alk. paper)
1. Kaska Indians—Yukon—Languages. 2. Athapascan languages—
Yukon—Revival. 3. Language revival—Yukon. I. Title.
E99.K26.M44 2010
497′.2—dc22 2010017786

Manufactured in the United States of America on acid-free, archival-
quality paper and processed chlorine free.

15 14 13 12 11   6 5 4 3

Contents

Illustrations

Preface

Some have carried it, held it close, protected.
Others have pulled it along like a reluctant child.
Still others have waved it like a flag, a signal to others.
And some have filled it with rage
and dare others to come close.
And there are those who find their language
a burdensome shackle.
They continually pick at the lock.
                    —Ofelia Zepeda, "Walking with Language"

It's difficult to imagine growing up without a language. Is it analogous to growing up without parents or grandparents? Is it the loss of something near and dear to our hearts, or is it something simply never realized, like growing up without siblings or pets? My mother never seemed to bemoan the fact that my grandfather, instructed to speak English at Haskell Institute, raised his children the same way—in English. This sociolinguistic practice has trickled down to my siblings and my cousins, most of whom are more interested and invested in learning globally significant languages like Spanish, German, and French, than in revitalizing their ancestral American Indian language—let alone someone else's ancestral language. On the other hand, the opportunity and the challenge of learning another language have always been celebrated in my family. From listening to recordings of language lessons to being surrounded by speakers of an unfamiliar language, the drive to investigate the linguistic similarities and differences—grammatically, socially, ideologically—has "walked" with me since childhood. As Zepeda's poem vividly portrays, walking with language—especially an endangered language—is difficult, an extraordinary challenge that is asked, and often demanded, of indigenous peoples. This book is a reflection on and analysis of the time I spent walking with an endangered language, one that may or may not be my own, but one that certainly called to me.

Beginning the Journey: Methods and Motivations

As an ethnography of language revitalization, the primary goal of this study is to show how the practice and ideologization of Kaska have influenced Kaska language revitalization, focusing especially on moments of *disjuncture* and the semiotic processes that coconstruct and mitigate such contradictions. By *disjuncture,* I mean the everyday points of discontinuity and contradiction—between social or linguistic groups, within discourses, practices, or between them, even between indexical orders—that interrupt the flow of action, communication, or thought. Most of the disjunctures I describe in this book are sociolinguistic, points where multiple, shifting, and conflicting language ideologies or semiotic practices collide—or move past one another (see chap. 2). To do this, I have combined various research methods in order to find out what adults and children know in relation to what they speak and what is spoken and expressed around them (see Hill 1993:88 on methodology; see also Ochs and Schieffelin 1979). Generally ethnographic, the methods include formal linguistic description and analysis, participant observation, tape recording, and interviewing. A psycholinguistic comprehension task was also developed and piloted. I do not report on that task here, but I do mention below the importance of comprehension tasks in relation to studying situations of language shift and revitalization.

Ethnographic, and more specifically linguistic anthropological, methods provide a way of assessing the impact of different social contexts on a people's language use and knowledge, with potential insights into an individual's retention or loss of specific linguistic structures. In particular, these methods allow for an analysis of interaction patterns and an evaluation of the role these play in the maintenance and acquisition of a (minority) language in a multilingual context. It is important to understand the ways in which these different contexts and patterns may either promote language retention or encourage language loss, in order to determine measures for stabilizing an indigenous language. Additionally, language ideologies are relevant to language development in that the ways in which individuals view competing languages may covertly undermine any effort to revitalize or maintain the heritage language.

Developmental psycholinguistic methods in general provide a way of assessing a child's or novice's linguistic knowledge synchronically and over time. They are useful for examining when children acquire particular linguistic structures or for simply identifying which structures have been acquired. The relevance of comprehension techniques for language shift studies are multiple. First, there is the problem of production reliability where speakers or language learners know more than they produce (McKee 1994). Participant-observation and socially occurring speech are both limited in this way, providing evidence for a subset of a speaker's grammatical knowledge. Second, younger adults passively use their linguistic knowledge when interacting with (older) heritage language speakers. They show evidence of grammatical knowledge through interactional competence and comprehension, not through production. Third, children are typically the generation that evidences the greatest shift. They primarily (or exclusively) use the dominant language, not their heritage language, for everyday interaction. However, they may still have opportunities to acquire knowledge of their heritage language, because adults and elders still know and speak the language. While not a part of this study, comprehension tasks provide an extremely useful means for examining a population's linguistic knowledge in contexts of language shift, especially where speaking is left to the elders and not the children. Thus, developmental psycholinguistic techniques can be used to examine what a child knows with respect to her or his heritage language, be it passively or actively used.

Thus, a combination of methods is necessary for understanding the complex aspects of language development and endangerment in such multilingual settings and for informing language revitalization efforts. Without knowing what people, including children, have or have not acquired, it is difficult—if not impossible—to develop a language program or curriculum that draws on their already-developing (or even adult) grammars. Furthermore, it is important to know how the heritage language is ideologically positioned across different contexts in order to promote local language practices and coordinate them with revitalization efforts in a productive way.

Without knowledge of these different linguistic realms, language revitalization efforts may achieve only minimal success. Most language revitalization projects focus on a part of this big picture. That is, the process of language revitalization is limited to the classroom or the home. In the past, educators and linguistic consultants often talked about the need to expand these contexts of use, to develop more teaching materials and "culturally oriented" activities such as language camps, and to focus on child language as well as adult language, but the literature frequently offered only a call to arms as opposed to tangible, applicable solutions (see Fishman 1991). However, recent scholarship and fieldwork practices have begun to provide resources for the development and implementation of language revitalization programs (see below). This study contributes to that scholarship, examining in detail the contexts affecting one particular instance of language shift to gain further insight into the dilemmas and strategies for successful language revitalization programming. It details over two years of aboriginal language revitalization in the Yukon Territory, Canada, focusing on the Kaska language in particular.

Aboriginal Languages of the Yukon Territory

Kaska is one of several Northern Athabaskan languages spoken in the Yukon Territory,[1] along with the following: Gwich'in, Han, Northern Tutchone, Southern Tutchone, Tagish, and Upper Tanana.[2] Besides these, Tlingit is also spoken. All of these languages are "endangered" or "obsolescing" to some extent. In Krauss and Golla (1981), all of the indigenous languages in the Yukon are listed as "moribund," except for Gwich'in (also called Kutchin or Loucheux).[3] The Han language in particular has undergone a radical shift, with the remaining speakers estimated at fewer than fifteen (Aboriginal Language Services [hereafter, ALS] 1991a).

According to the 1996 census (Statistics Canada 1996), of the 6,175 aboriginal respondents in the Yukon Territory, 770 claimed an aboriginal language as their "mother tongue," with 705 of these being in the category "other Aboriginal languages."[4] "Mother tongue" is defined as "the first language learned at home in childhood and still understood by the individual at the time of the census" (Statistics Canada 1996). Additionally, 185 respondents chose both English and an aboriginal language as their "mother tongue." Overall, 890 respondents claimed an aboriginal language as their first language, or approximately 15 percent of the aboriginal population in the Yukon Territory first learned and still understand a local aboriginal language. This is slightly lower than the overall Canadian percentage of 16.9 percent (DIAND 1995).[5]

Examining language shift within the Yukon, a comparison of census data for "home language use" and "mother tongue" clearly shows that shifts have occurred for the languages indigenous to the Yukon (see also Cook 1998 and Drapeau 1998 on tabulating language shift for Canada's aboriginal

Table P.1. Distribution of aboriginal languages across some Yukon communities

Location	Percentage of those who learned one	Percentage of those who used one at home	Percentage of those who have some knowledge of one
Carmacks	12.9	4.3	17.0
Mayo	9.2	3.1	14.1
Pelly Crossing	17.0	0.0	21.3
Old Crow	38.2	18.2	39.3
Carcross	10.3	0.0	12.8
Carcross Indian Reserve	12.5	0.0	12.5
Burwash	25.0	16.7	16.7
Ross River	40.0	22.9	40.8
Upper Liard	36.4	9.1	36.4
Two Mile Village	45.0	15.0	45.0
Two and One-Half Mile Village	0.0	0.0	33.3
Lower Post (B.C.)	0.0	0.0	16.0
Good Hope Lake (B.C.)	11.1	11.1	11.1

languages). Since data for the Yukon are sporadic, table P.1 provides percentages, not by language, but by community, or location, where available. The percentages refer to the percentage of people who learned, use, or know an aboriginal language. They are based on the total population for the statistical community, and not the aboriginal population only.

Except for Good Hope Lake, all communities show a degree of language shift when comparing column A (aboriginal language first learned and still understood) to column B (aboriginal language spoken at home). Since these are percentages derived from the total community population, not the aboriginal population alone, the percentages would be the same or higher when tabulated for the aboriginal population alone.[6] Additionally, Cook (1998:140) notes that existing speaker estimates are not very reliable or complete, stating, "I suspect that the number of bilingual communities, in which an Aboriginal Language is acquired and maintained as a second language, is growing." Overall, though, the above percentages show decreased in-home use of the Yukon's indigenous languages, resulting in a territory-wide shift from aboriginal languages to English.

Locating Kaska, Locating the Researcher: Description of Research Project

The research took place in the community of Watson Lake/Upper Liard, with visits to Ross River and Lower Post, from January 1998 to April 2000, followed by visits in February and March of 2005, and July 2008. The Watson Lake/Upper Liard area is located in the southeast corner of the Yukon Territory (see fig. P.1). There were approximately 975 speakers of Kaska in the Yukon at the time of research; approximately 67 percent were

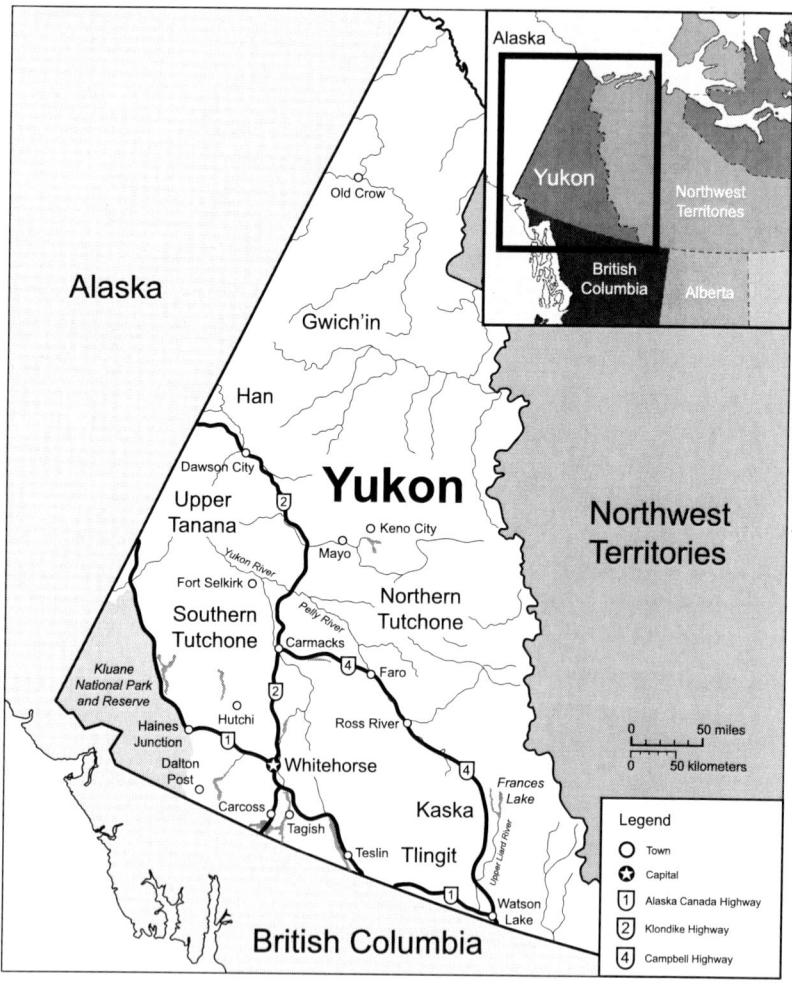

Figure P.1. Map of the Yukon Territory.

members of the Liard First Nation (see chap. 2). According to a 1989 language survey sponsored by Aboriginal Language Services (ALS 1991a), the most fluent speakers were *elders*, officially defined as members aged fifty-one years and up, and the least fluent speakers were young adults, aged sixteen to thirty-five years.[7] This exemplified a common trend across all of the First Nations in the Yukon Territory.

My introduction to aboriginal language revitalization in the Yukon Territory was facilitated by my husband, Dr. Gerald Carr, who was conducting fieldwork in Carmacks, Dr. Patrick Moore, who was working for the Yukon Department of Education at the time, and sponsorship through Aboriginal Language Services. Once in Watson Lake/Upper Liard, I situated myself in the community by volunteering at the Liard First Nation's Aboriginal Head Start (AHS) center and at the elementary school, as well as by working with the Kaska House of Language project sponsored by the Kaska Tribal Council. During most of my research, I lived with two different families, and I also visited with many others. A number of factors affected the collection of data, including my personal history and the types of social positions I could inhabit in Watson Lake and elsewhere. I have organized my discussion below of these factors in the following way: (1) personal, (2) social, (3) political, and (4) ideological. The combination of these challenges dictated the research methods appropriate for different contexts and molded the types and amount of data I collected.

The Aboriginal Head Start program positioned me as an educator and child development specialist, because of the research I had conducted on child language development as part of my training. For this reason, some parents began to express to me their concerns over their children's English competence, reacting to educators' comments about Kaska children's inability to speak "correct" English. As a result, parental fears that their children were not competent speakers of English often overshadowed any concern they might have about their children's acquisition of Kaska. Because I was positioned here as an authority, some parents looked to me to either dispel these misconceptions or to teach their children "better" English.

In contrast to this role, my participation in the Kaska language workshops positioned me as a teaching assistant (with respect to my literacy and writing skills) and as a student (of Kaska). I had limited authority in this context. Additionally, most participants were paid to attend these workshops, either through their own jobs or through workshop funding, and I was no exception. My own grant support and sponsorship by ALS placed me directly in the role of assistant, making me responsible for the preparation and administering of language materials. Furthermore, my (assumed) age in relation to the other participants (and my gender) positioned me as having minimal authority. This meant that I was expected to help out by serving food and beverages, fetching pencils and paper, attending to children and other youth, cleaning, driving individuals to and from the workshops during the day, note taking, and documenting Kaska—luckily, these tasks were all manageable ones for me.

My ability to write Kaska was valued by workshop organizers and participants and created a space for me in the community's language projects. Many people were fluent speakers of Kaska but did not write the language. Thus, their motivation for attending the workshops was to learn to write their language. On the other hand, I was able to write the language (as a result of my linguistic training) but did not speak it. My skills, then, as a linguist were complementary to their skills as speakers, creating a relationship between us that otherwise might not have been established (for further discussion, see chap. 4). Additionally, because of my involvement and interest in Kaska language projects and my continual presence in the community, my immediate presence did not drastically influence people's language choices.

Beyond gender and age, three other personal factors relevant to how I was positioned were: (1) my own identity as Native American, (2) my training under Dr. Mary Willie while a graduate student at the University of Arizona, Tucson, and (3) my knowledge of other Athabaskan languages, in particular, Navajo. Combined, these three factors led to an introduction to and acceptance by the staff of Aboriginal Language Services, a territorial-level funding program for indigenous language projects. The staff, in turn, introduced me to various First Nations members who invited me to become involved in community-level language work. The First Nations members, all women, involved in these projects accepted me because of my background as well. Some of these women had studied under Dr. Willie at the American Indian Language Development Institute (AILDI). These factors, however, affected my role only when I self-identified as her student or when those who knew me informed others of this dimension of my history. Not everyone had direct access to this knowledge, whereas my participation at the AHS and in the workshops was community knowledge.

Finally, my gender and the nature of my research led me to work primarily with women and not men. Being female, I was expected to work with and learn from women. Researching child rearing and language development also predisposed me to work with mothers and women involved in raising children. Hence, women were my socially appropriate teachers. As one elder remarked, "it is important that there are men teaching the boys, and women teaching the girls"; my experiences reflected this approach.

Socially based factors affected my research in a different way. In particular, I had to be flexible and creative in collecting data, because plans were often changed. Child absenteeism at school and at AHS was common. Children were often sick or out of town. They would accompany their parents or grandparents to Whitehorse to see medical specialists not available in Watson Lake. Some children did not always have transportation to AHS, although the director did her best to provide transportation for all students. Overall attendance in the program was somewhat random and unpredictable. Along with fluctuating attendance, families moved and changed frequently. Parents would move to Whitehorse or another community for a period of time from weeks to months, depending on their employment situation or medical needs. Children would be sent to live elsewhere for weeks or months, depending on the availability of family members within the community to provide temporary caregiving. Additionally, some children were in foster care, which moved them around from family to family every three to six months. Foster families were not always located within the same town as the birth families.

Another significant factor affecting the planning and execution of this research was that of community deaths that occurred during my fieldwork. When a Kaska band member passed away, all Kaska-run facilities closed, including AHS, and Kaska individuals who were not employed by the band had the option of taking the day off from their respective jobs to attend the needs of the deceased's family, especially when he or she was of the opposite clan, because the opposite clan planned and carried out the funerary potlatch. Ethics of respect dictated that people (especially aboriginal people) should neither be working nor conducting research at these times. In fact, because of the cultural and political ties between all Yukon First Nations, funerals in one town routinely caused the closure of band offices across the territory.

Band office and band facility closings were not limited to periods of mourning. Many government events led to office closures, which in turn resulted in the closing of AHS and the suspension of other language activities. The territorial government sponsors frequent workshops for band employees, as well as federal meetings pertaining to land claims and self-governing negotiations. All First Nations in the Yukon Territory are involved in these negotiations, and while many First Nations had settled, the Kaska had not. As a result, many members attended land claims meetings locally and in Whitehorse. Meetings could be scheduled at any time, day or evening, and required Kaska interpreters when elders attended. Additionally, there was a financial incentive to attend the various meetings, especially for

Kaska elders. This meant that a research schedule had to be flexible, working around the obligations and concerns of the community.

The frequency of such workshops proved to be the most challenging and interruptive factor. First Nations individuals were constantly being asked to attend three-day, four-day, and weeklong workshops, held locally or elsewhere. Those held in Whitehorse required two travel days, resulting in individuals leaving Watson Lake on Monday morning and returning Friday evening. Often, people spent the weekend in Whitehorse as well, playing bingo, visiting family and friends, and shopping. The Yukon government sponsored the majority of workshops and paid participants to attend. These workshops provided additional job training or were therapeutic "healing" workshops, providing a forum for every traveling motivational speaker passing through the North. Work—volunteering at AHS, visiting elementary school classrooms, and running Kaska language workshops—and research—visiting and interviewing people, recording verb paradigms, playing language games with children—had to be scheduled around these educational opportunities. Thus, a variety of individuals participated in different capacities at different times, resulting in a range of not-always-comparable situations or experiences.[8]

Conceptualized initially as a programmatic, formal study of language acquisition and socialization, my research emerged from these multiple positions, in dialogue with bureaucrats, language professionals, local individuals, and families. It has also, obviously, been interpreted through my own developing knowledge of Kaska, my profession, and the people who ameliorated my many errors and naive assumptions. Similar to Jeffrey Anderson's description of his own research methods, most of my research experience has been "dialogic rather than structured by detached interviewing or a preoccupation to 'gather data'" (Anderson 1998:44). My growing conceptualizations have arisen as a result of everyday conversations with people in the Yukon, from those who shared their homes with me, to tourists wondering about my preoccupation with and investment in endangered aboriginal languages. Paralleling Anderson's approach again, I have chosen at various points not "to include direct quotes or descriptions of actual events in order to maintain anonymity of persons [involved in this] rather politically charged issue" (Anderson 1998:44).

Finally, audio recording was expectedly controversial. In the Yukon, aboriginal language speakers are sought out by local aboriginal radio and television, cultural events such as storytelling festivals, and institutions like the Yukon Native Language Centre. Consequently, everyone I worked with was quite media-savvy. One might presume that such experience would breed comfort with audio and video recording, which it does at a certain level, but it also builds a consciousness for the situational appropriateness of recording. For instance, it was not allowed in the home at random. For recording to occur, a learning situation had to be constructed. Upon request, parents were willing to let me record their children and play language games with them. But they were not as willing to accommodate the recorder if they themselves might be recorded. Additionally, some parents would express their views on education, language ability, and such, but again, many, if not most, adults objected to being recorded, especially when speaking Kaska. Elders, on the other hand, were willing to be recorded as long as the topics were pedagogically focused, resulting in the documentation of information that they wanted preserved for their children and other younger relatives; traditional stories, personal narratives, descriptions of traditional practices, and the Kaska language itself were all recordable topics. These discussions often led to commentary on other topics too. In such cases, if an elder did not want to be recorded, she or he would simply turn off the tape recorder.[9]

Recordable contexts were often public, and the recorded material itself was intended to be public. In contrast, recording in private contexts, such as in family homes, or during private events, was not as acceptable. As suggested above, recording was especially associated with teaching. At a community language meeting, several comments were made linking recording with language instruction. One participant noted, "Our language was taken away, so our situation is not like French. This is why we lost our language. Some people spoke even when they were threatened. We need to sit down and work together to bring it back. We need to educate our children. . . . We need more materials, including tapes that show us how to pronounce the words." Other participants expressed the imperative to "keep recording stories" and "make tapes for kids." Any dialogue or information to be recorded that was not regarded as instructional was potentially problematic. Children's interactions were an exception, perhaps because the children themselves liked being recorded. (From shoving the microphone into their own mouths to performing a made-up song, they liked playing with the tape recorder and enjoyed listening to themselves on tape.) For this research, recordings were done at the Aboriginal Head Start, the Kaska House of Language workshops, and elders' homes or camps. The recordings were not regular, nor were they always audible. However, they did highlight the predominance of English across contexts and speakers, and the limited and often routinized role of Kaska in everyday interactions. It is the routinization of this endangered language—its continual transformation—in relation

Figure P.2. This photo of the sign that greets people upon their arrival to Kaska country welcomes the reader into the ethnographic scenario and provides an inviting glimpse of both the physical environment and, more symbolically, the fraught relationship between the Kaska language and the more dominant language, English. Photo by the author.

to ideological and social changes in the sociolinguistic environment that is the focus of this book.

Walking with Kaska

In chapter 1, I present the colonizing history of Watson Lake's Kaska community, through the eras of assimilation and reconciliation, through language suppression and language revitalization, highlighting key disjunctures pertinent to the current language situation. These disjunctures include economic and political disjunctures, segregation, disjunctures of identity, and, ultimately, sociolinguistic disjunctures. This chapter also describes the presence of aboriginal languages in everyday (adult) interactions and the emerging economy of aboriginal language in the Yukon territory. Disjunctures within this emerging "linguistic marketplace" are explored, and what becomes clear across different moments of interaction is the specialized nature of these languages and their association with specialized roles. Such linguistic specialization emerges in other (nonendangered) language contexts as well, ranging from the use of particular grammatical elements, such as the ergative object marker during Western Samoan fono events (Duranti 1994), to the use of entirely different linguistic codes, such as saying mass in Latin (see Keane 1997 for other cases of religious language). These are exactly the kinds of social factors easily overlooked by language planners, which, as I show, have significant effects on the sociolinguistic field and contribute to language shift.

Chapter 2 details the theoretical framework of "sociolinguistic disjuncture" and the challenges of disjuncture for endangered languages and the pursuit of language revitalization. The chapter begins by discussing the various factors used to determine the vitality of an endangered language and appropriate measures for reversing shift. It then highlights the remaining conundrums affecting language revitalization and turns to linguistic anthropology for an answer. Research on language shift, language socialization, and language ideology in particular complicates our purview of endangerment and revitalization, providing arguments for a more socially grounded approach to language revitalization. This approach is then theorized through the concept of sociolinguistic disjuncture, that is, the moments of discontinuity between practices, between ideologies, within and across these social domains.

Chapter 3 carries along this theoretical trajectory, focusing on interactions with children and other Kaska language learners. To reveal the sociolinguistic disjunctures across these interactions, comparisons are made between institutionalized educational contexts and family settings. This shows that while some children are acquiring an indigenous language passively at home (serving a goal of language revitalization), the institutionalization of the language erases the grammatical and communicative diversity of these family interactions (countering language revitalization efforts). Another way in which disjuncture emerges is through interlocutors' limits of awareness (Silverstein [1981] 2001). Currently, most Dene children's experience with socially occurring, spoken Kaska comes from the home and other family settings (mainly provided by their grandparents).[10] However, they also attend Kaska language classes at the local elementary school. In such institutional settings they experience Kaska in a very different way. Educators often present the language as an object of learning, as an artifact. Students learn lists of nouns, token expressions, and decontextualized scraps of cultural knowledge that serve only to fetishize the language. In the end, such educational events often interrupt, dislocate, or work against the goals of language revitalization by teaching children that their language is no longer a valid form of communication, even though their grandparents still converse in Kaska at home. Whether intentional or not, patterns of language use in the home, at school, and elsewhere have socializing consequences such that linguistic practices across different contexts can be contradictory or in conflict.

Another way in which language efforts can be at odds with the goals of revitalization is in the construction of language materials. Chapter 4 describes the ways in which indigenous languages are manufactured, by both "experts" (researchers, linguists, educators) and indigenous communities. Such "experts" are often concerned with documenting the grammatical knowledge of speakers before this knowledge is lost, along with the diversity it represents. They are also concerned with sharing these documents with the relevant communities. What many of these experts have not attended to are the ways in which they represent the indigenous language. Only recently has attention been drawn to actual page layouts, the use and amount of the dominant language appearing in indigenous language texts, the topics addressed in lesson books, and overall pedagogical styles (Meek and Messing 2007; Nevins 2004; see also Frawley, Hill, and Munro 2002; Hinton and Hale 2001). Documentation also raises the question, By whom is literacy highly valued? And for those who value literacy, which materials are they using, and when are they using them? While many communities support the production of some kind of indigenous language media, they do not all agree on the kind of media used, nor do they all have access to these media and their linguistic content. So, why do indigenous communities participate in language revitalization at all, given the disparities between practice and plan?

The concern over production extends beyond the "reversing of language shift" (cf. Fishman 1991, 2001); it is about asserting an aboriginal heritage and claiming the political power that comes with the recognition of this heritage by others. Chapter 5 focuses on the role of aboriginal language in government (noneducational institutions) and other nation-building ventures, analyzing how aboriginal languages are represented across different programs and bureaucracies. For example, within bureaucratic rhetoric the commodification of language is downplayed in favor of depicting language as a feature of identity rather than an issue of property. In the Yukon this has resulted in disjuncture. The Yukon government's slogan "We Are Our Language" was originally intended to communicate solidarity through the identification of language and culture with a people, but it has become ideologically divisive, marking heritage speakers as core members and erasing those large numbers of First Nations people who cannot speak an indigenous language or who speak a "nonstandard" variety. Subsequently, these representations map onto or break down in relation to bureaucratic designations (linguistic or otherwise) and group allegiances within First Nations communities. Certainly a language can be a means for collectively identifying as a group. However, counter to such a monolithic representation is the actual linguistic diversity pervasive across most, if not all, communities such that there is a mismatch between the actual ethnolinguistic identities that people enact locally and those imagined by governing agencies. Frequently the work of language revivalists and the agencies funding this work allow the linguistic diversity to fade into the background of their public, expert rhetorics (Hill 2002), creating another opportunity for disjuncture.

The final chapter links my findings about disjuncture to broader theoretical and applied concerns. By approaching language revitalization as a sociolinguistic process, the multivalent ways in which endangered languages are being performed, entextualized, and imagined emerge. My approach builds on the semiotic framework put forth by Judith Irvine and Susan Gal by analyzing language revitalization, and shift more generally, through the "ideologizing of [the] sociolinguistic field and the consequent reconfiguring of its varieties" (2000:77). I focus on the different interactional moments and linguistic experiences that mediate and are mediated by these reconfigurings and lead to disjuncture. The concept of sociolinguistic disjuncture is a way to talk about the breakdown between and across theories and practices. It is in these moments of sociolinguistic disjuncture that the sociolinguistic field is reconfigured and the course of language shift (re)directed, but also when opportunities for negotiating and containing disjuncture exist.[11]

Acknowledgments

While singular on cover and in copyright, this text has been composed through the labors and the support of many. Though brief, this is my heartfelt attempt to thank all involved for their commitment to this project and their faith in the author. For funding and support in the United States, I am indebted to the following institutions and departments: the Wenner-Gren Foundation (#6375), the Woodrow Wilson National Fellowship Foundation, the National Institutes of Health (PG# 1-F31-GM18263-01), the National Endowment for the Humanities (#FA-53427-07), the University of Arizona, the Department of Anthropology at the University of Michigan, and the University of Michigan. I would also like to acknowledge the tremendous support I've received from the University of Arizona Press, the three outside reviewers, the staff, especially Nancy Arora and my copy editor, Lisa Williams, and editor-in-chief Dr. Allyson Carter. I have also benefited from conversations with many audiences and colleagues far and near, too numerous to name; thank you. I would also like to thank those locally who have helped my ideas grow, especially Dr. Judith T. Irvine and Dr. Bruce Mannheim, and budding colleagues, especially Jean Balestrery, Erika Hoffmann-Dilloway, and Sherina Feliciano-Santos. For resources and support in the Yukon Territory, Canada, I am immensely grateful to Aboriginal Language Services (Yukon Territorial Government), Yukon Native Languages Centre, the Department of Education (YTG), Kaska Tribal Council, and Liard River First Nation. I am also extremely thankful to the aboriginal language teachers, administrators, linguists, and friends who have guided, instructed, and mentored me along the way, most especially Mrs. Ann Bayne, Mrs. Alice Brodhagen, Mrs. Leslie Carberry, Ms. Olive Cochrane, Mrs. Mida Donnessey, Dr. Jane Hill, Mrs. Leda Jules, Mrs. Aggie Magun, Mrs. Kathy Magun, Mr. Russell Magun Jr., Mrs. Linda

McDonald, Ms. Cheryl McLean, Dr. Pat Moore, Mrs. Barbara Morris, Dr. Susan Philips, Mrs. Jeannette Poyton, Dr. Keren Rice, Dr. Diane Riske-dahl, Dr. Scott Rushforth, Dr. David Samuels, Dr. Emory Sekaquaptewa, Mrs. Marie Skidmore, Mr. Mike Smith, Dr. Mary Willie, Mrs. Eileen Van Bibber, and Dr. Ofelia Zepeda. I am eternally grateful to the families and children who welcomed me into their lives—while unsurprising, it's still astonishing how much everyone has grown since this project began, including my own two children! Finally, my own family deserves recognition, a few apologies for distraction, and overwhelming thankfulness, especially to my husband, Gerald Carr.

WE ARE OUR LANGUAGE

Ruptured

Kaska in Context

In a small town located near the border of British Columbia just inside the Yukon Territory, a cluster of people converged on the First Nations community center, a single-story, one-room log-cabin-type building with a ramp leading up to the two front doors and steps leading to a side entrance. The building itself was located at Two Mile Village, a First Nations neighborhood two miles north of the Alaska–Canada Highway and Watson Lake's town center, an area historically designated as an "Indian settlement" by the Canadian government. Inside the hall, decorations were sparse: an electronic bingo board in one corner, a whiteboard in the center of the back wall, and a few windows scattered around, letting in nearly blinding streams of sunlight that illuminated delicate motes of dust suspended as if they were decorative beads sewn into yards of translucent ribbons of *babiche*. Filling the room were long tables and blue plastic chairs, whose stacking and unstacking punctuated many hall events. Outside, the sunshine danced across the frozen landscape of bejeweled snowdrifts and glittering patches of ice, patches frequently found around steps and in parking areas, areas now filling up with pickups, old American sedans, and a Yukon government van. Of course, in the throes of winter these light-filled moments were brief. In the southeast corner of the room was a kitchen, demarcated by an open wall—a useful arrangement for selling coffee and snacks on bingo nights. Across from the kitchen were two restrooms, one for men and one for women, with a couple of stalls in each. The plumbing sometimes backed up, and toilet paper wasn't always at hand, but these minor inconveniences were usually expediently remedied, often by First Nations employees who worked just across the road at the Kaska Tribal Office. If no one was available nearby, a quick call to the Liard band office just down the road or a quick trip to the store fixed these ordinary hassles.

On this cool November day, people were assembling here for a language workshop, a workshop designed to teach them how to read and write their ancestral language as well as to encourage conversation in this aboriginal language. Most of these people were adults, many of whom already knew the language, having acquired it as children. On occasion, children from the local schools visited, primarily attending the afternoon sessions when elders demonstrated various tasks, like moose-hide preparation, snowshoe making, or beading, but a few teenagers came regularly, substituting attendance at the workshops for attendance at their Kaska classes in the high school. The language workshop would last four days, beginning on Tuesday and finishing on Friday, and running from 9:00 in the morning until 4:00 in the afternoon, with periodic breaks throughout the day, and an hour for a potluck lunch at noon. The workshops were sponsored by the Kaska Tribal Council (KTC) in cooperation with Aboriginal Language Services (ALS), a Yukon government program supporting language revitalization initiatives across the territory (see Appendix A for a list of acronyms used in this book). The workshops were facilitated by several individuals, including an ALS employee, two linguists (Patrick Moore and me), KTC representatives, and several elders.

This workshop day began like many others, with Pat and me searching for the key to unlock the community center and then unloading the equipment—tape recorder, camera, blank tapes, copies of previous recordings, boxes of papers, and materials for the afternoon activity, all as workshop participants began to arrive. On occasion, we would also provide transportation for elders who had no other means of transport. This was the third workshop we'd had, with three more to follow in the new year, so the routine was finally becoming routine. The most regular participants were elders, women between the ages of thirty and fifty, and a handful of high school students. Attendance fluctuated during the week, ranging between twenty and thirty participants at any given time, but most of the elders, unless their health was compromised, tirelessly came to every workshop and shared what they could with the rest of us. This week we were learning about snowshoes, sewing, and optative verbs, along with the usual listening and writing exercises.

The morning exercises began with a prayer in Kaska from a prominent elder, an elder who often performed at the Yukon International Storytelling Festival. Following her opening oration, the workshop's itinerary was handed out on a yellow piece of paper, a table in landscape style and all in English except for the phrase *Dene k'éh zedlé'* (Kaska only), underscoring the cultural activities at 1:00 each day but Wednesday, that day and time being reserved for optative verbs. After the fifteen-minute overview of the week's activities, the Kaska lessons began, starting with fifteen minutes of conversation, followed by a listening exercise. This time we discussed being hungry and liking moose meat and learned to distinguish between the orthographically represented sounds of "tl" and ejective "tl'." While seemingly simplistic, these exercises were quite complicated because of the various dialects spoken by the participants and the range of competencies, both orally and textually. After another hour elapsed, coffee and snacks were served, allowing time for elders to visit with one another, and for a few dedicated smokers to step outside for a quick drag—somewhat ironic, given that on bingo night the hall would be drowned in cigarette smoke. After the brief respite, we regrouped to discuss traditional values, focusing on respect in particular, and then participated in another listening exercise, distinguishing between long and short "a," orthographically represented as "ā" and "a." After our potluck lunch of moose meat stew, bannock, bagged salad, and a tart soapberry dessert, we began to work on snowshoes, watching and listening while an elder demonstrated and described his technique. By 3:30 p.m., most everyone was exhausted, elders and youth alike. The younger participants cleaned up, while elders packed up their belongings, sometimes only the papers acquired throughout the day, and other times their beadwork and personal notes. Carefully shuffling out of the hall, onto the freezing walk before us, each one of us looked forward to the next three days.

Admittedly, these workshops were ambitious events intended to both teach and document Kaska, to encourage everyone to read, write, and speak some variety of Kaska, and to avoid discouragement, of which there was ample opportunity, from forgetting to elicit a particular dialect version for a list of terms to overemphasizing (or perhaps even privileging) documentation and writing rather than speaking and narration. By the end of these workshops, we were all worn out, though satisfyingly so. These workshops instilled a sense of pride in the community and a feeling of accomplishment for having taken steps toward preserving and revitalizing one of the territorially recognized aboriginal languages. However, if the primary goal of language revitalization is to produce new speakers, these workshops did not achieve that end. The people who were the most active and regular participants were the ones who already knew the aboriginal language. Given that, how were these workshops successful language revitalization events? What were we accomplishing? Moreover, what could we accomplish? What should the goals of language revitalization be, and how might they be attained?

An institutional accomplishment of these workshops has been the economic demarginalization of both aboriginal peoples and aboriginal languages. As a response to a tragically oppressive history of contact between First Nations peoples and European-based nations, the workshops attempted to restore continuity, practically, epistemologically, and linguistically. They served to remedy disjunctures—two in particular, a linguistic disjuncture and an economic disjuncture—salient to elders, bureaucrats, and academics.

To understand this accomplishment, it is necessary to begin with the historic upheavals that economically and demographically marginalized First Nations peoples and contributed to aboriginal language endangerment. While language endangerment is first and foremost about the often violent replacement of one linguistic code by another, it is also about the rupturing and replacement of sociocultural practices and everyday interactions, resulting in the disintegration of the speech community or social networks that sustained the previous code. Textbook cases of endangerment are found throughout the world, from Papua New Guinea and Japan to Scotland and Canada (Nettle and Romaine 2000). All of these documented cases entail a history of colonization where the dominant (colonial) language supplanted, or is supplanting, indigenous linguistic varieties. In the Yukon, as in most of North America, this replacement happened through boarding schools. This review excludes from consideration accounts of immigrant languages, though social pressures affecting immigrant language shift are relevant in later chapters.

After a brief historical overview of the colonizing practices and beliefs impacting and subjugating aboriginal peoples in Canada, I discuss colonial ideologies of "Indians" and their languages that persist in contemporary public discourses in the Yukon. Next I discuss Canada's attempts to mitigate this history of colonialism, reflected through these discourses, and to economically and ideologically demarginalize First Nations peoples and languages. Articulated through the concept of "reconciliation," a related aspect of this commitment to redress past wrongs has been the creation of economic opportunities in relation to and through support for aboriginal language revitalization.

Colonizing Practices

All cases of colonization have entailed assimilation, practices aimed at erasing various social differences between colonizer and colonized by incorporating indigenous populations into "mainstream" society through marriage, employment, and education. The disjunctures resulting from rupturing indigenous practices have emerged in various ways, such as the categories used to depict types of Indians: "traditionalists" and "assimilated" Indians, "rural" and "urban" Indians, "status" and "non-status" Indians. Underscoring all of these practices of assimilation has been a focus on language. Early linguistic domination happened in several ways, through both direct and indirect colonial practices, from forced assimilation to genocide.

A key component of such colonial domination has been institutionalized education. In the United States and Canada, boarding and residential schools proliferated. From the late 1800s to the early or mid-1900s, American Indian children were taken or sent to schools run by or through the federal governments (for a detailed history, see Lomawaima and McCarty 2006; see also Littlefield 1993; Lomawaima 1993; McCarty 2002; Szasz 1977, 2005). Many of the students who attended these schools have written or spoken about their experiences (for example, Johnston 1989; Lomawaima 1994). A common theme in these narratives is the stripping away of native heritage by changing students' clothes, hairstyles, religious practices, and language, replacing them with those deemed by adult educators and legislators to be more appropriate. Importantly, the language deemed appropriate for native students, which would be the key to their educational success and future economic success, was English. These institutions are an obvious example of the kinds of ruptures experienced by indigenous peoples as part of colonization.

Ruptures also resulted from legislation governing status. In Canada, enfranchisement was the process by which Indians gained the rights of Canadian citizens. However, in doing so, they lost status as Indians. For instance, men could become enfranchised through property ownership, literacy, or exhibiting "moral" behavior, even obtaining a university degree or working in certain professions. Women lost their status if they married a non-Indian man. Conversely, if an Indian man married a non-Indian woman, then often she would gain Indian status. When the concept of Enfranchisement was incorporated into the Indian Act, the primary legal vehicle for regulating Indian identity in Canada, it was a critical move in the erasure of Indianness. The rupturing effect of the regulation of status was twofold. First, it symbolically alienated particular individuals from their own communities, and second, it perpetuated the ideological separation of these communities on a national scale—a legislative rupturing through the official regimentation of difference, and thus sanctioned discrimination.

Enfranchisement paralleled the U.S. Dawes Act (1887), criticized for demographically eroding the native population base while dispossessing them of their remaining land holdings. In both countries, the legislation was passed under the guise of protecting "Indians" and "Indian land" but effectively opened the door for the increased settlement of Indian lands by non-Indian settlers. It also instituted the public registration, or federal documentation, of Indian bodies and superimposed the European ideology of "blood" purity over indigenous descent-based reckoning systems. Most U.S. tribes today determine citizenship partly or wholly based on the rolls resulting from the Dawes Act and an assessment of "blood quantum" (Strong and Van Winkle 1993, 1996; Sturm 2002). However, unlike federally recognized U.S. tribes, who almost universally define citizenship through the concept and fractioning of "blood quantum," Canadian First Nations show greater variability in the conceptualizing and reckoning of blood as part of their official procedure for determining First Nations citizenship or status. In either situation, the legitimation of membership through the quantification of "blood" has resulted in the rupturing of biological relatedness, and thus the perpetuation of each federal nation's colonial legacy.

Whether or not a person has citizenship in a federally recognized political body (tribal Nation or First Nation), assessment of Indian ethnicity is still largely based on popular, conventionalized phenotypic characteristics associated with American Indians, to such an extent that Jack Hitt was able to write and have published in the *New York Times Magazine* a piece entitled "The Newest Indians" (August 21, 2005), discussing what one might call "born-again" Indians, people who either "look White" but maintain certain ancestral Native American practices or people who recently discovered, and had institutionally legitimated, their Indian heritage. Linguistically, reactions to this "identity crisis" range from the revitalization or re-creation of heritage languages (Hinton 2002) to the reincorporation of a style of greeting or introduction into a community's repertoire, such as the introductory routines performed at powwows and other public gatherings (Ahlers 2006). This need to revitalize or re-create certain language practices returns us to the history of colonization impacting the indigenous peoples of the Americas, where one of the crucial steps toward assimilation has been the linguistic colonization of these peoples (Lomawaima and McCarty 2006:114–115; see also Errington 2003). The legislative and ideological separation and erasure of indigenous bodies and peoples pair with a linguistic separation and erasure.

Linguistically this ideological separation was reinforced within the education system through the promotion of one language, English, over any other linguistic code. This linguistic separation was accompanied by the underlying assumption that Indian students were "primitive," "one-dimensional," "silent learners."

> Just as communities were assumed to be deficient in pedagogical theories and methods, Native individuals were assumed to lack the verbal, cognitive, even motor skills necessary to succeed in schools. . . . The ideology that juxtaposed "civilized" against "primitive" justified . . . forced assimilationist schooling. Stereotypes about Native learners—as "silent," "stoic," or "visual"—have strategically reinforced the necessary difference and distance between "civilized" and "primitive" students (Lomawaima and McCarty 2006:16–17).

Lomawaima and McCarty go on to note that "the schooling paradigm has often targeted 'difference' as

> uncivilized, disadvantaged, or worse; it has defined difference as a problem. The alleged attributes of Native students' difference constitute a lexicon of marvelous abundance: . . . students who possess "less developed" visual perception . . . and "severe linguistic inadequacy" . . . are among the fundamentally "disadvantaged" children from "cultures of poverty" (Lomawaima and McCarty 2006:20).

This logic ideologically supports a disjuncture between native children and non-native children. All of which suggests that native students could acquire only one language competently (if at all), and that language should be English, just as historically a native person could "acquire" and maintain only a single citizenship, and that citizenship should be American (either U.S. or Canadian).

This predilection toward monolingualism then pitted native parents who supported the acquisition of their aboriginal first language against institutional educators who promoted the acquisition of the national language over any other variety, highlighting the growing linguistic chasm between parents and their children. Some parents also became involved in furthering this chasm, encouraging their children to learn English and to excel in state-run schools rather than to maintain their heritage language (Blair and Fredeen 1995; see also Hinton and Hale 2001; McCarty and Zepeda 1998). Building on the logic highlighting differences, the chasm between languages and between students is resolvable were all students to speak a standard variety of English and to participate in their education in similar ways. Ideologically, if assimilation were successful—and erased the Indian from the student, as it were—then the disjuncture, in the guise of ethnic and linguistic differences, would be erased. The problem would be solved; native students retooled as English- (or French-) speaking North "Americans" would no longer struggle educationally or socially, resulting in national unity.

In the Yukon Territory, the period of colonization has been briefer than it has been for other aboriginal peoples in North America such that contemporary discourses on indigeneity emphasize revitalization and preservation rather than re-creation. This also means that even though children and youth are acquiring varieties of English, they remain exposed to some varieties of aboriginal languages, because boarding schools and a strict state-run educational system came late to the territory. However, this also means that current generational differences are exceptionally salient. This unsurprising salience provides another opportunity for the ideological mediation of differences. Viewed as linguistically discontinuous by some and as socially congruent by others, differences in language practices reveal both rupture and repair. To unpack these perspectival differences, we will begin with a bit of history.

The next section historically situates the current sociolinguistic situation found in the town of Watson Lake, followed by a brief recounting of pertinent historical events in the Yukon Territory. This history covers the fur trade, the gold rush, and the construction of the Alaska Highway. It is drawn from ethnographic and historical sources, as well as from personal narratives told by local elders. Following this is a discussion of the impact these events have had on the indigenous languages of the Yukon Territory and especially on Kaska. Finally, I describe the current social and economic environment of the Yukon as it relates to the emergence of aboriginal language projects, focusing on the Watson Lake area and the families who participated in this research in particular.

Finding Watson Lake

My first impression of the Yukon Territory reminded me of my brief encounter with Iceland during a short layover while on my way to Sweden; from the airport, the place appeared small, cold, and desolate, both in terms of its remoteness and its scrubby landscape. Whitehorse displayed similar attributes, but with the bonus of a mountain-filled horizon. I arrived in the territory on the shortest day of the year. The shock of the darkness was substantial, given that I had just flown up from Arizona. The winter temperatures would further stun me, once I began to navigate the darkness. In preparation for relocation to the Yukon, I had purchased a military-style, down-filled winter parka (good to about −30 degrees or so) at a local Army-Navy store in Tucson; unsurprisingly, they did not have much of a winter selection. I came to fully appreciate this parka, and especially the tubular nature of my parka's hood and the wreath of coyote fur outlining it, both of which minimized the impact of the cold on my complexion and my breathing. While I have been above the arctic circle, nowhere have I experienced such penetrating coldness and constantly frozen nose hairs.

Similar to Whitehorse, though more lush as a result of greater precipitation, the climate in Watson Lake is one of extremes.[1] One of my many trips to Watson Lake entailed a brilliantly sunny drive down from Whitehorse—clear roads, blue sky, warm temperatures (my winter parka lay in the backseat of my borrowed compact, along with my all-leather, calf-high, steel-shanked Timberland boots)—only to have my winter gear pressed tightly to my body for the drive back during a whiteout, where the only other vehicles on the seemingly unplowed highway from Watson Lake to Teslin were semitrucks and one sedan with Alaska plates. Winter is longer and darker than summer (179 days compared to 109 days), with plenty of snow and rain year-round—there is a very good reason why people pack snowshoes when out in the bush. I experienced the depth of a snowdrift firsthand when walking home one day from the elementary school. In an attempt to show politeness to a passing vehicle, I stepped off the plowed road onto what appeared to be the unplowed shoulder, only to find myself panicked and drowning in snow. Recalling a similar personal experience in Sweden, I turned onto my side—as if floating on top like a swimmer—and rolled back into the plowed road (without looking both ways first).

Watson Lake is located in the southeast corner of the Yukon Territory near British Columbia and is positioned at the intersection of the Alaska Highway and the Cassiar/Campbell Highway. It serves as a major hub along these travel routes. Whitehorse, the capital of the Yukon, is 283 miles to the west, along the Alaska Highway. Travel in the other direction leads to Edmonton, Alberta, 1,001 miles away. Following the Cassiar Highway south eventually leads to Vancouver, British Columbia, over 1,300 miles away. Two additional Kaska-affiliated towns are Ross River (Yukon Territory), 231 miles north of Watson Lake on the Campbell Highway, and Good Hope Lake (British Columbia), nearly 100 miles south of Upper Liard, down the Cassiar Highway. Despite the distances between these communities, residents frequently traveled between them, thinking nothing of driving for hours to go shopping, play bingo, or just visit friends and family. Community members, especially elders, often traveled hundreds of miles, in all kinds of weather, to attend funeral potlatches in other towns.

The town of Watson Lake was initiated by the settlement of a "stampeder" on the way to the Klondike gold fields in 1897 but developed only when the U.S. Army built an airfield there as part of its "Alcan Project" (the Alaska Highway). Reflecting the policies of the time, First Nations peoples in the area were pushed into places away from town centers. This resulted in the Indian settlements of Upper Liard, Lower Post, Two Mile, and Two and One-Half Mile, which surround Watson Lake.

Four hotels in Watson Lake housed travelers year-round, with an additional one opening only during the peak tourism months, May to August. Three of these hotels had restaurants. There was also a Chinese restaurant between one of the hotels and the government-run liquor store. One grocery store (which recently burned down) and three gas stations, centrally located, served the community. Two of the gas stations rented videos that were predominantly in English, along with a few French and foreign-language movies. One also functioned as a bus depot, laundromat, and fast-food establishment. Since this gas station was also located near the high school, it served as a local hangout for pre-teens and teenagers. Another gas station and mini-grocery were located at a public campground just east of downtown. Just west of town was a sawmill.

Also downtown were the post office, some shops selling clothes and tourist memorabilia, the Northern Lights Centre, Radio Shack, a bank (and an ATM), and the dentist's office. These were all along the Alaska Highway. Along the Cassiar Highway to the north were the high school, the Liard First Nation's band office, and a community recreation center. The hospital, doctors' offices, and the elementary school were also located just north of downtown. Additionally, a number of day-care centers, a couple of auto repair shops, two more laundromats, a few churches, two hardware stores, and the Kaska Tribal Council offices were scattered around Watson Lake.

Southeast of Watson Lake, along the Alaska Highway, was the community of Lower Post, and to the west Upper Liard, both predominantly First Nation communities. Facilities in Lower Post were limited to an elementary school and a community center that housed the band office. Upper Liard had a restaurant/gas station, a Catholic church, a golf course, an adult learning center, and the Aboriginal Head Start/Child Development Center.

Demographic Context

The total population in the Watson Lake–Lower Post–Upper Liard area, based on the 1996 Canadian census, was approximately 1,378, with the population of First Nations peoples estimated at 470, or 38 percent of

Table 1.1. First Nations population comparison

	Watson Lake area	Yukon Territory	Canada
First Nations population (FP)	470 (580)	6,175	799,010
Total population (TP)	1,253 (1,378)	30,655	28,528,125
Percentage (FP/TP)	38 (42)	20	3

the population (table 1.1). This was rather high compared to the national average of 3 percent First Nations people, and the territorial average of 20 percent. (The numbers in parentheses include the population for Lower Post, British Columbia, because it is a First Nation Athabaskan community that is part of the Watson Lake area.[2]) Again, the data show that the Watson Lake area had a greater population of First Nations people than did either the Yukon Territory or Canada. The table also shows that the Yukon Territory had a higher population of First Nations people than the country as a whole. Given this, the First Nations population was a greater minority population territorially than nationally, and the Watson Lake Athabaskan population was an even larger minority population. This suggests that the local First Nations people could have more political, economic, and social control and authority than other First Nations within the territory and across the country.

Most First Nations individuals in the Watson Lake area identified as Kaska and were members of the Ross River, Dease River, or Liard First Nation. The Kaska Tribal Council linked together all Kaska First Nations, including those across the border in British Columbia, for purposes of land claims negotiations, language planning, and other enterprises requiring interaction with territorial-level governments.[3] The British Columbian counterpart, the Kaska Dene Council, looked out for the Kaska First Nations' interests in the provincial government of British Columbia.

Within Kaska communities, recognition and membership have been managed in two general ways, by non-native governments that controlled the defining of "Indian" identity, and by traditional aboriginal culture, which determined identity in a variety of ways, not least of which was through kinship. As mentioned above, federally controlled definitions began with the Indian Act (see Indian Act, section 11, and Bill C-31), which stipulated that Indian status could be determined through either one's mother or one's father as long as one parent was an officially recognized member of an Indian band.[4] Status Indians are people who are registered with the

Table 1.2. Kaska language distribution for the Watson Lake area

	Aboriginal population	First learned and still understand Kaska* (%)	Use Kaska in the home (%)	Have knowledge of Kaska (%)
Watson Lake	220	n/a	n/a	n/a
Two Mile Village	100	45	15	45
Two and One-Half Mile Village	40	0	0	33.3
Upper Liard	110	36.4	9.1	36.4

* The phrase "language first learned and still understand" refers to "the first language learned at home in childhood and still understood by the individual at the time of the census. Sometimes referred to as mother tongue" (Statistics Canada 1996).

federal government as Indians according to the terms of the Indian Act, and non-status Indians are people who are not registered. Today, the simple distinctions of status and non-status have been replaced by much more complicated legal classifications (see below). Clan membership, which is defined by the community, has been strictly matrilineal. Like other Northern Athabaskan groups, the Kaska people have had a moiety system, with everyone having a designation as either Crow or Wolf. If your mother was Crow, then you were Crow. If your mother was Wolf, then you were Wolf. This was important when choosing a partner, of course, since the moieties were exogamous (Honigmann 1954). Beneath the level of the moiety were family groups, which also served as economic units.

Family group affiliation has also paralleled culturally recognized linguistic divisions (dialects) within the community (McClellan 1975). There were at least three family dialects represented in the Watson Lake area: the "original," the Pelly Banks, and the Stone Mountain dialects. In addition to these linguistic distinctions, there were two other prevalent choices: a standard variety of Canadian English and a Kaska-inflected variety of English. (In addition to these two varieties of English, a small Francophone community was present, along with other English varieties, including a U.S. variety.) In everyday interactions, community members might use both English dialects as well as their own Kaska dialect. However, it was clear that English was rapidly replacing Kaska. Table 1.2 shows the distribution of Kaska use for the Watson Lake communities (from the 1996 Canadian census data) around the time of this research. A comparison of columns B, C, and D reveals that a number of individuals learned Kaska first and still understood it, but few still used it in their homes.

Table 1.3. Comparison of percentages of aboriginal language acquisition

	Aboriginal language first learned and still understood (#)	Aboriginal language first learned and still understood (%)
Watson Lake area	85	34
Yukon Territory	960	16
Canada	208,615	26

Unfortunately, census data on the Kaska language for Watson Lake itself were, and are, not available. However, my own research indicates that all individuals who first learned Kaska and still understood Kaska were older adults and elders, with variable usage in the home. A number of younger adults had knowledge of Kaska but refrained from speaking the language. However, the Two and One-Half Mile numbers are problematic in this respect. Of the thirty individuals who I knew were living there, thirteen, or 43 percent, first learned, still understood, and had knowledge of Kaska.

Extending this comparison beyond the Watson Lake community, we see that the Kaska language had more speakers and/or passive users than did most of the aboriginal languages in the Yukon Territory or in Canada overall. The percentages given in table 1.3 illustrate this.

A similar distribution, at least in relation to the other aboriginal languages spoken by or affiliated with First Nations people in the Yukon Territory, was found by ALS (1991a). Their reports show that, percentage-wise, the Kaska language had more speakers and passive language users than many of the other indigenous languages within the Yukon Territory. While statistically the Kaska language situation appeared and appears more hopeful, the fact that Kaska was not being spoken or acquired as frequently as English places this language on the endangered list. There are a number of reasons for the endangered condition of Kaska and the other aboriginal languages. The rest of this chapter lays out the historical and sociopolitical events that have contributed to the marginalized status of First Nations people in the Yukon and the loss of speakers among these languages, focusing on Kaska in particular.

Sociohistorical Context

Prior to the 1830s, the indigenous populations of the interior Yukon Territory had little if any contact with non-native populations or individuals. In "precontact" days, trade with the interior was controlled by coastal

Tlingits. When Russian traders entered the scene, seeking fur for the lucrative European market, they were halted by this coastal power. Through these active networks, however, European trade goods and diseases were introduced to populations who never laid eyes on their importers. The first non-native individuals to venture into the territory (coming from the east) were employees of the Hudson's Bay Company (HBC) (Coates 1991:21; see also Cruikshank 1990; McClellan 1975). With the arrival of the Hudson's Bay Company in the 1840s, interaction between non-native and native fur traders began. The local communities suddenly had an opportunity to directly exchange their goods and services for commercial goods provided by the HBC, including hardware like guns and ammunition, as well as an abundance of commercial alimentary products, such as flour, coffee, sugar, and other grocery items.

These goods quickly became staples, a culinary reflection of the HBC's transformative impact on First Nations peoples. Talking about her mother during one of the Kaska House of Language workshops, Auntie Beatrice recalled making trips to the local HBC store.[5]

> (She) make something, we pick 'em up. . . . Work on a hide, sell hide.
> (She) just trade it for groceries. No money that time, can't use money.
> Mom just buy flour and anything with it. Thin one they just make vests.
> But they don't make much. Sell it too cheap. Fifteen dollars.

A few families also planted gardens, growing rhubarb, turnips, potatoes, and the like, although this never supplanted traditional subsistence. The following quote illustrates such alimentary maximization. Reflecting on her childhood and her mother's practices in particular, this same elder recalled:

> Fish, dry fish, dry meat, mom picking berries in August.
> Cranberries, lots of different blackberries he pick, he dry them.
> We got dad, mom make a little garden like that, big as that place.
> Turnips, we got potatoes, beets, cabbage, lots, big.
> Moose guts, you know, he clean it, he spread them all over winter time.
> Dishes, when you wash dishes, you throw that soap in it.
> Anything grows huge. Rhubarb, we got lots.
> First time she make this big, pretty soon that far. Oh anything grow.
> We don't buy potatoes. Mom try save them. Some dry, some get moldy.

That time you can't jar nothing, no jars, not very many pot either.
You have to work everyday, pull garden.

As a result of contact with Europeans, Kaska people expanded their culinary repertoires through incorporating new subsistence practices.

The HBC established two trading posts on traditional Kaska land: one on Frances Lake and another on the upper Pelly River (Coates 1991:24). In a collection of narratives produced by the Kaska Tribal Council, Mrs. Liza Magun, a Kaska elder, retold an account of when some Kaska people first encountered skukāni (white person/people). It seems likely that the skukāni she talked about are the ones from the HBC party led by Robert Campbell, who set up the Frances Lake HBC post in 1839–40.

Long, long ago they say people at Frances Lake saw the first white people.
They say those people long ago didn't know about many things.
They were living on wild game: caribou meat, gopher and things like that.
That's all they lived on. They didn't know about tea, didn't know about tobacco. They only drank soup made with caribou blood.

They came to the white people and were astonished to see them.
They didn't understand them.
Then those white people put tea in a pot on the fire for them.
They poured tea and put some sugar in and offered it to them as well as other kinds of white people's food.
They dipped tea out for them and put in sugar.
That white man took some and told them, "drink it," and they did that.

The white traders stirred tea and bannock and everything in front of them.
They gave them flour and everything.
The Kaska learned quickly and they were able to do it themselves right away. One boy understood them after only a short time and spoke to the white people, they say. He caught on right way, they say.
That was the first time that they saw white people, they say.
(Mrs. Liza Magun 1999:434–443; translated by William Atkinson)

This narrative reflects not only the ease with which Kaska people adjusted to the shifting sociocultural and economic landscape—"The Kaska learned quickly and they were able to do it themselves right away"—but their ability to accommodate the shifting sociolinguistic landscape as well—"One boy understood them after only a short time and spoke to the white people, they say. He caught on right way, they say."

During the initial invasion of non-native fur traders, the native population held dominion.[6] They were familiar with the landscape as well as fur-trading practice.[7] Demographically they were also dominant (Coates 1991). As a result, Yukon aboriginal languages, including Kaska, were not impacted. Instead, multilingualism was promoted and valued.

In another narrative, Mrs. Mary Charlie recounted a story about a winter where starvation was rampant, affecting the HBC employees as well as the native population. In her account, a Kaska man takes the two HBC men some caribou meat and finds only one of them still alive, having survived off the flesh of the other HBC man (Charlie 1999). This story is intended to show the ability of the native people to survive under duress, and the weakness and immorality of the foreigners under the same conditions. It also effectively reveals the dependence of the non-native population on the native population, important because, as the non-natives assumed a role of dominance, they increasingly rationalized their role as one of helping the native people, who, it is said, could not take care of themselves.

According to Coates (1991), the shift in economic power in the Yukon Territory and the resulting marginalization of the native population occurred with the Klondike gold rush in 1897 (see also Cruikshank 1990; McClellan 1975; Osgood 1971). When news of the riches broke, an estimated 100,000 non-natives from North America and Europe flocked to the Yukon to find their fortunes. Many, encountering a harsh, forbidding environment, turned back. Those who actually made it to Dawson and the gold fields found that most of the stakes had been claimed, and many of these fortune seekers also abandoned the effort. A number stayed, however, resulting in an increase in overall population and a sudden, permanent, shift in native to non-native ratios, with non-natives greatly outnumbering natives. By 1901, after the rush, the total Yukon population was 27,219, with a native population of 3,322, or 12.2 percent (Coates 1991:74). Roughly a century later, aboriginal people still constitute only about a quarter of the population.[8]

The Klondike gold rush also gave birth to the Yukon's mining industry. In contrast to the fur trade, the non-native population controlled mining from the start. They allowed native participation in only a limited capacity. First Nations individuals were hired as casual laborers, deckhands, packers, woodcutters, guides, and "meat harvesters" (Coates 1991:41–43). Most of these jobs were temporary and/or seasonal. For example, deckhands were needed only when the steamboats ran, which was only when the river wasn't frozen, that is, in the summer.

Additionally, the gold rush "determined the two-sector economy of the Yukon Territory," mining versus hunting and trapping (Coates 1991:46), with First Nations people linked to hunting and trapping ventures and non-natives with mining. This meant that the high-paying, full-time jobs of the mining industry were given to non-natives, a practice that was largely the result of non-native racialized views of First Nations peoples. "[Only] a small number of Indians actually worked in the mines, especially at the small copper properties near Whitehorse. But few managers, most of whom carried decidedly negative stereotypes of Indian labour with them from the south, willingly substituted Native workers for the readily available and skilled, albeit more expensive, white workers" (ibid., 49). For the Kaska communities, mining was not a local enterprise. And, although they remained relatively isolated from the invading non-native population and their racial attitudes, some sought employment or temporary jobs from non-natives. In one interview, a young man recalled helping his grandfather work on the riverboat during the summer months.

Joe: We used to well my grandfather used to work a running river-boat, and they were building a bridge on the Thompson Highway.

Barb: Oh yeah.

Joe: Yeah.

Barb: Oh neat.

Joe: Yeah, I used to sit there and bail water from the boat ((laughing)) cuz it get so deep.

Apart from mining-related employment opportunities (such as running a riverboat), Kaska families had contact with non-natives at the local trading post. Auntie Beatrice also talked about her father and his occupation, when asked about whether he went to the post to trade:

(My dad) too busy, he was going to help us, learn us how to school, busy trapping.
Summer time he cut wood for winter, fish, no time.
He just got enough time to sit down a little bit.
He cut trail all over Watson Lake, for trapping, make tent frame.
Lot of work, make cache.

All over he make cache.
No time to teach us school, too busy.
He cut wood for old people too.
With crosscut saw, three old people there, six I think.
He cut wood for all them.
He just get little money.
Big pile, winter time he haul it. Really big dog.
Lot of work those days.
Mom told me that story. I was too small, didn't know.
(. . .) (Older brother) used to help him.
Knock those wood, with a little axe.
(Older brother) he's more work.
He cut wood with saw even, he's a lot older.

Additionally, many of the Kaska elders' historical narratives depict a context where there was minimal contact between the Kaska people and non-native individuals. As described by Coates, most of this early contact occurred at trading posts and during seasonal work, such as working on the rivers on a steamboat.

The event in Kaska history that significantly changed First Nations peoples' existence was the building of the Alaska Highway in 1943 (Coates 1991; Cruikshank 1990). The construction of the highway brought the non-native population to their doorstep. This provided certain economic opportunities for native men, such as guides for survey crews, laborers, equipment operators, and for women, such as launderers, seamstresses, housemaids, and waitresses. With these new employment opportunities and economic viability, the aboriginal communities along the highway suddenly found themselves participants in a larger economic system. The intruding Canadian government resolved to incorporate the aboriginal populations into the now-dominant, "nontraditional" economy and to make them independent and self-reliant—overlooking the fact that they had been just that, up until these intrusions (Coates 1991).

This desire to acknowledge and incorporate First Nations peoples into the Canadian system prompted the development of territorial and federal programs aimed, paradoxically, at assimilating the native populations into Canadian society, yet maintaining a degree of social and physical distance between the two. Coates argues that this segregation resulted from two ideologies: (1) to protect the "childlike" Indian from debauchery, and (2) to maintain non-Native "purity" and "cleanliness" (1991:93). The method with the greatest impact came from the institutionalization of education, especially in the form of residential schooling, and its associated assimilationist ideology. The goal was to strip all Indians of their language and their identity as natives, thereby transforming them into Canadians.

Four residential schools were built around the territory, one each in Dawson, Whitehorse, Carcross, and Lower Post. The Lower Post residential school was the one attended by many of today's Kaska elders and younger adults. It opened in 1949 and closed in 1975 (Coates 1991:155, 205). Catholic, French-speaking nuns and Spanish-speaking priests ran the school (Mrs. Leda Jules, pers. comm.). However, rather than focusing on education, much of the students' time was spent maintaining the school buildings and gardens (Burnaby 1999). As part of these assimilationist tactics, children were restricted from speaking their first language(s); for Lower Post, this meant Kaska and/or Tlingit. If a child was caught speaking his or her first language, punishment ensued. One Kaska elder recounted an episode where she and a friend were speaking Kaska and joking around. A nun overheard them, assumed they were making fun of her, and punished them by making them scrub the dormitory staircase (three floors) with toothbrushes. On another occasion, this elder and her friend were tied together at the waist for an entire day. This was punishment for always "buddying" around together and for not interacting with children whom they did not know. This imposed assimilation included English-only communication, cleaning rooms until they were spotless, darning socks to perfection, and cutting their hair, activities symbolic of the dominating culture and nonnative practices. Residential schools were reserved for status Indian children only, children who were registered as Indian by the federal government (Burnaby 1999). All other children were sent to public schools. Illustrating the government's efforts to maintain a separation between aboriginal and nonaboriginal populations, this racially segregating practice ironically was motivated by attempts to "incorporate" (assimilate) First Nations peoples into Canadian society.

Another area that clearly illustrates this racialized segregation is the way in which communities were and are arranged. For example, residents of towns such as Watson Lake are predominantly Anglo, or at least nonnative. Most of the indigenous population is removed to communities outside of the town, places like Two Mile, Upper Liard, and Lower Post. This division is a historic artifact resulting from the federal government's initiative to settle the aboriginal population on reserves (see Coates 1991). Thus, Lower Post and other native-dominant communities are the remnants of old Indian reserves, now technically labeled "Indian settlements" by Statistics Canada. This segregation inevitably led to racial conflicts (and still does today). "Watson Lake, for example, was notorious for the tensions between the white and Indian sectors" (Coates 1991:222). Describing in 1962 the interaction between natives and non-natives, Dr. O. Schaefar states:

> Lower Post now appears to have the reputation of being extremely lawless. No doubt because of this, workers from Cassiar and Canada Tungsten and others flock there. The Lower Post Hotel is their hangout . . . it appears the Lower Post Hotel is being used as a "brothel." The Lower Post Indians have only been in contact with civilization for the last 25 or 30 years and they certainly have not built up an immunity to liquor. Because of this the Indian girls and women can, after a few drinks, become the victim of unscrupulous "White Trash." (quoted from Coates 1991:225)

This representation, of native peoples having only recently encountered "civilization," is a mainstay of occidental historic discourse (Deloria 1998). Ironically, it is natives' embracing of "civilization," that is, liquor, that produces and reinforces the negative stereotypes portraying indigenous peoples as "drunken," "debauched," "dirty," and "diseased." A similar description to that for Lower Post is given for the state of affairs at Upper Liard in 1966:

> Upper Liard is a village of problems. The people are apathetic, unskilled and often unemployed. Children are poorly cared for. Severe drinking is wide spread, reaching down to the younger school age group. While the adults drink, night after night, the school children wander the village, sometimes until day break [sic]. Violent strife frequently breaks out in manifestation of the ever present hostility between factions and families, husbands and wives. There have been killings. We have reason to expect more. (quoted from Coates 1991:227)

Though this description dates to the 1960s, the same image, of First Nations peoples as wild, uncontrollable, and immoral, still surfaces today. Kaska people were no exception to this uncivilized-and-inebriated-Indian representation.

Such imagery has served only to reinforce the arguments for the need to teach native peoples English and rid them of their "barbarous tongues." As noted above, the role of institutionalized education, and the focus on English, was the amelioration of these attributes in order to facilitate native children's acquisition of contemporary, "western," and "civilized" knowledge and practices. Such imagery continues to fuel some of the rhetoric surrounding native children and public education, although in new guise. Transformed, the revised imagery reflects a concern with reparations and healing, of abused children who have become adults, and of suffering juvenile delinquents.

In response to this rhetoric, there has been growing support for the creation and incorporation of aboriginal language classes in the public schools and other public institutions. An appeal for the revitalization of aboriginal languages and cultures has been put forth to heal aboriginal peoples, physically and psychologically (see chap. 5).

Ethnohistorical Dimensions of Kaska Language Shift

Two important observations relating to today's indigenous language situation stem from the history of the Yukon Territory. First, the active implementation of segregation and assimilation forced the Yukon's indigenous population to change and adapt to new economic conditions. They did not succumb to these pressures because they thought they could not survive otherwise, but because the Canadian government decided that they, the First Nations peoples, could not survive within the Canadian system in any other way. The effect this had on language was clear. The aboriginal languages spoken in the Yukon, and the Kaska language in particular, were forced into obsolescence or dormancy.

Second, the underlying social construction of native peoples as either "childlike" or "savages," a historic image that has been produced and reproduced up into the present (Berkhofer 1978; Cassuto 1997; Deloria 1998), deterred individuals from wanting to claim native ancestry, what Eva Garroutte has called a "legacy of insecurity and pain" (Garroutte 2003). It is likely, then, that this shame carried over to speaking their heritage language (Foley 1988; House 2002; Kroskrity 1993; McCarty, Romero, and Zepeda 2006). That is, Kaska and other First Nations peoples may have refrained from speaking their respective languages because of the negative stereotypes that surrounded their identity as "Indians," and subsequently their languages. In a passing conversation, a young woman who thought of herself only as Kaska commented to me that she didn't know she was an "Indian" until she went off to school. It was then that she learned that she was included in this negative, racialized stereotype and was supposed to be ashamed of her heritage.

For the indigenous languages of the Yukon, and Kaska in particular, these ideological associations have served to suppress indigenous language use in public and private contexts. In public, individuals were ashamed to use their own language because of the negative attention it invoked. A Northern Tutchone speaker remarked to me once that while in Dawson a non-native person came up to her and a friend and told them to stop "speaking Indian." They obeyed his instruction. Additionally, I was often told that it was impolite to "speak Indian" around those who did not under-stand the language, especially around non-natives. The focus on politeness overlies another explanation. A number of native speakers told me that non-native speakers, upon hearing a native language being spoken, would interpret the discourse as being about them and, in particular, as mocking them. As a result, native speakers refrained from using their language in public and around non-native speakers, in order to accommodate others' insecurities and lack of knowledge.

In private, heritage language use was also diminished, replaced by an emphasis on speaking English. This replacement stemmed in part from peo-ple's not wanting their children to experience the same disciplinary action and scrutiny that they had experienced as young people. One young adult surmised, "A lot of people, I guess, say they were forbidden from speaking their language and stuff, that's probably because that's the only thing they could speak at the time, [their] language." Additionally, one young elder remarked that "if anything, it was through residential school that we lost our language." More specifically, this shift from speaking Kaska reflected the hope that if their children learned English well at home, they would never have to endure a residential-school-like atmosphere. The displace-ment of the heritage language by English in the home has resulted from this practice. When younger adults were asked about not speaking their heritage language, they often stated that they didn't speak their language well enough and/or were shy about speaking it. Shyness was by far the most common explanation for choosing to speak English (as opposed to Kaska) in contexts where elders and other speakers were present.

Whether First Nations peoples refrain from using their heritage lan-guages out of shame, politeness, or shyness, the fact that they do so is reso-nant of their history, including a long history of oppressive contact with non-natives and their awareness of the derogatory ideological associations that non-native people had maintained with respect to First Nations peoples.

The Rise of Language Revitalization in the Yukon

During the 1970s, Canada officially abandoned its policy of aboriginal assimilation and began seeking a new framework of relationships with its indigenous peoples. By the 1980s, the Canadian government's platform had become the promotion of a multicultural society and a celebration of Can-ada's cultural diversity, indigenous and otherwise (Penikett 2006). This new federal position, known as reconciliation, is expressed most fully in the five-volume report from the Royal Commission on Aboriginal Peoples, released in 1996. This report includes many recommendations toward reconciling the relationship between Canada and its aboriginal peoples and integrating them into Canadian society while recognizing their cultures as unique. Specifically regarding language, it led to the development of Aboriginal Head Start programs (which were intended to put aboriginal languages on an equal footing with English in the preschools), outlined the intention of the government of Canada to begin providing aboriginal language services and programs, and otherwise worked to put aboriginal language issues at the forefront of political consideration and in the minds of Canadians at large (Royal Commission on Aboriginal Peoples 1996). Reconciliation even reached a point where it could address the painful topic of residential schooling. In 1998, the government endowed a foundation to support victims of boarding school abuses, and in 2008 the prime minister of Canada issued a formal apology to all former residential school students.

The shift to reconciliation was a response to intense lobbying by Indian activist groups in the 1970s. The National Indian Brotherhood (now known as the Assembly of First Nations) lobbied successfully for control of local schooling, which allowed for the reintroduction of traditional religion, customs, and language into educational curriculum. With this came an end to the church-run and government-run residential schools that had done so much to eradicate aboriginal languages. In 1985, through an amendment to the Indian Act known as Bill C-31, some of the most repressive of the remaining Indian Act era policies were retracted, the most important regarding the definition of Indian status. Designed to bring the Indian Act into accord with the Canadian Charter of Rights and Freedoms, Bill C-31 mandated the equal treatment of men and women, the prevention of loss of status due to marriage, and equal treatment for children born out of wedlock and within. It also restored status for many who had lost it through the policy of enfranchisement, including their descendants. Through the amendment, Indian bands were regaining control of their own membership.

Change in the Yukon was also a result of Indian activism. In 1973, the Yukon Native Brotherhood, which evolved into today's Council of Yukon First Nations, traveled to Ottawa to present their position paper "Together Today for Our Children Tomorrow" (Council for Yukon Indians 1977). This "statement of grievances" argued for aboriginal self-government and tied the right to preserve aboriginal cultural identity and language directly to the land claims process. In 1993, after twenty years of negotiating, Canada's first modern Indian treaty was signed. This treaty, the Umbrella Final Agreement, lays the foundation for each of the First Nations' land claims and self-governing agreements, replacing the Indian Act in this area. The UFA was an important treaty in the history of aboriginal–state relations in North America. It provided land—more land than all the Indian reserves in Canada combined, and a large enough land base to support traditional subsistence practices—as well as settlement funds, mineral rights to 26,000 square kilometers of territory, and a guaranteed voice in the decision-making bodies that managed natural resources in the Yukon. It also laid the foundation for aboriginal self-government. Significantly, each of the newly formed First Nations would be free from the control of Indian Affairs, dealing directly with the federal government, not quite on a government-to-government basis as with true sovereignty, but in the way municipalities relate to the federal government in Canada. In the Yukon, First Nations receive funds to operate their governments and are in turn free to administer to their own people, to govern their own locality, and to have shared jurisdiction in areas such as education, economic development, and health and social services (Penikett 2006). Additionally, one of the many issues addressed in this treaty is the thorny issue of enrollment. Definition and control of membership now rests with the First Nations governments, who have created constitutions that define both requirements for membership and processes for modifying these requirements.[9]

The UFA also contains explicit provisions for aboriginal language. Section 2.12.2.9 states that "each Board shall consider including in its annual budget funding to allow the Board to provide its members with cross cultural orientation and education, and other training directed to improving its members' ability to carry out their responsibilities, as well as funding for facilities to allow board members to carry out their responsibilities in their traditional language." Furthermore, the chapter on the Heritage Board, in section 13.1.1.2, states that among its objectives is "to promote the recording and preservation of traditional languages, beliefs, oral histories including legends, and cultural knowledge of Yukon Indian People for the benefit of future generations" (121). The Heritage resolutions also call for working with aboriginal people in the interpretation of cultural materials, proclaiming that "oral history is a valid and relevant form of research" (122). Regarding self-government and native language, the agreement states directly in section 24.2.0 that language, culture, and spiritual beliefs and practices are all legitimate topics for negotiation in the ongoing settlement process (260). Furthermore, First Nations may negotiate the transfer of programs and services pertaining to the "design, delivery and management of Indian language and cultural curriculum" (section 24.3.2.1, p. 261). This is important now, as the First Nations are beginning to take over the existing programs. In the future, each First Nation is expected to have its own program in this area.

These provisions were influenced by language revitalization activity undertaken in the Yukon during the negotiating years. In the 1970s, researchers such as John Ritter and Julie Cruikshank, who were working on various language projects with Yukon native peoples, helped form the Yukon Native Languages Project. The project was officially started in 1977 and was sponsored, as it is today, by the Council of Yukon First Nations (CYFN). The project itself became known as the Yukon Native Language Centre (YNLC) in 1985. Since its inception, it has been involved in recruiting native speakers for linguistic documentation and for training as native language teachers. This latter goal became possible with the passing of the Education Act, which opened the door for aboriginal languages in local classrooms. YNLC also initiated a program of teaching literacy to First Nations people who were still fluent in their ancestral languages. To this end, literacy workshops were held, and repeated, for groups of elders from most, if not all, of the eight officially recognized Yukon aboriginal languages. The impact of YNLC on aboriginal languages was significant. For many elders, YNLC provided them with their first experiences with preservation work. Dozens of elders from all over the Yukon have been recorded talking, singing, and telling stories in their own languages. With this work they gained a familiarity with performing for a tape recorder or video camera, creating a new site and method for the reproduction of aboriginal language practices.

Although YNLC was controlled by the Council of Yukon First Nations and funded, ultimately, by the Yukon government, national politics would lead to another government-sponsored program for native language revitalization. In the 1980s, Canada was finalizing its Official Languages Act, which provided an opportunity to legitimize Canada's many aboriginal tongues. The Yukon government seized the opportunity and negotiated an exclusion to the Official Languages Act that would *not* make French and English official languages but would create an atmosphere in which French, English, and any aboriginal language would be recognized as legitimate. The result was the Yukon Languages Act (1988) and a funding agreement with the federal government on "the importance of further measures to preserve, develop and enhance the Aboriginal languages of the Yukon, to recognize the status of those Aboriginal languages and to provide for Aboriginal languages services" (quoted in Leslie Gardner and Associates 1993:1). With this came the establishment of Aboriginal Languages Services, within YTG, five years of funding, and an evaluation and the option for renewal after this period (Leslie Gardner and Associates 1997:27). The initial period of the agreement ran from February 24, 1989, to March 31, 1993, and was funded with $4.25 million. The second period extended the program through fiscal year 1998 and provided $5.9 million. The first funding agreement cites objectives such as "ensuring the perpetuation, revitalization, growth and protection of Aboriginal languages" and "responding to the language needs of Aboriginal communities in the Yukon" (Leslie Gardner and Associates 1993:2). It also provides funding specifically for consultation for program planning, for linguistic and historical research, training of teachers, translators and interpreters, and translation of government materials. Since then, the agreement has been renewed, but the funding has been slightly diminished, down to $5.5 million (with an additional $26,000 each year from YTG) for the 1998–2003 five-year agreement.[10]

Unlike most other indigenous (minority-language) communities, the language situation in the Yukon Territory was one where the government had institutionalized the preservation and revitalization of support for local aboriginal languages. Rarely do we see such a commitment by a dominant regime to the language concerns of marginalized aboriginal communities. However, there is much more to revitalization than simply lifting the sanctions against particular practices and providing funding for their renewal. Attempts to address these concerns were made in the specific programs and their guiding philosophies (see chap. 5).

Changing Economic Conditions

With both the institution of self-governing among the First Nations and the creation of aboriginal language programs, new employment opportunities were created for native people. Unlike the existing job opportunities, such as mining or fire-crew work, which could be temporary, seasonal, and unpredictable, the new government positions offered permanent employment and more secure, higher-paying positions. More importantly, they were positions where First Nations people controlled the capital, especially the cultural and linguistic capital.

Language-related employment opportunities ranged from full- and part-time positions in the territorial and First Nations governments and in schools, to recurring temporary "consultant" and translator jobs for government workshops. For example, in 1998 and 1999 Aboriginal Language Services employed a staff of five people, three of whom worked in the main office in Whitehorse, one person in Carmacks, and another person in Watson Lake. Three of the permanent employees were from Yukon First Nations, including one from Liard First Nation. ALS also provided funding to pay honoraria and travel expenses for elders for many of the events they participated in around the territory, as well as elsewhere, and paid other individuals for temporary work on language-related projects.[11] One year ALS even funded an educational trip for three elders to attend the American Indian Language and Development Institute, held at the University of Arizona every summer. ALS also contributed significant financial support for the Kaska House of Language workshops. Through the Department of Education and in collaboration with the Yukon Native Language Centre, the territorial government also created jobs in the public schools specifically designed for First Nations individuals who still spoke their languages. In 1998, the Watson Lake school district maintained three native-language teacher positions, two full-time (one at the high school, one at the elementary school) and one part-time (at the elementary school). Additionally, the Aboriginal Head Start program/Child Development Center employed a part-time native-language instructor, and the Yukon Territorial Government would provide additional funding to hire elders to facilitate native-language classes in the schools. At the high school, in particular, one elder came regularly to assist the native-language instructor. All of these jobs were local.

Beyond language-related jobs, the settling of land claims across the Yukon created a vast network of government departments and programs in need of staffing. Consequently, the main employers of First Nations people in Watson Lake were the Liard (River) First Nation (LFN) and the Kaska Tribal Council (KTC). Most of their employees, in fact, were Dene. In contrast, all other local businesses and government-run facilities (excluding the schools) were owned and operated by non-native persons, employing, almost exclusively, non-native people (this residual segregation is much less salient in other Yukon communities, especially Whitehorse). One exception to this employment pattern was the sawmill, in which LFN held a 10 percent share, a share that required the sawmill to hire a certain number of LFN members. Kaska men could find employment there, but usually only in the lower-level entry jobs. Thus, employment opportunities for LFN members, outside of the band office, the KTC, or the school, were still slim. Most work for men involved temporary relocation outside of the territory, such as to Fort Nelson to work on oil rigs, or equally distant mines and logging operations within the territory. The persons participating in my study or consulting with me in some capacity fit this pattern of employment. They made up 15 percent (38 of 250) of the total aboriginal population for Two Mile, Two and One-Half Mile, and Upper Liard. While the employment distribution is fairly representative of the community, the samples by sex are not. According to the 1996 census, the community overall had a larger population of men (150) than women (95) (Statistics Canada 1996). Many of these men, however, were employed outside of the community and did not reside in the Watson Lake area year-round. The distribution by sex is more representative of the territory's distribution, which had a larger population of women than men.

Most of the people with whom I worked or interviewed were employed (approximately 70%). The women who were unemployed were either elders (retired) or students. The unemployed men were all elders. Across the sexes, employment appeared comparable. While I was there, though, the local sawmill went out of business. This changed the employment balance slightly, with women having a higher rate of employment than men. This is more typical of the unemployment patterns throughout the Yukon Territory and points to the fact that men tended to be employed in seasonal jobs or, at least, in less stable industries (Statistics Canada 1996). The largest employer of both sexes, however, was the local First Nations government, 69 percent of women and 55 percent of men. The rest of the women were employed by YTG, and the men were in industry.

The fact that LFN was the largest employer of Dene people is not surprising, given the expansion of government that occurred in the territory and the rather slow pace of aboriginal economic development in the 1990s. However, this pattern may also be reflective of the difficulty many native people had finding work outside of their own First Nations. For women, the second major employer was the YTG.[12] Interestingly, none of the men were employed by the YTG, whereas 31 percent of the women were. On the other hand, 45 percent of the men were employed in primary, resource-based industries, either the logging/forestry industry (at the local sawmill or as a logging truck driver) or oil drilling industry. None of the women had employment in these industries, whereas all of the native-language-related positions were held by women then.

These economic trends pertain to language revitalization in two ways. First, the concentrating of the First Nation workforce into First Nation government positions might suggest that it would be a simple matter to use Kaska as the language of business and everyday interaction within the band office. Yet, even though it had been recommended that all band employees use Kaska, few appeared to do so, or did so only in the privacy of their offices. One parent stated: "I think they should use Kaska more than they do, if everybody's so concerned about our culture and all that. I mean you can't just go to meetings and bitch about it and not practice it. Ya know, like at the band office, there, they should encourage their workers to use Kaska and . . . then they'll have influence on people . . . they should practice in a place like that." Such scenarios were not uncommon, even in the educational contexts set aside for Kaska language use such as the Aboriginal Head Start (see chap. 3). However, such sentiments reveal that while Kaska language use is supported in theory, in practice fewer and fewer individuals are managing to shift back to using Kaska in contexts that support its use. In Watson Lake, there were no businesses where the language of the work environment was Kaska, and even in local government the language of business was English. Official documents, like treaties and settlements, were written in English and French, and all negotiations with federal and territorial governments were in English. The schools provided a similar experience. The business of teaching and learning was conducted in English, while the Kaska language itself was taught as a *subject*, something that was talked *about* (see chap. 3).

To participate not only in the greater Canadian economy, but even in the local system, one must speak English or French (and French was rarely spoken in the Yukon). This in turn affected language socialization discourses in that parents emphasized learning to speak "correct" English over learning to speak Kaska. As one parent noted in response to a question about teaching children English in school, "Well, yeah, good proper English, even I could use some." Not only does this reflect an emphasis on learning English, this statement highlights the fact that people were aware of and differentially evaluated the varieties of English constituting their sociolinguistic landscape. This also harks back to the earlier pedagogical discourses framing native students' educational experiences depicting them as "primitive" and "severely linguistically inadequate." The priority for the moment, for many, was to competently learn and speak a standard variety of English, not any other "foreign" or "primitive" language, and not Kaska, even if Kaska's "linguistic capital" was on the rise. Such sentiments are difficult to overcome, and they present one of the many challenges facing language revitalization.

The second way in which these trends relate to language revitalization is through the reframing or redefining of the linguistic marketplace. Part of the motivation behind language revitalization is the revaluation of indigenous languages, largely through increasing their marketability. This can be and has been accomplished in several ways. One way is through the institutionalization of indigenous languages. By incorporating Kaska language classes into the public school curriculum, opportunities for developing and teaching a Kaska curriculum arise, which then requires personnel to create educational materials, to train people to teach with these materials (along with designing their own materials), and to teach. The implications of these new economic opportunities were significant and are discussed below in more detail (see chap. 4). The most significant change, however, was in the employment of elders; they were institutionally sanctioned by bureaucrats and linguists as authorities on the territory's aboriginal languages, as repositories of linguistic and cultural knowledge, and as themselves subjects of revalorization.

Transforming the Linguistic Marketplace

Two significant social dimensions affecting Kaska language practices were the identification (and employment) of elders as language experts (see chap. 4 for further discussion) and the language socializing discourses of these elders. While one of the effects of the creation of language-related jobs was a new labor force and market, in tandem these two dimensions led to a new social hierarchy, with the irony being that the institutionalization of Kaska created a new linguistic regime (Kroskrity 2000) that excluded younger generations of potential Kaska speakers. This section focuses on the socializing narratives of elders, shared both in private and in public settings. The predominant theme circulating through these narratives is the concept of á'i and its interpretation in relation to everyday practices and communication. Á'i is an expression understood on the one hand as taboo, and on the other as respect. It entails ideas of appropriateness and success, and guides people's behavior, linguistic and otherwise. While not directly employing the rhetoric of language endangerment, these discussions of á'i highlighted the shifts taking place and a recognition of the loss of knowledge generally. Framed another way, this concept identifies everyday disjunctures, and the ultimate disjuncture—younger generations' failure to acquire this knowledge (see Meek 2007 for a more detailed discussion).

On several occasions, at the House of Language workshops, on previously taped interviews with individual elders, and in *Haa Shagoon* videos, the ways in which people understood the concept of á'i had been expressed. In my language research, elders often requested that I tape-record some of our interactions, because these interactions were in fact socializing or educational interactions. The recordings were meant to facilitate acquisition—of both linguistic and cultural knowledge. One occasion in particular illustrates the conceptualization of á'i, directly in terms of behavior and indirectly in terms of language; two of the elders recorded predominantly Kaska varieties, and the other elder spoke a variety of English with some Kaska phrases to exemplify her points.

In a rented SUV, rather than the borrowed, now broken-down, K-car that I'd used during the summer months, I had carefully driven out toward the airport about ten miles (from downtown Watson Lake) on a sheet of ice intermittently covered with packed snow, to pick up Auntie Beatrice. It was the usual frosty February afternoon—snow creaking beneath my worn-out, leaky hiking boots and blinding sunlight forcing me to squint as I carefully avoided the slick patches of ice leading up to Auntie Beatrice's doorstep. Her two-story, split-level home appeared brilliantly blue, like the February sky itself, against the frozen white landscape in which it was buried. All of the summer's activities were immersed now in several feet of snow, making the yard appear lumpy with tips of branches, chicken wire, and timber poking through at random. I lightly tapped on her door before pushing it open with a gentle shove and calling up the steps to her. She had been waiting patiently for my arrival and now descended the steps with her kerchief covering her hair, her snow boots providing stability for her feet, and her sunglasses protecting her eyes. Unlike the eager neophyte standing on her landing, she knew how to dress for this weather.

Together we headed back to downtown Watson Lake and the band office, an unremarkable building set next to Tags, a gas station and convenience store, to pick up the second elder, Auntie Adele. With Auntie Adele was her granddaughter, a high school student who had the afternoon off from school. After awkwardly clambering back into the seemingly luxurious rental vehicle—a four-wheel drive SUV with heated leather front seats—we made our way back out to Two Mile (in the direction of the airport, but only two miles from downtown Watson Lake). I had worked with these women on several occasions, at both formal and informal events. At these various events, all three had expressed serious concerns about the lack of knowledge First Nations children seemed to have regarding their First Nations heritage, reiterated yet again during this visit.

> Auntie Beatrice: It really hard.
>   These days nobody sayin' (this).[13]
>   Kids they got good time ((laugh)).
>
> Auntie Adele: "No," they say.
>   I think they need to learn it, eh?
>   They need to know these things, you know?

And why do children need to acquire this knowledge? As Auntie Beatrice elaborated,

> That's for kids growing up (so) they know
> And (when) they go in the bush,
> If they (get) hard time,
> Something gonna help them.

A mainstay of elders' personal narratives is the anecdote of a "hard time" that illustrates their resourcefulnes in the bush, followed by a comparison with today's youth. These stories display a concern that youth will not only be deprived of their cultural heritage but will not be able to survive in the bush should hard times return. Further along in this exchange, the sense that linguistic and cultural knowledge was slipping away from children inevitably became foregrounded in elders' discussions about the Kaska language. As on so many other occasions, the recorded discussion that day would center on knowledge and practices of respect necessary for a balanced existence, healthful lifestyle, and survival.

We pulled off the iced-over dirt road and parked in front of Auntie Martha's home, a single-story house with two bedrooms, 800 square feet at most. From the outside, it looked like many of the other homes in the area, covered with aluminum siding with smoke streaming out of the smokestack on the roof but originating from a pitch-black iron woodstove inside. The band had installed a ramp up to her front door to accommodate her decreased agility, but it also came in handy when other elders visited. Having announced our arrival by politely stomping up the ramp in an attempt to remove some of the snow from our boots, we entered Auntie Martha's home without loud knocks or doorbells ringing. She was sitting at her kitchen table, waiting, with her cane to one side and the coffeepot behind her on the kitchen counter keeping the nearly twelve cups of coffee warm for visitors. We contributed some orange juice and fresh fruit. After shedding some of our layers and our boots, everyone gathered around the kitchen table, with the exception of Auntie Adele's granddaughter. With teenage-perfected ennui, she casually moved over to the sofa, picked up the remote, and turned on the television, her attention confined to this more technologically advanced form of entertainment and the barely audible voices resonating from it. The rest of us were busy setting up the tape recorder, getting out our notebooks and pencils, and serving beverages. Finally settled into our chairs around the kitchen table, I began the discussion by asking the women how elders recognized elder status. Arising from this query, the women pointed out that part of being an elder entailed passing on knowledge, by telling stories to or recording stories for younger people so that this knowledge would be preserved.

> Martha: Dene desūhdi yéndedāhi t'eni, they get old.
> Dene-jōn í-légehdi dene too old dene ehday.
> *People have a hard time getting up when they get old. People-getting-old, that's what they mean by elder, when people become too old.*

Adele: Dene gugáni, dēhį̄, kola echo' enja' gededí;
        Ihį yā ghāde meyēgehdí gediya?
        People like us, they say (we're) already elders;
        How do they say they know?

Martha: Dahyegah dene enlīn meyēgedí sā gehdī-na.
        You know dene enlīn dzenḗs, eh?
        You know, sā léndent'ą̇i, igháde lēgehdī.
        Łúngodiwōł.
        When people become (elders), they just know so they say.
        You know a person's birthday, eh? You know, when the sun comes back,
        (that's) how they know (one's age).
        It goes back to where it began ((like hands on a watch)).

Adele: Hmm.

Martha: I guts'įh dene cho' edē gehdī.
        From that they become elders.

Adele: Mhm.

Martha: Dene cho' dē̄ gudeji yagháde dene meyudíha.
        I guts'įh how many years yagháde dene gudíha long time
        ago, eh?
        Elders tell stories so that a person can learn.
        From this, so many years from now people will have knowledge from
        long time ago, eh?

Adele: Mhm.

Martha: Emā gecho' you're old enough to work kíntla ezés.
        Dene k'éh meyíntla.
        When one's mother gets old you're old enough to work so you worked on
        hide.
        Indian way you worked on it.

Adele: Mhm.

Martha: T'āk yédé (???) gah yédé ghą nḗntl'úí ne-mom yéh géndahi.
        Your mom would go around with you when you set snares for rabbit,
        using feathers.

Adele: Mhm.

Martha: Spring pole snare yéh kulédénłá'í, tl'ūł k'i tl'ūł (???) gah
        dogah. Gucho' łą̇́ hard time tl' ą̇́, they die. Ł ą̇́ hard time
        gucho' nésejá' tl' ą̇́, kḗgedéhtéh.

*And spring pole snares, you put them on the pole, rope also, rope (snare?)
for rabbit. When our elders had a really hard time, they died. After our
elders became elders, they all died off during really hard times.*

As the discussion of elders progressed, the topic shifted to the concept of
á'i. As mentioned above, many elders were concerned that young people
were not learning or did not understand what this term meant. This concern motivated the following commentary.

Martha: Yeah, á'i gēhdia i kḗt'ē yếdé ghą gudēhdéh.

Ts'édāne meyēgudíhi dega, k'úk kah megēgun(e)gets dega
lēdī, k'úk kah megēgudíhi-gedai, yéhdī léhdī. Á'i yāgíhdia
á'i? Á'i gíhdī yḗdé ghą gudendéh dé kola etie.

*Yeah, á'i they call it that, like that, so let's talk about it so that children
can learn about it and she ((Barb)) can write it down, so that if they see
it on paper, they can learn what somebody says X means. So, á'i, what
do they mean by á'i?*

Beatrice: Yeah, something on the ground (???) you can't, á'i, somebody's coat maybe on ground, then licked ((if step over it
or on it)), even mittens just one, you can't walk over, put it
in the corner, mom say.

Barb: So, don't leave your stuff lying all over?

Beatrice: No, put it in one place so nobody walk over (it).

Adele: Even kids?

Beatrice: Even kids.

Adele: Even kids do it.

Martha: (???)

Beatrice: That's for kids so they won't get hard time growing up, so
they know and they go in the bush, if they get hard time,
something gonna help them.

Adele: Mhm.

Beatrice: Put in corners, even blankets and take 'em out, put them on
pole.

Adele: Mhm.

Beatrice: Gee, you know, time when no washing machine.

Adele: Mhm.

Beatrice: (???) nāts'út'ūt boys got washtub for them, nobody put his
clothes in there with them.

Adele: Oh?

Beatrice: Gee, hard time.

Martha: Gee, young girls (today) they don't care, eh?

Adele: Mhm.

Beatrice: Our clothes we wash it alone, in old pail or something,
boys got good tub, they don't even put mooseskin in (tubs
used for boys).

Adele: Mm.

Beatrice: "Á', Á', the boys' tub lāt'ā," they say.
"Á', Á', that's the boys' tub," they say.

Adele: Mhm.

Beatrice: Oh, too much, eh? Even old moccasins.

Martha, Adele: Mhm.

Beatrice: Kē ts'āhdé' they call it, they throw (them) in the fire when
they finish so nobody walk over them. Sometimes I can't
just take it.

Martha, Adele: ((laughing))

Martha: Indian way too much //sometime//

Beatrice: //Cache we got little.//
"Édénléh, édénléh," they call it. "Don't walk on it," they just
holler.
"No," I said, "I didn't walk on it."
"Just pull it out," they say, "put on rope, take it down (too)."
Oh too much.
Even flour, even on a sleigh like that, pile of stuff.
"Ah no, no, no, don't walk over, go around," they say.
They put it, their stuff, on brush.
"Don't walk over it," he say. "Á'i," they say.
Rope more worse. Soon as we finish they pile 'em up.

Adele: Any kind of rope?

Beatrice: Mhm.

Adele: Mmm.

Beatrice: Even dog harness, "Á'! Á'!"
           The dog harness, don't walk over long (piece), on a trail.
           We campin'; they put all the rope on the brush and put
           brush on top so nobody walk on it, even axe.
           "Don't touch my axe, don't walk over it," they say.
           Somebody walk over the axe.

Adele: You can't touch anybody's things, eh?

Beatrice: Gee, I find my own axe; sometimes I don't see (it).
           I make mistake, I walk over my own axe ((laughing)).
           There you can't trap with beaver trap.
           Gotta put it under tree, "Don't walk over! Don't touch it!"
           You set trap, you push stake, I pull it out.
           "No, no, no, just pull it straight (???)."
           Oh my, sometimes I just look up.

Martha: What (???)?

Beatrice: Yeah, beaver meat worse.
           Gotta hang it up, smoke it, all hang up, his head and his feet.
           They tell me, "Put it long ways in the bush, put it (like
           this)," they say.

Martha: Do it even—

Beatrice: Even they cut mooseskin that round, łágat'ás.
           They burn 'em (the scraps from cutting it out) so nobody
           walk over it.
           It really hard.
           These days nobody sayin' (this).
           Kids they got good time ((laugh)).

Adele: "No," they say.
           I think they need to learn it, eh?
           They need to know these things, you know?

Martha: //???//

Beatrice: //We set tent.//

Martha: Łáne hard time gehtáni yā nitl'á.
           Really hard time after they were raised.

Beatrice: Nobody walk around the tent.

Barb: Around the tent?

Beatrice: Just outside, he don't go around like that, just go one way.

Martha: That first time, i ts'édāne old woman eday nénētsék géhdī.
           That first time, when children become women, they sew.
           ((When you first become a woman, you sew and wear a
           puberty hat.))

Adele: Ts'at cho yegeh, kánégénlām?
           Under a big hat, did they do that to you?

Martha: Mhm.

Adele: Oh.

Martha: Gút'ē pile of skin; (you) can't see nothing, can't look up, eh?

Adele: Oh my goodness, how big nets'adé' dédáhcho-a?
                               how big was your hat?

Martha: Big, you know, like tent, eh?

Adele: Just like a tent?

Martha: Mhm, á'i, you can't look at your brother or nothin'; bad eh?
           Now girls don't care.

Adele: Yeah.

Martha: They throw away their things; they don't (care) ((laughing)).
           They throw out everything, *(that's why everything)* more bad.
           Gúja'.
           It happens.
           Endia, no good, dūlá̧ á' genzen yéh.
           Ya know, no good, because they don't have respect.

Adele: Yeah, well, dūlá̧ engédíh yéh lēget'ini, deda.
           Yeah, well, they act (like that) because they don't know, ya know.

The á'i practices alluded to in this passage are culturally relevant across the
Yukon and less stringently adhered to by younger generations (a source of
irritation and concern for the elders). For instance, a strong cross-sex sibling avoidance rule (see McClellan 1975) provokes Martha's comment that
it is taboo for a girl to look at her brother, and her observation that "now
girls don't care." The many injunctions to not step over personal belongings
(and conversely, to not leave them scattered about so that others may step
over them) reference spritual contamination protocols. The elders here,

both women, are discussing specifically the men's items that women were not supposed to touch or step over, such as rope, sleighs, dog harnesses, axes, and traps (a woman may have her own trap or axe but should not touch her husband's, especially while menstruating) (for further discussion see Honigmann 1949, 1954; Wheelock and Moore 1997). These practices of respect and the concept of á'i were also important topics at the House of Language workshops and during elders' visits at the Aboriginal Head Start and in school classrooms. On these occasions, elders often contrasted their own childhoods with the lifestyles of their grandchildren to highlight practices of respect and the importance of these practices for today's generations (see Meek 2007).

Sa'a dédzētsedle gudehę duga kēdzīla', my cousin yéh
"Egudehę duga ses lídehlé'," gwodī.
Tses lídzedele, etsā mets'í no'gwehdi'á'.
MacDames dēstsedle kēsdī.
Egudehē ts'í líndzededēlí meduga tu' élé lídzedeléhí tses élé
lídzedeléhí kēdzet'in.
Dédu ts'édāne dúłą̄ nē(ge)déts'ek gujá'.
Guheni la wēdé' Mom ts'edéts'ek-la.
Dene gudedéh, dene zedlé' (???).
Ts'édāne dúłą gégeyes, lā gutie.
Dédu lā ts'édāne k'éngeyese, dene gudedéh gólí.
Dúłą gólí dene gudedéh genezen.
Dúłą á' genezen . . .
K'éngeyes, egudehę nélīn nētsedzī gólí.
Géneyes dúłą á' genezen.
Gujá'.
Guheni dēdzētsédle dúłą gédzeyes-la.
Néguna'in éh kula dene etsedzi, dene etsedzi kula ts'edéhts'ī-lą.

Long ago when we were small, we worked for an old lady, my cousin and (me).
They told us, "Bring back wood for that old woman."
We brought wood down to her like they told us to.
I remember when I was small at MacDames.
When we returned to that old woman, we brought water for her and wood.
That's what we did.
Now children don't listen.
We (current elders) always listened to our mothers.
When people talked (???)
children didn't run around, that's how it was.
Now (children) run around even when people are talking.
They (children) don't show respect when people are talking.

They aren't respectful. (. . .)
They run around even when those old ladies are eating.
They run around without thinking (about the elderly women).
That's the way it is.
When we were little, we didn't run around.
While a person ate, we sat down.

The importance of acting appropriately, especially around elders, emerged in almost every conversation pertaining to Kaska linguistic and cultural practices. Such statements not only were educational but underscored elders' authoritative role within the community. Their own narratives legitimated their authority. As Martha noted above, "Dene cho' dẹ gudeji yagháde dene meyudíha. I guts'įh how many years yagháde dene gudíha long time ago, eh? (*Elders tell stories so that a person can learn. From this, so many years from now people will have knowledge from long time ago, eh?*)." Their knowledge of traditional practices emerged as a form of specialized knowledge, acquired by elders from their elders. This knowledge now included the Kaska language. Having resulted from the process of language shift, the specialized nature of this linguistic knowledge was reinforced by both the growing generational differences in language use and the institutionalization of aboriginal languages. While an index of a Kaska speaker, Kaska language practices were becoming socially (re)construed as indexical of a social difference, of a hierarchical difference.

Disjuncture: Endangered Languages as Specialized Knowledge

The influx of non-native peoples into the Yukon initiated a series of ruptures threatening the economic and cultural survival of its indigenous peoples and established an ideological marginalization of Yukon "Indianness" within the Canadian political sphere. This ideological marginalization has had a devastating impact on aboriginal languages, pushing them into endangerment. The assimilationist policies of the Canadian government, spurred by still-persisting popular representations of aboriginal peoples as childlike and savage, were enacted most successfully through residential schooling in the Yukon, which quickly relegated the local languages to passive language status. However, since the 1970s, encouraged by the federal policy of reconciliation and empowered by land claims settlements and self-governing agreements, language revitalization and aboriginal languages themselves have been firmly institutionalized across the territory. Today much programming exists that provides educational opportunities for learners, economic opportunities for speakers, and an ideological demarginalization of aboriginal languages themselves.

An important aspect of this demarginalization has been the revaluation of elders and their knowledge in the linguistic marketplace. Ironically, this valuation reinforced a linguistic stratification emerging in relation to the ongoing language shift, indirectly indexing the link between the Kaska language and the practices of elders. Through it, the Kaska language itself has become a form of specialized knowledge, removing the aboriginal language further still from everyday communicative events.

This sociolinguistic disjuncture surfaces as a linguistic discontinuity between generations and as a hierarchization of languages, with Kaska emerging as the language of elders (Meek 2007). This hierarchization is sociolinguistically contradictory for language revitalization, because it ideologically privileges particular speakers rather than encouraging all possible speakers. In other endangered-language situations, such hierarchization may work in tandem with feelings of shame, incompetence, or shyness, further discouraging other, usually younger, potential speakers from conversing in the endangered language. For Kaska, the social and generational sociolinguistic differentiations are but two disjunctures influencing Kaska language revitalization. Ideologies of interaction and the regimentation of language practices in classrooms also play a part in mediating the transformation of an endangered sociolinguistic landscape, as we shall see in chapter 3. Before moving on to the classroom, the next chapter orients this ethnography theoretically, in relation to the literature on language endangerment and revitalization and the concept of disjuncture.

Endangered Languages and the Process of Language Revitalization

Loss and revitalization have become enduring themes for indigenous communities around the world. In native North America the loss is articulated through discourses on language. Loss stems from a forced assimilation that targeted indigenous languages through institutionalized education. Such colonial practices severely altered the sociolinguistic landscape. While historically American Indian languages were acquired in the home, and dominant languages were learned at school, today in situations of language revitalization, with minor exceptions, the reverse is true; dominant languages are being acquired at home, and endangered languages are being learned at school. Such shifts in the sociolinguistic landscape are changing the ways in which people communicate and experience endangered indigenous languages. Revitalization became a central theme as assimilation was replaced by government support for indigenous languages. Unfortunately, even with this support, language revitalization has proved to be a difficult endeavor. For various reasons, articulated in the literature, language revitalization projects seldom realize their ultimate goal: to create new (first language) speakers. Clearly, endangerment is not simply a result of past assimilation projects; today's atmosphere of multiculturalism and aboriginal rights is equally a path for the ongoing march toward language death. To interrupt this march, it is necessary to understand language revitalization challenges not in terms of failure and success, but as a function of contemporary sociolinguistic landscapes. We need to ask in what ways current social practices and ideologies reinforce, rather than prevent or reverse, indigenous language loss.

Language endangerment and revitalization need to be analyzed in relation to the sociolinguistic practices and beliefs that affect change, construed more generally as intentional processes of social transformation. As such, an intricate analysis of the social practices, beliefs, and contexts through which language and ideologies of language emerge and through which these practices and contexts are defined furthers our understanding of language shift overall. Much of the language revitalization literature has centered on language-specific analyses of the grammatical elements that undergo shift in language endangerment and on minority language situations, and related research offers educational and technical guides for doing language revitalization. Such scholarship has not extensively addressed the role of the social environment. This book elaborates on the social complexities of language shift by focusing on the disjunctures affecting the process of language revitalization.

Language Endangerment and Revitalization

In 1992 Michael Krauss, a prominent linguist working at the Alaska Native Language Center, forecasted that over 4,000 of the world's languages would disappear by the end of the twenty-first century (Krauss 1992; see also Robins and Uhlenbeck 1991; Wurm 1991; Zepeda and Hill 1991). Concerned with such a dire prognosis and its implications, linguists became more concerned with language endangerment and revitalization, resulting in a substantial increase in scholarship (Grenoble and Whaley 1998) and publicity.[1] This increase in publicity, with the goal of raising public support, is reflected in current radio programming, such as "Watch Your Language" on *Worldview*, Chicago Public Radio in September 2006; articles in popular magazines, such as the *New Yorker*'s article on the last native speaker of Eyak (Elizabeth Kolber, June 6, 2005); or Walter Benn Michaels's reflection on language shift in the *New York Times* (October 1, 2006); as well as more popular books, such as Mark Abley's *Spoken Here: Travels among Threatened Languages* (2003). Also increasing are the scholarly books, reflecting a range of perspectives from language maintenance and language death (Bradley and Bradley 2002; Crystal 2000; Dalby 2003; Janse and Tol 2000; Leap 1981a; Nettle and Romaine 2000; see also Dorian 1989), to language revitalization (Fishman 2001; Grenoble and Whaley 2006; Hinton 2002; Hinton and Hale 2001; Leap 1981b; Reyhner 1997; Tsunoda 2005; see also Fishman 1991). Other related terms found in the literature include language shift, language loss, language re-creation or reclamation, language rehabilitation, language preservation, language obsolescence, and language extinction.[2]

Within this literature, two themes or questions predominate: Why should we care that languages are dying? What steps can be taken, and what are the complexities involved in saving endangered languages?

The first question has been addressed by much of the scholarly and popular literature, with answers articulating—or lamenting (Moore 2006)—particular aspects of loss, from a loss of knowledge and diversity (for example, Hale 1998; Maffi 2001; see also Hale et al. 1992) to a loss of "the opportunity to appreciate the full creative capacities of the human mind" (Mithun 1998:189) and a violation of human rights (Skutnabb-Kangas and Phillipson 1994). To further underscore the direness of language endangerment for a broader audience, expressions of loss and urgency often include rhetorical themes of enumeration, valorization, and ownership (Hill 2002; see also Errington 2003). As I discuss in chapter 4, these themes are usefully deployed in bureaucratic rhetoric to justify resource allocations for aboriginal language revitalization in the Yukon Territory, Canada. The question itself encourages such articulations, because of the contexts within which it is posed. It requires those concerned with language endangerment to validate their concerns through a practical and moral framing familiar to a general ("western") audience, forcing the audience to buy into a common ideological ground with the government.

With respect to the second question, several factors have been discovered that complicate the undertaking of language revitalization, the ideal goal of which is the production of new first-language speakers. Few language revitalization projects have achieved this result. In Dorian (1989), a range of case studies is presented and compared, highlighting factors such as social context, geographic location, language contact and interference, the range of speaker fluency and the number of speakers, types of language death, and patterns of grammatical change across endangered language situations. Fishman (1991) identifies stages of shift in relation to media, the attitudes of people, degrees of linguistic competence and performance, and the sociocultural context, especially hierarchical dimensions. Adding to this earlier literature, many of the chapters in Grenoble and Whaley (1998) emphasize the social and ideological dimensions of language endangerment. While this research programmatically emphasizes "the sociocultural dimensions of endangered language contexts," "sociocultural" typically refers to large-scale, macrosociological settings. Precious little of this research engages directly with local political, economic, and ideological dimensions. Some authors state explicitly that they are not going to undertake an analysis of the ideological dimensions but acknowledge the importance of doing so and incorporate such dimensions into their programmatic frameworks.

Most recently, in their guide to language revitalization, Grenoble and Whaley (2006) discuss nine factors enumerated in UNESCO (2003) for the assessment of a language's vitality in order to develop successful language revitalization practices. The factors are the following (Grenoble and Whaley 2006:4):

Factor 1: Intergenerational transmission
Factor 2: Absolute number of speakers
Factor 3: Proportion of speakers within the total population
Factor 4: Trends in existing language domains
Factor 5: Response to new domains and media
Factor 6: Materials for language education and literacy
Factor 7: Governmental and institutional language policies, including official status and use
Factor 8: Community members' attitudes toward their own language
Factor 9: Amount and quality of documentation

Successful revitalization, as indicated by these factors, is dependent upon speakers (1–3), sociolinguistic practices (1, 4, 5), materials (5, 6, 9), and support (7, 8), and unsurprisingly these factors will move in and out of our analytic purview. All of these factors, especially in terms of domains of practice, affect and reflect aspects of language socialization.

In terms of strategies, various types of assessment, resources, media/technology, literacy practices, educational contexts, and teacher training are all significant components of language revitalization (Grenoble and Whaley 2006). The roles and involvement of "community-external" and "community-internal" participants are an additional consideration, along with attention to people's attitudes. Within and across each of these components, potential problems exist. People may disagree on the applicability of writing, texts, and literacy. For some, such practices may be antithetical to local language ideologies that promote orality as the primary method for maintaining or revitalizing a language (Brandt 1982; Pecos and Blum-Martinez 2001; Sims 1998, 2005), while others support the development and use of literacy materials as an integral part of indigenous language education (for example, Charles 2005; Hinton and Hale 2001; Hornberger 1997; McCarty 2002; Meek and Messing 2007; Morgan 2005). The creation of written materials has its own challenges, from determining effective dictionary entries (especially for verb forms in polysynthetic languages, such as Athabaskan languages) (Munro 2002) to standardizing an orthography (Rice and Saxon 2002), which again involves a range of concerns, from which symbols to use to which linguistic varieties (dialects) to represent. Within either existing or emerging educational contexts—which may or may not include literacy and writing practices—arises the issue of training, not only for the instructor but any person involved in curriculum development. As linguists are well aware, an ability to document and analyze the grammar of an endangered language variety does not necessarily transition into an ability to design curriculum even though linguists are often called upon to create or to assist in the creation of indigenous language education curricula. As indicated throughout the literature on language revitalization, there are numerous potential pitfalls. Amidst these pitfalls, a few cases of successful language revitalization have been reported (Maori, Hawai'ian, and Hebrew). Some of the factors contributing to their success, as noted above, are numbers and proportion of speakers, positive responses to new domains and use of new materials across domains, and support—political, material, and ideological. Additionally, linguistic homogeneity (as in only one indigenous language to revive) and isolation (both geographic and social) have facilitated the success of these language revitalization cases (see Hinton 2003). Thus, we would predict that the likelihood of success would be greatly increased were many or most of these factors realized.

The Kaska language situation is an apt language revitalization situation for examining more closely these factors. The number and proportion of Kaska speakers (factors two and three) are substantial. Between 30 and 50 percent of the people living in the First Nations neighborhoods in Watson Lake acquired Kaska as their first language, retain knowledge of the language, and use the language interactionally in everyday contexts (see chap. 2). The sociolinguistic situation is fairly uniform, with English and Kaska being the primary languages used in the Watson Lake area. In relation to other local aboriginal languages, the other territorial languages—with the exception of Tlingit—are Northern Athabaskan languages [Mithun 1999:347]), and all of these aboriginal languages are categorized within the Athabaskan-Eyak-Tlingit language family (Mithun 1999:347). Outside of the Yukon Territory, other Athabaskan varieties are prevalent and still in use, such as Slave in Alberta (Patrick Moore, pers. comm.). Along with linguistic or grammatical uniformity, First Nations people tend to live in the same neighborhoods ("Indian settlements"). Locally, they are physically and socially isolated, a condition reinforced geographically by the remoteness of the Yukon Territory itself.

Domains of practice (factors four through six) are fluid in the sense that people can be overheard speaking Kaska at the grocery store, while dining at the Chinese restaurant, in their homes, or out at their cabins.

Furthermore, domains have increased due to the establishment of new language policies and programming (see chap. 1) that led to the creation of texts, an aboriginal language curriculum, and radio and television programming (see chaps. 3 and 4). While the Kaska language does not have a grammatical text equivalent to Keren Rice's *A Grammar of Slave* (1989), there exists a vast and growing scholarly literature on Athabaskan languages, including Kaska. In light of these positive factors, Kaska language revitalization should be successful, yet there are realistically no new first-language speakers. Is English really that insidious? Is bilingualism unimaginable? What is happening within and across domains such that Kaska language revitalization is as yet unrealized?

All of the language endangerment and revitalization scholarship by linguists provides significant insights into the linguistic process of language endangerment, loss, and revitalization, but in the end, as Michael Walsh succinctly pointed out, "what is clear is that the process is profoundly political" (2005:293). Missing from our understanding is a detailed investigation of the social, political, and ideological conditions that mediate the above factors and within which these linguistic and interactional changes are taking place.

The View from Linguistic Anthropology: Language Shift

Research by linguistic anthropologists on language shift and social transformation has complemented the technical linguistic literature on language endangerment. It has emphasized the social and cultural processes through which shift happens, focusing in particular on the construction of hierarchical roles and authority, their relationship to language practices, and the theoretical frameworks underpinning these practices (see, for example, Anderson 1998; Blot 2003; Collins 1998a, 1998b; Errington 1998; Gal 1979; Hill 1985, 1993; Hill and Hill 1986; House 2002; Jaffe 1999; Kroskrity 1993; Moore 1988, 2000; Patrick 2003; Scollon and Scollon 1979; Tsitsipis 1998; see also Heller and Martin-Jones 2001; Mufwene 2003, 2004). Most of this scholarship has focused on the interactional changes, social practices, histories, and ideological positions that underscore an indigenous language's shift toward loss. That is, the emphasis has been on the political-economic context, the hierarchization of languages, and the disempowerment of speakers in contact situations. With few exceptions (such as Jaffe's work on Corsican [1999]), this scholarship has approached shift unidirectionally toward loss and domination. It has been less positively concerned with the sociolinguistic conditions of endangered languages or varieties in relation to maintained elements and shifts toward growth and empowerment, however minimal.

With respect to endangered Native American languages, much of the recent research—while still reflecting dimensions of loss—has shown that various interactional or sociological elements are being maintained even though the grammar of historical expression has changed (see, for example, Anderson 1998; Field 2001; House 2002; Samuels 2001, 2004; see also Kroskrity and Field 2009). One example is Margaret Field's research on Navajo. In her 1998 dissertation, Field investigated the interactional practices of children and caregivers across various settings, showing that the same pragmatic practices were in use regardless of whether an adult or a child spoke Navajo or English. The differences in the interactions were at the level of the code; they were not pragmatic. Even though the children were shifting from speaking Navajo to speaking English, Field showed that language socializing practices preserved Navajo routines and pragmatic elements (see also Field 2001). Similarly, House (2002) reveals the ways in which a community-internal Navajo philosophical framework guides the pedagogical and curricular approaches developed for Diné College (formerly Navajo Community College). While many younger people, and students, may not be as competent in Navajo as older generations of speakers, they continue to be immersed in and educated through the tenets of SNBH (Sa'ąh naagháíí bik'eh hózhóón), a philosophy emphasizing balance and harmony. This trend is a more general pattern found in anthropological research on Native American identity—a person can be Native American without speaking his or her ancestral Native American language.

Thus, endangered language research in linguistics and language shift literature in anthropology have grappled with different aspects of the same dilemma. In linguistics, as Hinton (2003) has pointed out, language endangerment and revitalization research tends to overlook interactional practices and their preservation, instead focusing primarily on lexical and grammatical changes. In the anthropological literature on language shift, the predominant focus has been on the negative relationships between the ideological, historical, or institutional aspects of shift and linguistic practice. Bringing together and building on these literatures, the following chapters expand these foci by considering the multiplicity of perspectives and interactional practices within and beyond Kaska speakers, and the ways in which these sociolinguistic practices are mediated by and emerge out of other practices and ideologies. Each chapter grapples with the multifaceted dimensions of language revitalization by investigating particular domains of practice cross-generationally and cross-contextually, analyzing in particular the fluid ways in which different contexts and interpretive moments move between the recognition and empowerment of particular kinds of speaking bodies (and generations) and the diminishment, toward erasure, of others.

Language Revitalization as Socialization

Theoretically, language revitalization recognizes all generations of speakers, but categorizes them according to (endangered) language ability (see Krauss 1998 for example). Part of this categorization entails the recognition of those persons who will need to acquire the language in order for it to be reversed or reborn. The reversal or rebirth of a grammar or code is achieved through its renewed use by some community or network of speakers, especially by novice and child speakers. Thus, language revitalization is ultimately a process of language socialization because it involves the intentional socialization of new language speakers (including community-external researchers such as the author)—grammatically, interactionally, materially, politically, and so forth. It is also a process involving both continuity and change, maintaining (consistently or not) various elements, practices, or interpretations while transforming others.

Within linguistic anthropology and sociolinguistics, language socialization research addresses the question of change and continuity through investigations of the everyday practices through which (often) novice interlocutors acquire, maintain, and alter their social worlds (see Fader 2007; Field 1998a; Garrett 2000; Kulick 1992, 1993; Meek 2001; Mertz 1996, 2007; Moore 2004; Ochs 1988; Philips 1983; Pye 1988, 1992; Schecter and Bayley 2002; Schieffelin 1990; Scollon and Scollon 1979; Zentella 1997; see also Garrett and Baquedano-López 2002; Ochs and Schieffelin 1995; Schieffelin and Ochs 1986a, 1986b). While much anthropological investigation attends to the "results" of socialization, as in the habits of adults, language socialization research attends to the practices that scaffold these results—the habits of experts (the socializers) when interacting with novitiates (the socialized). Being intent on understanding the processes by which social knowledge is acquired, and the ways in which language facilitates this acquisition, means that this tradition of scholarship has always been concerned with processes of transformation and continuity, on change and reproduction. Language revitalization fits well within its purview.

The concept of language socialization covers two general ideas: (1) cultural socialization through language use and (2) language development (socialization) through linguistic practice, including everyday use as well as instructional and specialized uses. In their seminal monographs, Elinor Ochs (1988) and Bambi Schieffelin (1990) each addressed the role of the social environment in children's language development. Ochs focused her analysis on the grammatical development of children and the influence of the sociocultural environment on this development. For example, she showed that children's lack of use of the ergative marker in Samoan was not conditioned by their lack of grammatical knowledge (they had not acquired the form yet) but was conditioned by their social knowledge (they were not sanctioned to use it). Only those individuals in positions of authority (for example, men in fonos; cf. Duranti 1994) could legitimately use the ergative marker. On the other hand, Schieffelin focused her ethnographic investigation more centrally on the interactional and ideological elements socializing children into particular ways of interacting and relating to one another. For example, her research revealed a gendered dimension to the interactional styles performed by girls and boys at the encouragement of their caregivers. While girls were encouraged to be generous and to reciprocate, boys were instructed on how to make refusals and demands; they were being socialized to deploy different affective stances based on their genders. Both scholars emphasized the importance of social contexts in relation to the development of linguistic knowledge and language practices by novices.

Taking this a step further, Don Kulick (1992) explored a shifting bilingual situation where children were acquiring an indigenous language, Taiap, and a nonindigenous language, Tok Pisin, although Taiap was losing ground to Tok Pisin. He showed that in part this linguistic shift was happening because of the parents' own language behaviors (speaking Tok Pisin) and because they were unaware of the children's bilingualism (see also Kulick 1993). His research highlighted the relevance of a language socialization approach for understanding situations of language shift. His investigation illustrated Ochs and Schieffelin's observation that "grammatical development cannot be adequately accounted for without serious analysis of the social and cultural milieu of the language acquiring child" (1995:91; see also Ochs 1988:17, 129; Philips 1983:3–4; Schieffelin 1990:14; Schieffelin and Ochs 1986a:2; Ochs and Schieffelin 1984), or the language-developing learner. Given that language revitalization is often practiced and conceptualized around grammatical development, any serious analysis of the process of language revitalization crucially entails an examination of the social and cultural milieu of the language-acquiring person and language-practicing speaker, to elucidate the impact of different social factors on an endangered language's use as well as to show the impact of different patterns of use on the structuring of social contexts (cf. Ochs, Schegloff, and Thompson 1996).

To elucidate such relationships (between the linguistic and the socio-cultural), Michael Silverstein (1976, 1979) introduced and reformulated the concept of indexicality (see also Hanks 1999). His concept of indexicality and, more recently, his notion of indexical order (2003) allow for the inclusion of sociocultural constraints or conditions on the interpretation or analysis of a linguistic event, or utterance, and move the analysis beyond formal grammatical or semantic renderings to include both pragmatic presuppositions and ideological affectations. These concepts take into account the appropriateness and the effectiveness of sociolinguistic practices (Silverstein 2003:213–214). They extend—and demand—a sociolinguistic investigation of the situatedness of the communicative event and of its transformative impact. While much of the linguistic anthropological research acknowledges that linguistic forms and practices are both constitutive of and constituted by the contexts and ideologies through which form finds expression and can be rendered meaningful, minimal attention has been paid to the "duplex quality of language use" (Silverstein 2003:227). It is this "duplex quality"—the presupposed and the entailed, the taken-for-granted and the emergent, the code itself and contexts of use—that poses the ultimate challenge for language revitalization. The taken-for-granted can no longer be assumed, rendering the meaningfulness of interactions in an endangered language emergent at best and uninterpretable at worst for most interlocutors. Thus, language revitalization involves the reconstitution not only of some grammar, but of the indexical orders that link a grammar to a complex of meaning emergent through a world of experience. The partial reproduction or continuity of these worlds of experience becomes lost, erased, or forgotten when the indexical links are shattered; the emotional scars of residential schooling and assimilation fade, the significance of taboo practices becomes muted, ways of knowing are silenced. As endangered languages are reconstituted, so are the contexts within which they are used; the appropriateness and the effectiveness, intertwined, of such linguistic phenomena sustain infinite possibilities for both successful interaction and communicative collapse. The opportunity for contradiction abounds; but where might these contradictions reside?

Language Ideology and Disjuncture

Two theoretical avenues that speak to this question are language ideology and modernity, with a focus on disjuncture in particular. All situations of language endangerment and revitalization have points of discontinuity or contradiction, moments where practices and ideas about language diverge.

I call this phenomenon *sociolinguistic disjuncture* (cf. Foucault [1968] 1972; see also Appadurai 1996). Sociolinguistic disjunctures can appear between ideas and practices, between practices, or between ideas shared by a group or across groups—between indexical orders. They are not only the discontinuities apparent to individuals socialized into some "master narrative" (Daniel 2000) or the results of globalization and shifting "[macro]-scapes" (Appadurai 1996:33).[3] They are the everyday disruptions or inconsistencies that cause people to pause and reconsider a pronunciation, a word choice, an educational technique, or the punch line of a joke. An example of sociolinguistic disjuncture can be found in Silverstein's discussion of the conditions for using T or V (informal and formal second-person pronouns) when he notes that the form used "is never 'wrong'; it just breaks or resets a pattern of established pair-part usage (at the first-order of analysis), . . . as it invokes (makes relevant to the course of interaction) new identities or sociocultural aspects of participant and context" (2003:210). Such disjunctures create opportunities for resetting patterns, for reschematizing some system of semiotic value, for transforming everyday communicative practices and expectations. Identifiable through speech errors, practices inspiring verbal correction, or expressions of confusion, sociolinguistic disjunctures are most salient in such moments of awareness (cf. Silverstein [1981] 2001) and the ideologization of these moments.

Three semiotic processes identified by Irvine and Gal (2000; Gal and Irvine 1995) that may participate in the ideologization of these experiences, equating certain (kinds of) people with certain (kinds of) languages, and vice versa, are: iconization ("rhematization") (the isomorphic equating of one social type with one characteristic or practice, as with the ideology linking indigenous peoples with primitive, uncivilized behavior), "fractal recursivity" (the partial extension of an iconic relationship to another level or type of relationship, such that this primitive quality extends to evaluations of indigenous peoples' inability to speak [animal-like sounds] and to learn English [dysfluent, "severe linguistic inadequacy"]), and erasure (the omission or deletion of other aspects of some relationship, the negative counterpart to iconicity, exemplified by the non-acknowledgment of bilingualism and scholarly aptitude among indigenous peoples). Each of these processes narrows the interpretability and salience of different sociolinguistic phenomena; they constrain the ways in which people may conceptualize relationships between linguistic form and social practice (Irvine and Gal 2000:36). Not only do language ideologies come to signify through such semiotic processes (Woolard 1998:18–19), processes that relate ideas about language to other (often macrohistorical) social, political, and economic conditions (see chapters in Schieffelin, Woolard, and Kroskrity 1998; Kroskrity 2000), but language ideologies also gain significance through and are conditioned by the disjunctive interactions that inspire or evoke them—an interaction that inspires an interlocutor to discursively engage some semiotic process in his or her accounting of some linguistic event. (Said the Native American student to his professor, "Of course I'm going to write my dissertation in my native language—English.") During such interactions, the ordering or layering of signification may be (re)produced, the adumbration of meaning and interpretability may be transformed, or both. As later chapters illustrate, such semiotic processes mediate the ideologization of linguistic differentiation (and assimilation), flowing through the discourses and practices that are reconstituting the Kaska language.

Of further interest for research on language revitalization are the different interactional moments and linguistic experiences that both lead to and transform disjuncture. In this way, disjuncture creates opportunities for reconfiguring the social world through a raised awareness of the current configuration. Since language socialization, and socializing discourses generally, hinges on the maintenance and construction of various iterations of continuity, a crucial dimension of socialization is the identification of sociolinguistic disjunctures and their remediation, their "erasure." By examining the different interactions and linguistic conceptualizations involved in the transformation of an endangered linguistic landscape, the ways in which sociolinguistic disjunctures emerge and affect such transformations can be investigated. Language endangerment and revitalization in particular are significant processes for illustrating disjuncture, and ultimately transforming language ideologies, because of the conscious attention to language and linguistic practice that is found in these contexts.

Most importantly, sociolinguistic disjunctures impinge on or alter practices of language development and socialization, practices that are integral to the maintenance and survival of any language. *This means that language endangerment is not just a repercussion of colonial assimilationist tactics—it is an effect of contemporary sociolinguistic practices, ideologies, and disjunctures.* Through an investigation of the process of language revitalization, we can begin to understand where the difficulties, the disjunctures, arise and the ways in which they pertain to and are involved in language shift. That is, sociolinguistic disjunctures mediate and are mediated by practices of signification, resulting ultimately in both change and continuity.

An earlier study addressing the contradictions arising in relation to language shift is Jeffrey Anderson's (1998) ethnohistorical account of Northern Arapaho language shift. He illustrated in detail the multifaceted, complicated amalgam of views, situations, and particular histories and biographies related to Northern Arapaho language shift that resulted, perhaps inevitably, in contradiction. Anderson located these contradictions or disjunctures comparatively between: different histories of language (linguists, anthropologists, elders), different generations, different pedagogical and socialization practices, different pressures and concerns emanating from within the community (versus emanating from outside), different conceptions of knowledge and "ownership," and different conceptions of language and language varieties (Anderson 1998:81–82). He argued that conventional linguistic and anthropological models of language shift were unidimensional and univocal; they missed the multivocality of Native Americans, especially within their own communities, and the history of language shift within native communities, especially in relation to other sociocultural changes. He suggests that language shift is "shaped by contradictions generated in a particular contact history" and notes that "language shift need not be isolated from the other cultural changes or from ethnohistory, or confined to a single level of social forces, power, discourse, or interactive context. An ethnolinguistic approach can pay attention to the dialogue, argument, and parallax of indigenous and social scientific perspectives" (1998:103). The "parallax" of indigenous and social scientific perspectives is an integral part of Kaska language revitalization as well (see chaps. 4 and 5 in particular).

Another example of sociolinguistic disjuncture can be found in the ways in which linguistic practices are configured and reconfigured in relation to language ideologies (for example, House 2002; Jaffe 1999; Kroskrity 1998; Kulick 1992, 1993), such as the socializing narratives that influence children's use and conceptualization of community languages. Don Kulick's (1992) ethnographic account of language shift in a Papua New Guinean community of speakers of Taiap and Tok Pisin illustrates this phenomenon. In this case, Kulick shows that the ideological or conceptual framework already available to community members reframed the sociolinguistic landscape by associating Tok Pisin with certain positive cultural valuations such as masculinity, maturity, and modernity and linking Taiap, the indigenous language, with negative characteristics such as femininity, children, and backwardness (Kulick 1992:20). Because of this conceptual reframing, caregivers began intentionally and unintentionally to encourage the use of Tok Pisin over that of Taiap. From the adult point of view, children appeared to speak Tok Pisin more than Taiap. This research revealed that adult speakers attributed the linguistic shift—from Taiap to Tok Pisin—to child speakers, unaware of both the children's occasional use of Taiap as well as their own switches to Tok Pisin (Kulick 1992, 1993). The adults were unaware that they were socializing their children to choose Tok Pisin over Taiap as their primary language of communication. A disjuncture arose between practice and theory; adults theorized children's practices in contrast to their own, reinforcing the growing language shift by misrecognizing children's use of the ancestral language and erasing Taiap from children's imagined or perceived repertoires.

Another example of disjuncture pertains to the ways that indigenous languages fit into local systems of value. For example, the Tewa people of Arizona, living on the Hopi reservation, use only their ancestral language during religious kiva ceremonies (Kroskrity 1993, 1998) such that the Tewa variety of ceremonial speech functions "as a local model of linguistic prestige" (Kroskrity 1998:108). This model of linguistic prestige corresponds with a trifold ideology of "regulation by convention," "strict compartmentalization," and "indigenous purism," sentiments that support and strengthen Tewa language practices in general (Kroskrity 1998). While these sentiments have done much to maintain Tewa language use historically, current generations of speakers are shifting away from using Tewa as their primary language of communication (Kroskrity 1993). Such changes in conjunction with the conservative ideologies that work to maintain "stylistic consistency in a highly conventionalized liturgical speech level" (Kroskrity 1998:108) might result in the Tewa language, mundane or otherwise, becoming an esoteric code for private events. Such a change would work against the goals of language revitalization, because it would limit Tewa linguistic performance to Tewa ceremonial leaders. That is, the liturgical variety (and value) of the Tewa language would continue while replacing or erasing more mundane varieties of Tewa. Speaking Tewa would then emerge as a specialized practice restricted to those with specialized training.[4] The disjuncture for language revitalization in such a case appears in relation to the goal of language revitalization: to increase the number of speakers. People across the board, from linguists to indigenous community members, are conceptualizing the shifts in practice in relation to their particular theories, rather than changing their practices or shifting their theories. Other documented cases of aboriginal or indigenous language shift and endangerment also exemplify this predicament (see, for example, House 2002; Meek 2007; Moore 1988; Nevins 2004).

These examples of sociolinguistic disjuncture illustrate that the forces of language shift are not located only in the past, in oppressive boarding school practices, nor are they confined to aspects of public policy that still favor adoption of a majority language for all minority peoples. Attention to these components alone cannot fully account for the continuing slide of endangered languages. Instead we must focus on all (or several) aspects of the sociolinguistic environment, as a totalizing, holistic phenomenon that has both positive and negative effects, both intended and unintended consequences. Within the programs and policies themselves lie significant disjunctures that impede success such that by framing language loss as a sociolinguistic issue, we can begin to understand the ongoing transformation of indigenous language practices and the processes that perpetuate the decline of endangered languages. For this reason, anyone concerned with language endangerment and revitalization, and more generally minority languages and language shift, should also be concerned with the ways in which speakers are being socialized into and through particular experiences of sociolinguistic disjuncture.

Growing Up Endangered

It was late May. The snow had finally melted; the ground had firmed up, and driving the Al-Can Highway was no longer a harrowing, life-threatening experience, at least not until the tourists in their huge RVs would begin to arrive. The monthly Kaska language workshop was in progress, day three, and directionals were the topic of the day. Crowded into a smallish classroom at the high school, windows gazing eastward with sunshine streaming in, we waited for the session to begin. No children or teenagers were present yet, with one exception, a one-year-old who was babbling away next to her mother and grandmother. "Daa, daa, adaa," she said over and over again while sitting upright in her stroller smiling at everyone. This continued until finally her grandmother turned to her, and harshly said, "Yā endia? Łá̧ gudendéh! (What are you saying? You talk a lot/too much!) Yā endia? Łá̧ gudendéh!" then remarked to the rest of us that "she drives me crazy."

Along with expecting children to be quiet and attentive in the presence of adults, especially elders, some Kaska elders discouraged parents from conversing with their children until the children were considered old enough to understand. Unlike the "hardening" effect of talk on Kaluli children in Papua New Guinea (Schieffelin 1990), Kaska language socialization emphasizes taciturnity and the inappropriateness of very young children as conversational partners (Pye 1992; Scollon and Scollon 1979:187–189). Such different social expectations have different interactional consequences. For an indigenous language, the consequence may prove to be detrimental, particularly if utterances, especially children's utterances, are used to gauge a language's viability and the means to a language's survival.

Figure 3.1. The high school/Yukon College building and downtown Watson Lake area, near the "signpost forest." Photo by the author.

Shifting Socializing Contexts, Shifting Language

For endangered languages, the language that interlocutors choose and the manner in which they use that language vary predictably with age, as noted by Krauss (1998, 1996), Crawford (1991), and others. The most fluent speakers of indigenous heritage languages are typically the elders, the oldest living generations. What Krauss and others have explored less closely is how this linguistic distribution significantly relates to sociolinguistic practices. They recognize that minority populations must learn the dominant language to be economically competitive, educationally equal, and socially accepted within various dominant culture contexts. This partially accounts for the preference for using English over Kaska. However, the choice to speak Kaska is not merely a factor of age or ability but is influenced by other dimensions of the sociolinguistic landscape: ideologies of language, patterns of interaction, and individuals' social roles and status within their own communities. As the excerpt above illustrates, interactional conventions influence linguistic practices, constraining or encouraging some speakers. Such conventions will affect the ways in which language learning can and does happen, potentially resulting in a disjuncture. For Kaska language revitalization, a disjuncture between a theoretical tenet of socialization and a practical dimension of language development arises, because some Dene adults' beliefs about appropriateness contrast with children's and other learners' acquisitional needs. Even though Dene children, of course, do not always adhere to the socializing tenet of taciturnity, their opportunities to speak Kaska are constrained because they are discouraged from initiating conversations with adults and elders, those individuals who are the most competent speakers of Kaska (see chap. 1; see also Meek 2007).

On the other hand, classroom routines do interrupt this tenet to some extent, but interactions between Kaska language teachers and students are largely limited to scripted educational routines, influenced by institutional and noninstitutional conventions, and interpreted through local ideological frameworks. These routines lead to another sociolinguistic disjuncture, a disjuncture between styles of speaking. As exemplified below, children are taught a school style of Kaska, while adult interlocutors use a different style.[1] As with "baby talk" or "foreigner talk" (Ferguson 1964, 1971), some adults switch to a different style of Kaska when conversing with children. I did not discover an analogous switch by Dene adults when English was the predominant conversational code. Such a shift in style could also account for situations where older generations claim not to understand younger generations whose acquisition of the indigenous language was facilitated by classroom learning.

Thus, the focus of this chapter is on the sociolinguistic conventions mediating adult utterances across different language revitalization contexts in order to examine a fuller range of the elements affecting language learners' Kaska acquisition. While children and youth may not be acquiring the same grammatical knowledge of the Kaska language as adults (if any), they may, however, be experiencing and reproducing the social conventions and discourses that mediate such grammatical knowledge, evidenced in part by their practices among peers. These practices and conventions also affect the ways in which children have access to or opportunities to acquire linguistic knowledge of their heritage language at home, in the classroom, and elsewhere, practices that are further influenced by institutionalized educational conventions. Intertwined with the institutional conventions are familial expectations. Because the Kaska language teachers in the classrooms were also relatives and neighbors of most of the Dene students, we would expect school and nonschool interactional conventions to have moments of disjuncture and intersection, emerging as mutually constitutive along various axes of practice, and discordant along others. Nor would it be surprising to find that from the overlapping and blending of conventions is emerging a style of Kaska that differs from styles found elsewhere. The rest of this chapter explores the situations wherein people articulate elements of Kaska grammar resulting in the maintenance of certain communicative practices, the erasure of other elements, and the emergence of a new style.

The situations described below range from an evening at an elder's cabin with her family to Kaska language classes at AHS, the elementary school, and a Kaska language workshop. The focus on particular situational moments allows the incorporation of other semiotic modalities influencing adults' and children's practices and the ideologization of the Kaska language beyond that of real-time recordings. The descriptions depict real contexts, based on my field notes and tape recordings. However, in order to preserve participant privacy, some people's practices, and especially children's, are portrayed through a fictionalized account of everyday experiences. The point of this approach is to highlight the sociolinguistic elements of the different contexts that are a part of most Dene children's everyday experiences, while maintaining their anonymity.

Directing Language: Kaska Language and Socialization

Having ample time to sit and observe adult–child interactions at the Aboriginal Head Start during my eight months in residence there, as well as in homes I visited and lived, I noticed immediately the unaffected style that those parents, grandparents, teachers, and other adults used when addressing young children. Affective elements ("ooh," "aah," "ham," "ehehe") appeared most frequently as signals of encouragement, with little articulated elaboration beyond "very good," or "łáne etie." On the other hand, older children and adults often switched to a mock respect style of speech when playfully teasing younger children determinedly engaged in some adult activity, such as drumming. On several occasions, one of the more precocious preschoolers would "practice" drumming during playtime at AHS. While he drummed, some of the girls would dance, sing, or play hand games in accompaniment. His mother noted that he would do this at home as well, having received a smaller drum as encouragement for his budding talent (the usual-sized ones, around a foot in diameter, are used by Dene drummers at various social events). His determination and focus did not go unnoticed by either adoring elders and female relatives or skillful younger male drummers. The younger drummers would gently tease him by asking him questions, such as whether he could teach them to drum so well or make them a drum as nice as his own. While socially disjunctive in some ways, the playfulness of the interaction was marked by the interactional inversion of authority, by treating the youngster as an expert. Such teasing indexes the chronologically mediated schematization of interaction while also interrupting this chronological mediation. Such teasing routines also reinforce the pragmatic conventions mediating interaction and generally promote Dene practices (on Native American teasing, see Philips 1975; on indirectness, see Field 1998b; Rushforth 1985; Scollon and Scollon 1979). However, the teasing unfolded in English, not in Kaska.

Because of the grammatical form of expression, such routines are discontinuous with the process of revitalizing Kaska grammatical conventions, but socially they preserve particular interactional habits. Similar to Field's findings for Navajo (1998b, 2001) and Philips's observations at Warm Springs (1983), certain communicative, in this case pragmatic, elements are being maintained in spite of the overall language shift. Such findings suggest that other sociolinguistic elements are also being preserved in the face of language shift. Another pragmatic element present across such endangered language contexts is directives. Across school and nonschool contexts, directives in second-person (singular, dual, or plural) imperative form were typical Kaska expressions addressed to children. Not uncommon, an example from Field (1998a:84) illustrates the use of directives in Navajo and English between a parent and her child.

(3.1) Use of a Navajo directive in parent-child interaction

M: Ni Ronald, pick up all those toys, now
you.

R: Oh

M: Hurry up, pick (up) all those toys.

R: No.

M: Box biih naanijaah.
box into.it back. 2p.put.pl.objects
Put them back in the box.

R: Huh?

M: Box biih naanijaah.

R: No.

M: Nora, help your brother to put those toys back in the box.

As the mother switched between English and Navajo throughout this interaction, she maintained a referential and pragmatic parallelism between her utterances. Such translational pairing can be found throughout Kaska language learning contexts between speakers and learners. The Navajo utterances also underscored the imperativeness of her request. On occasion, directives in Kaska also carried a greater illocutionary force than those in English. I found this useful when accosted by a young man demanding a cigarette. I kept politely deflecting his request ("I'm sorry but I don't have any cigarettes") to no avail in English. Frustrated, I blurted out in Kaska "Ts'īk endúé!" which resulted in an apology as he shuffled away. An interesting grammatical dimension of directives illustrated in the Navajo exchange pertains to the verb stem. In this exchange and those I recorded and heard in Kaska, especially around children, handling verb forms were used, like *naanijaah* (put plural objects back) above. Kaska language teachers could be overheard saying, "Esyénhtsūs" (give me [that] clothlike object [piece of paper]) when telling a child to hand in his or her assignment, or "Meyénlē" (give her them [the crayons]), or "Nédé'én'á" (put it down [the ball]). For Athabaskan linguists, these verbs are a distinct and unique category of Athabaskan grammar (Axelrod 2000; Basso 1990; Carter 1976; Hoijer 1945; Poser 2005; K. Rice 1989; S. Rice 1998; Rushforth 1991; Willie 2000; Young and Morgan 1992), a distinction noted as well in the language lesson books for aboriginal languages in the Yukon. The fact that they are still an expressive part of the sociolinguistic landscape in spite of language shift deserves further inquiry.[2] From handling verbs to translation pairs, directives were a salient part of a language learner's socializing experience.

In describing various Northern Athabaskan groups' noninterventionist, individualistic approach to communication and learning, ethnographers have noted that directives, while expressed, are seldom elaborated; people are expected to observe and learn on their own without detailed instructions (Christian and Gardner 1977; Honigmann 1949; Scollon and Scollon 1979; Underwood and Honigmann 1947; VanStone 1963). Beyond translation, certain directives were not given further elaboration in Kaska language classrooms or at home. Elaboration happened during storytelling events. Such events taught children and others directly and indirectly about history, social values, cultural practices, and language. During such events, elders and older adults shared their own personal biographies, historical narratives, and more formal legends. These events also reflected their familial educational experiences growing up, of sitting and listening to their grand-parents and other elders "tell stories." However, when children were part of the audience, the narrative often addressed more explicitly the ways in which children and youth should behave, especially toward elders. In the following narrative, the elder switched between Kaska and English, using English to translate her Kaska statements as part of an effort to maintain the audience's (children's) attention and to facilitate comprehension. The ages of the children ranged from 1;6 to 5;6 years old (see Appendix B); Ileanna was 2;7 years old, Jason was 5;6 years old, Michael was 2;7 years old, John was 1;6 years old, Adam was 5;2 years old, Tina was 4;0 years old, Larry was 4;2, and Joy was 3;11 years old. This excerpt illustrates the instructional function of narrative and the unelaborated form of directives.

It had been about a month since the last "Elders' Day." Now, in mid-February, the children were getting restless from being indoors as the winter temperatures (−40 degrees) and the darkness persisted. To liven up the situation, Mrs. Adele Johnny had been invited to talk to the children, a group that included a couple of her own grandchildren. Armed with a cup of coffee brought to her by one of the teachers, and seated comfortably at the adult table, but with her chair angled toward the Circle Time rug, Mrs. Johnny was ready to face an active bunch of preschoolers. Given no top-ical·direction, Mrs. Johnny began talking in Kaska about her childhood.

(3.2) Interaction between two elders (Adele and Ann), two teachers (Bertha and Barb), and children during Elders' Day at AHS

1. Adele: Yā wǫ gudusdéh? są géhdi? Heh, heh.
           What did she say I should talk about? Heh, heh.

2. Ann: Her? ((referring to a teacher))

3. Adele: Ham.
           Yes.

4. Ann: Anything dah gudendéh, kul(a).
           Talk about anything, ready.

5. Adele: Łáné détséle kú, ts'édāne eslīni—
           When I was really small, (when) I was a child—

6. Ileanna: Hi.

7. Barb: Do you know what she said?(???)

8. Adele: When I was, long time ago when I was this, you know,
           little child ((banging of blocks and toys in background))

9.   Dene cho' den(e) dets'į́'į́' lén-łéndedé͗'li, e ts'édāne ts'édān(e)
When adults people came together, the children children

10.   kḗnéht'éde kēndzeht'ē
everyone (all of us) we did like this
((children sitting in semicircle around Adele))
((noise of toys being dumped out of bin))

11.   Ełígé', ełígé' (:02). ełígé'one place dene nédzédēts'i'. Guchō
(in) one, one, (:02) one one place people, we all sat, our parents

12.   négúdúdḗhí, ts'édāne nḗgédéts'ek la.
they would be talking (while) we listened.

13.   Dułą́, dułą́' kádzéntąh.
We didn't play around at all.

14. Barb: You didn't play?

15. Adele: Mhm

16. Barb: Did you hear that? ((to children)) When she was little,
she didn't play, like what you've been doing all day long,

17.   ask her what she did.

Adele began her narrative emphasizing the importance of sitting and listening, rather than playing, when adults came together and talked. In an attempt to maintain an uninterrupted narrative flow, I attempted to quell a potential disruption, only to have my English statements disrupt Adele's narration, resulting in Jason's brief control of the interaction.

18. Jason: I's a (???) later on

19. Barb: What do you think?

20. Jason: I falled off and bumped my ankle.

21. Barb: Yeah, but what do you think your grandparents did when
they were little?
If they didn't play, what do you think they did?

22. Jason: I was crazy.

23. Barb: Mmm.

24. Adam: Me too.

25. Barb: Yeah, you're both crazy, come on let's listen

Instructed to listen, yet still squirming, Jason and Adam redirected their attention to Mrs. Johnny. In the meantime, this interruption inspired other children to begin their own conversations, which prompted Adele to wonder whether she should just switch to English.

26. Adele: Yeah, maybe I should just talk to them in English; think so?

27.   Dułą́ négédéts'ek gēt'ē. ((to Ann))
It seems like they don't hear (understand).
((children talking in background, not paying attention))

28. Ann: Kę́giht'ē-la.
They are like that.
((Barb trying to get kids to pay attention))

29. Adele: Ī, Ī gádáscho de, etáne ēdests'es-seg'la, ī ī dédácho-já?
How old is he now?
That one, that one, when I was that big, I really listened (well), that one, that one, how old is he now? How old is he now?

30. Barb: How old are you?

31. Jason: Five.

32. Barb: Five.

A little frustrated but not yet deterred, Adele hooked the children's attention by indirectly asking a question that many children find reasonable, "How old are you?" and then incorporated one child's answer into the restarting of her narrative.

33. Adele: Kádáschode, kádáscho esjá dé, e, e, elígé' ts'édāne zǫ́ze súgésdí la,
When I was that big, when I was his age, I would be teaching that one little child,

34.   Ech'ele gutie súnessin ma' môma kį́hłay, kēsgúh kēsgúh ką́gut'ē la,
(and) I took good care of my younger brother (while) my mother worked, that's the way it was,

35.   dene k'éh.[3]
Indian way.

36. Ann: Mhm.

37. Adele: Ts'édāne dułą́ dułą́ kāgéntạh.
Children didn't didn't play.

38.   Łát'āde kāgéntạ̄h, kūla etie ts'édāne yéh kāgéntạ̄h de
Sometimes they played, when children were good they played.

A growing rumble began to emanate from the floor yet again, prompting me to interrupt the narrative once more in an attempt to regain the audience's attention.

39. Barb: Are you really listening? ((to children))

40. Jason: I'm five (???).

41. Barb: ((to Adele)) Do you want to explain what you said to them?

42. Adele: I said when I was five years old—

43. Bertha: Now listen, listen.

44. Adele: Jason.

45. Ann: Ēdénts'ek.
             Listen.

After several commands of "listen" in both English and Kaska, Adele's narrative started once more, but this time in English.

46. Adele: When I was five years old like um five years old like you already I had to learn to help help my mom and dad look after little little baby like that ((referring to the one-year-old child sitting near his brother, Jason)), we never play aroun' we, we had to help, we don't play aroun', sometimes we play aroun', we play aroun' with other— ((a child interrupts))

47.   Listen, sometimes we would play aroun' with other kids but um a lot of times when we were home we help our mom an' mom and dad look after the other kids, you hear? ((to children))

48.   Do you help your mom and dad look after your brother? ((to Jason)) hunh?

49. Michael: Mhm. ((He has a baby sibling at home.))

50. Adele: Do you?

51. Jason: I do.

52. Adele: You listen? ((to Ileanna, who nods yes))

53.   Good girl. Good girl.

Even using English the children were showing signs of distraction. To confront this, Adele changed her narrative style yet again to include more questions and addressed these questions directly to her audience.

54. Adele: Yeah, well, well, I was, well, I was taught to be respectful too, you know.

55. Den-denétsí(d)le wólé 'á, dene géhdī lā, dene cho' guts'į́h egudedéh, de' cho'.
Even young people are told to have respect, elders say this to us, adults.

56. Dulą́ deneyų́ késtān (???)guts'į́h łénde(h)déłí, ełą́ne dzedéhts'i, ts'édāne
We didn't (???) different people, strangers, when they come to (visit) us, we really sat (still), (us) children

57. When strangers come, when other people come to visit, ((child interrupts))

58. Well, um it's just out of respect for people, ((child screeches))

59. and (you) don't run around all over, (???) we have to sit down in one place and listen. ((child screeching))

Interrupted again, the teachers attempted to reengage the children in the event through indirect requests and direct orders to listen and sit down. Amidst the chaos, Adele attempted to curtail the uprise by continuing her narrative, noting that when she was young, children spoke only when questions were directly addressed to them. Otherwise, they were silent.

60. Bertha: Do you hear that? ((to children)) And did you talk while you were sitting down in one place? ((to Adele))

61. Adele: No. ((child still fussing))

62. Ann: Ēdénts'ek!
Listen!

63. Adele: The only, the only time we would uh maybe speak up was when they ask us questions, but uh no often they would the elders would just come and tell stories and we'd listen.
((all children become distracted, so we stop and try to get children paired up with adults))

64. Ann: Hey, Jason, senda'!
sit

65.   Okay, come on, senda'!
                    sit

66. Adele: Yeah, when we were little like you kids we don't we
             don't do—

67. Michael: Aaaah

With some order restored, Adele lectured the children on practices of
respect, including being quiet and listening when an adult talked to you.

68. Adele: We don't disobey, ya know, somebody tell you you
             gotta do something, we do it, even (???) everywhere;
             we say, kids, they have to learn how to be respectful to
             everything; you can't pull flowers; when somebody talk
             to you, gotta listen, ya hear?

69.   You listen to your grandma when she talks to you? ((to
             Joy))

70. Joy: Mhm

71. Ann: Joy, no.

72. Adele: Joy.

73. Joy: mm

74. Adele: Oh, that's good.
             When you grow up, that's how you got to teach your
             kids, you gonna have kids when you grow up?

75. Ann: Turn around babe, look at your grandma, she's //talking.//

76. Adele: //Oh yeah.//
             When you grow up you have to teach your kids what
             you learn when you're small, you've gotta learn every-
             thing you could about our ways
             ((some adjusting of kids and quieting))

77.   When I was little we used to live only in camps, we we
             never had house, we don't have running water, nothin',
             we travel aroun' with not skidoo, we travel aroun' with
             dog team, (it) was really good used to be, we used to
             have lotta dogs, they hi—they hitch up our dogs and
             we, me an' my brother we go inside the sled, they tie us
             in with big big feather blanket when we go wintertime,
             we, even, fifty sixty below we travel 'roun, yea', so it's

78. Ann: Don't mark the paper up. ((to Joy))

79. Barb: Michael, senda'.
            Michael, sit.

80. Ann: Ejú', déndén'á.
            Don't, bring it back.

Adele's narrative was interrupted one last time while the teachers tried to restore the audience's attention. John, a one-year-old, began to color on the table, and Joy, almost four years old, tried to carry the two-year-old Ileanna around the room.

81. Barb: (???)

82. Adele: John.

83. Barb: Look, you're teaching John to do things he shouldn't do. ((to Jason))

84. Ann: Entą́h! ((to Tina))
            Across from you!

85. Jason: Bla, bla they called me too, bla. ((to Barb))

86. Ann: John!

87. Jason: John, don't color the table.

88. Ann: Well, you started his way.

89. Barb: (???)

90. Tina: Sit. ((to Joy))

91. Barb: (???)

92. Ann: Hey, Joy, nédé'ênhtéh, sék'āde dénht'ā?
            Hey, Joy, put her down, what's wrong with you?

93. Ileanna: ((squeaking))

94. Ann: No. ((to Jason, coloring the table again))

95. Jason: Okay.

96. Joy: Coloring, géhdi.
            Coloring, they say.

97. Barb: Listen.

98. Jason: John.

A few more minutes passed while the children settled down and the narrative began once more, introduced by a child's question, "Is it finished now?" and the response "Endúé (not yet)." By this point, Adele had resolved to finish her narrative in English:

> 99. When I was really small (we picked) grass by the shore, we pull it out and clean out the roots, and we use the roots for hair and dress up doll. We dress up and make legs and arms out of the—um—the grassy part, and we use the roots for hair, and we used to sew a little for the—for our little grass dolls or we make 'em swings, we have lot of swings, we used two swings for babies, small babies, that's um that's how we used to babysit.

The exchange began with both elders, Adele and Ann, speaking to each other in Kaska. Adele initiated the interaction by asking Ann what Barb had said she should talk about (line 1). Ann replied using Kaska followed by the beginning, in Kaska, of Adele's narrative about her childhood. English interspersed her narrative, providing translations or summaries of her statements in Kaska. For example, in line 8 Adele translated into English the historical nature of her narrative and applicability to her immediate audience, and then continued in Kaska (lines 9–13). During conventional storytelling events where the audience is composed primarily of older children and adults, English phrases frequently filter in and out of the narratives (see Moore 2002). However, when addressing children, the switches are often used to attract, maintain, or restore the children's attention. In this case, the children Jason and Adam began to lose interest quite early (lines 18–24). So in line 26, Adele asked Barb and Ann if she should speak English rather than Kaska, with side commentary to Ann in Kaska (line 27) about the children's ability to listen and to understand. Responding in Kaska (line 28), Ann simply pointed out that these children "are like that." While Adele initially provided her narrative in Kaska followed by English translations, she eventually switched to English. Even then, however, the children displayed difficulty in being able to sit and attend to her narrative.

The pragmatic elements both articulated in the narrative (metapragmatically) and practiced as part of the narrative show that while directives may be instructionally or discursively impoverished in some way (though in context they are clearly interpretable such that the children sat and knew where to sit when directed), elders' narratives often enhance the instruction. For example, the directives "senda'" and "ēdénts'ek" entail requests for silence and attention, mediated by an ideology of respect. Adele's narrative articulates this expectation by describing her own behavior as a child, including how she and other children sat during such events. She also related these behaviors to the concept of respect. As the elders stated in chapter 1, children need to learn about respect and the concept of á'i, not just for their own health and well-being but for the community's. Learning about respect includes learning about interaction. And a respectful interaction between younger and older interlocutors is an interaction that is arbitrated by the older or oldest interlocutor. Disjunctures emerge when practices deviate from such conventions.

Each interruption in this narrative event indicates a disjuncture, a moment signaling adjustment. In such moments, practices are changed either in alignment with conventions or in their modification. The disruptions experienced above may have been interpreted in several ways, such as a sign of hunger, or fatigue, or particular seating configurations. The conventional explanation suggested by the adults' responses attributed these disruptions to the children's ability to comprehend. While the children's ages and their overall development complicate an analysis of the narrative event above in terms of the children's ability to comprehend Kaska, it is clear that elders often analyze these interruptions or children's inattention as reflective of the children's lack or loss of ability to comprehend Kaska rather than as reflective of the children's ages. The real-time disjunctures were ideologized in a socially cohesive way (language loss), but at the same time highlighted a generationally located disjuncture in linguistic practice—children don't understand Kaska, while adults do. The fact that elders' narratives often describe their educational experiences from their own childhood suggests that such remarks about the behavior and knowledge of these younger generations are also highlighting another disjuncture, one between the ways in which elders had been raised and current socialization practices; a disjuncture in social practice—as children "we" sat and listened, displaying respect to adults and elders, but today's children lack this knowledge. In what ways, then, are these disjunctures significant to the process of language revitalization? Or, more precisely, what aspects of these disjunctures and their ideologization affect linguistic practice in contexts of Kaska language development?

"Dene K'éh Gúdzededéh": Early Language Development and AHS

Preschool programs for indigenous students in Canada have concentrated on preparing students for the transition from home life into institutionally controlled primary school environments. Historically, state-sponsored

early childhood education programs targeted underprivileged populations, including aboriginal groups, with the goal of helping these children
assimilate into mainstream society successfully. The programs focused on
aboriginal populations have shifted from assimilationist and then integra-
tive to community-oriented indigenously based models (Goulet, Dressyman-
Lavallee, and McCleod 2001; Howe 2000; Prochner 2000, 2004; see also
McCarty 2002, 2005). Sometimes described as interventions (e.g., Aboriginal Head Start [hereafter AHS] 1998), these early childhood education
programs emphasized the involvement of aboriginal peoples, as volunteers
or employees in the programs and as cultural and pedagogical consultants.
The Canadian Aboriginal Head Start program in particular states this
explicitly as part of its program principles:

> Aboriginal Head Start will . . . :
>   3. support parents and guardians as the primary teachers and care-
>   givers of their children;
>   4. empower parents to play a major part in planning, developing,
>   operating and evaluating the project;
>   5. recognize and support the role of the extended family in teach-
>   ing and caring for Aboriginal children;
>   6. include the broader Aboriginal community as part of the proj-
>   ect throughout all of its stages, from planning to evaluation.
>   (AHS 1998:10)

The primary goal of this is to "demonstrate that locally controlled and
designed early intervention strategies can provide Aboriginal preschool
children in urban and northern settings with a positive sense of themselves,
a desire for learning and opportunities to develop fully and successfully as
young people" (AHS 1998:9).

Underarticulated in this passage are the ways in which young children's
success will be evaluated and, more tacitly yet, the conventional notions of
personhood that underwrite educational practices and expectations that
lead to success. Conceptions of success (and personhood) emerge in the
areas and topics covered in the curriculum, the "program components":
culture and language, education, health promotion, and nutrition. These
components focus on two areas: school readiness and healthful lifestyle.
One possible interpretation of success, then, would be a child who easily
adjusts to primary school, has an appreciation for his or her own heritage,
and does not develop late-onset diabetes. In terms of language, Aboriginal
Head Start programs vary greatly—an expected observation, given that
the curriculum is individualized; "Aboriginal Head Start projects will be

developed by local Aboriginal communities . . . [and] provide Aboriginal children with appropriate curriculum and resource materials and activities that focus on their spiritual, emotional, social, intellectual and physical development. . . ." (AHS 1998:27). The curriculum in particular emerges through the coordination of "Elders, cultural teachers, traditional and knowledgeable people in the design, development and delivery of the Project" (AHS 1998:23). Each project is locally designed and managed, resulting in a linguistically and culturally diverse range of AHS programs. While the primary language of instruction for most AHS programs is English, the 2000 Aboriginal Head Start review notes that across all of these programs "[a] total of thirty Aboriginal languages are used in the presence of the children" (AHS 2000:8). In 1998 and 1999, the Upper Liard Aboriginal Head Start program was no exception.

The morning begins with the Head Start director, Ms. Viola, carefully navigating the ruts and ridges of the neighborhood roads at Two Mile, Two and One-Half Mile, and Upper Liard in a pale blue Chevy minivan. At Upper Liard, having picked up most of the children already, Ms. Viola pulls into the last driveway, gets out of the minivan, and retrieves the penultimate student, Kianna, from the First Nations–owned brown split level. Once all are neatly tucked and seat-belted into the van, it lurches forward on a short jaunt to the preschool. As soon as the van arrives, the last student, Joy, appears on the preschool steps, eagerly waiting to enter. Living next door to the preschool has its advantages. The children clamber up the stairs into the building where they deposit their belongings—coats, bags, lunchboxes (for the kindergartners), and boots—shoving them into their cubbies and then racing through the hallway into the play room. Hanging in the hallway, the children speed past a poster stating, "Dene k'éh gúdzededéh" (We speak Kaska), the only Kaska script to be found in the building. In the playroom, some of the boys grab fire hats and coats, a few of the girls head for the play kitchen and a couple of the younger children attempt to climb up the colorful plastic play structure in order to go down the slide. Amidst the shrieking, the adults—I, the director, the Kaska language teacher, and the teaching assistant—move down the hallway where the director's office and the classroom with the circle carpet, books, stereo, and adult-size table and chairs are located. After setting our belongings down, I head back down the hallway, past the entrance, towards the kitchen to make some coffee for the adults.

At the time of this research, AHS was located in a building that had previously been used as a senior citizens home. Tucked away in an Upper Liard neighborhood, the AHS house had vinyl siding with a wood ramp and wood steps leading up to the door, a single-story construction with a full basement (see fig. 3.2). The children occupied the main floor only. The basement remained empty except for miscellaneous discarded furnishings and a washing machine and dryer, which the AHS staff used to clean dish towels and children's clothes when the occasional "accident" happened. The smell of smoked moose hide was always present. Behind the building were the remains of a partially constructed ice rink; beyond this was forest.

For the majority of the day, the children played and learned in two adjoining main-floor rooms. In one room, bookshelves and toy bins were located, as well as a table and chairs for the staff and a mini-stereo system on a nearby children's table. On one wall hung a construction-paper tree introducing the children (photos with names below). Another wall had a poster with pictures of the children playing at AHS. The second room housed a Little Tikes slide, a wooden clothes rack with dress-up items such as firefighting and police attire, and a kitchen play set, complete with microwave, dishwasher, and cordless telephone. Two children's tables with chairs were also located in this room, used at various times for play, snack time, and art activities. Decorating the walls in this room was the English alphabet. Another room, located across from the kitchen at the back of the building and next to the children's bathroom, held most of the art and craft supplies, including two easels for painting. This room displayed the children's drying artwork. As noted above, the only item displaying Kaska script was in the hallway, a poster stating "Dene k'éh gúdzededéh" (We speak Kaska). At AHS, children's exposure to the Kaska language was predominantly oral, an aspect of the indigenous pedagogy being realized through this program.

As expected, given the five components of the national AHS program, this Aboriginal Head Start program emphasized Kaska language and culture. To facilitate this, a part-time Kaska language instructor and a teaching assistant of Kaska descent were employed.[4] Occasionally, Kaska elders and other community members were invited to visit and speak to the children, another dimension of the AHS programming. The AHS language instructor was also one of the language instructors at Johnson Elementary, teaching part-time at both locations.

A typical day at AHS began around 8:30 a.m. and ended around 3:00 p.m. Most of the children were picked up by the AHS minivan, although some parents were expected to drop off their own children. Only children of Kaska descent attended, with the exception of the director's child, who visited when he was unable to attend his own day care in town. Upon arrival,

Figure 3.2. The building where the Aboriginal Head Start program was located during the author's initial research. Photos by Molly Malone.

the children usually had free-choice playtime, then they convened for Circle Time, where they discussed the weekly theme, such as color terms, animals, body parts, and so forth.

During Circle Time, Ms. Viola introduces the word "blue," and then goes around the circle, asking each child to say his or her name and favorite color. In the privileged spot next to her teacher, Kianna happily states her name and her favorite color, pink. Joy is next but is too busy chatting with the boy next to her to take notice. An abrupt reminder from Ms. Viola ("Joy, pay attention, it's your turn") redirects Joy's attention to the task at hand, and the circle of sharing continues. Following this sharing routine, Ms. Viola leads us in song, using our fingers to act out the lyrics, and then back to our theme and the identification of blue in our clothes. I'm the only one not wearing any blue. Next Ms. Viola sets out blue X's on the floor and a creative game of tag begins; Kianna rolls to an X while Joy crawls; some others are hopping. Almost everyone safely moves to a blue X, and the tagging continues.

Fifteen minutes of Kaska language followed these events. The language teacher, Mrs. Albert, held up flash cards (the same ones used at the elementary school) and identified the pictures in Kaska, and the children repeated the Kaska phrases after her. Unsurprisingly, Kaska language instruction at AHS followed the same model as that for the elementary school—flash cards and repetition. On the "blue" day, Mrs. Albert led the students in the following exercise.

(3.3) Flash card exercise at AHS
a. tū	water
b. t'u	milk
c. bēs	knife
d. suně	flour
e. gedā kēgé'	moose print
f. gah elígé'	one rabbit
g. sas lígédet'ē	two bears

Mrs. Albert held up the picture, named the picture twice, and then the children repeated her utterance. On occasion, a child would pipe up before Mrs. Albert, and he or she would be rewarded with applause and limited praise: "Boy, at least somebody's paying attention." The fifteen minutes up ("Kula'"), children either colored or played until snack time. On occasion, one of the staff would read a book to the children. After snack time, the teacher had the children do some kind of craft, such as painting. For the "blue" day, the children made blueberry muffins, which they later enjoyed with their lunch. After lunch, the children played outside or indoors.

Such unstructured activities created opportunities for pretending. As part of this play scenario, they frequently inhabited the roles and practices of their parents and other relatives. Like the little percussionist above who played his drum while the other children pretended to stick gamble, these children often re-created events and practices they observed elsewhere, including Dene practices and discourses.

It was finally temperate enough for playtime outside. With boots and jackets on, we exited through the back door and entered into the magical world of the outdoors. Birdseed littered the ground outside, attracting several feathered scavengers delighted by the feast. Inhabiting the role of "father," Michael decided to hunt these dzų́dze in order to provide food for his "family," composed of Joy, "the mother," and Kianna, "the child." Picking up a nearby stick, he delicately inched closer to his game. Both Joy and Kianna shrieked at Michael's actions, ordering him to stop so that they could feed the birds rather than scare them away. Abandoning his stick, Michael joined the girls in their activity, only to watch the birds, startled by the sudden crying of an infant from inside, take flight. "It's my edédz[r]," Michael remarked, to which Joy responded, "She should stop crying because of the bears. Babies are good bear food."

Such code-mixed pronouncements were not unusual, although the Kaska element was frequently a noun form, such as *edédzé* "younger sister." On more than one occasion at AHS and elsewhere, Michael used Kaska nouns. While I was looking at a book with four-year-old Joy and the nearly three-year-old Michael someone started crying in the other room. I asked out loud who was crying, and Michael responded, "My edédz[r]," referring again to his baby sister using the Kaska noun for "younger sister" (edédze) in conjunction with the English first-person singular possessive, "my." (The Kaska first-person singular possessive morpheme is es- or se-, depending on a speaker's dialect.) In conversation, he also referred to his aunt as *ené*. During the play session described above, Michael had begun singing and drumming, to which Joy and two-year-old Ileanna had responded by pretending to stick gamble and sing. When the girls stopped singing, Michael told them, "nénjen" (sing again), directing them to continue singing. Later he told one of the girls, "nén'á"(put it down), directing her to put down the toy she was holding—an object not in keeping with the stick-gambling scenario.

Simple picture-pointing games also inspired children to use Kaska words, whether in response to questioning or not. Along with efforts to improve my own Kaska pronunciation (and vocabulary), I spent many hours at AHS reviewing the language lessons with children, elaborating upon the images and elicited words, and developing or coordinating simple games that reinforced both the images and the words. In trying to assess some of the preschoolers' vocabulary, the language teacher and I created a picture-pointing task where a student would view three pictures, hear one utterance, and then identify the picture he or she thought most appropriate. For fun, however, I would play a similar game using only two pictures. Ashley (5;6 years old) and I had been playing such a game. Throughout our game, Ashley often changed the conversational focus (the task), usually prompted by one of the pictures presented to her. In this case, she was looking at a picture of mittens (lābāt) (the target picture) and a picture of snowshoes (āh), and obviously thought that my utterance corresponded with the picture of the snowshoes rather than the mittens.

(3.4) Interaction between Barb and Ashley

1. Barb: Are you ready? I'm gonna say another word.

2. Ashley: U:m

3. Barb: Lābāt

4. Ashley: [la:ba:h] ((repeating Barb's utterance))

5. Barb: Lābāt

6. Ashley: [la:ba:h] ((repeating Barb's utterance))

7. Barb: Look at both pictures carefully.

8. Ashley: 'kay, [ləbá:h].

9. Barb: Lābāt

10. Ashley: [ləba:h] ((repeating Barb's utterance))

11. Barb: What's that mean?

12. Ashley: That's uh boots. ((explaining picture of snowshoes))

13.   Go in there. ((indicating the coat room))

14. Barb: Yeah, what's lābāt mean, though?

15. Ashley: [ləba:h]?

16. Barb: Yeah, do you know what lābāt are?

17. Ashley: In snow, walkin' in the deep snow. ((talking about snow-shoes still))

18. Barb: That's what you use these for, right, how 'bout these?

19. Ashley: Mm.

20. Barb: What are these?

21.   Ashley (???) Mitts.

22. Barb: Yeah.

23. Ashley: I show you, more boots over in the other room.

24. Barb: Boots in the, well, how 'bout later? Let's finish playing our game.

25. Ashley: Mhm.

26. Barb: Do you like animals?

27. Ashley: Yeah.

28. Barb: //okay//

29. Ashley: //???// us a horsey, that's a gun, my grandpa shoot big, he shoot big guns.

After this last comment, Ashley returned to playing the game. The next two flash cards depicted a glass of water (tū) and a blanket (ts'édé').

30. Barb: Tū.

31. Ashley: [tu:]

32. Barb: Which one's tū?

33. Ashley: ((points to the picture of water))

34. Barb: Very good, what does it mean? Do you know what that means?

35. Ashley: One.

36. Barb: Tū, what is this a picture of?

37. Ashley: Water.

38. Barb: Very good, tū is water.
              Okay, here you go, whoops. ((handing Ashley the picture))

39. Ashley: I'm gonna stand up.

40. Barb: Okay, you can stand up, that sounds like a good idea.

41. Ashley: I see dzy̨dze. ((walking toward window))

42. Barb: //What?//

43. Ashley: //There's// dzy̨dze.

44. Barb: Where?

45. Ashley: I see 'im fly away.

46. Barb: Dzy̨dze?

47. Ashley: Mhm.

While framed by the picture-pointing event, Ashley spontaneously produced the Kaska word *dzy̨dze* (bird) in lines (41) and (43) upon seeing a crow outside the window. Even though the earlier dialogue suggests that she did not understand my Kaska utterance for "mittens," nor did she necessarily enjoy the game, her self-prompted articulation of the Kaska word for "bird" suggests that she was engaged in the interaction, perhaps just not the visual stimulation I provided. Children also produced colloquial Kaska expressions, mono- or disyllabic forms that were used as directives. At the year-end AHS picnic, John (1;10 years old) went around to the adults and elders present, offering them potato chips by holding up the bowl and saying "Ná'" (analogous to English "here"). Similarly, Michael used both *ná'* (here) and *dé'* (gimme) when either offering or requesting items. During a drive to Ross River, Michael's mother and grandmother reported that Michael said, "Pop dé'" when asking for the pop can that his mother had in the front seat of the truck.

Flash-card routines reinforced the lexemic focus of these sociolinguistic practices. And, beyond flash cards, the language teacher often elicited statements from the preschool students by demanding, "Say X," or querying "What's this?" in conjunction with other routinized interactions from the elementary school curriculum discussed below.

Having spent the first part of the hour observing Rose sew the top of a moccasin as she explained the items and tools necessary for beading, the children had begun, as usual, to grow restless during the Elders' Day visit. To reengage them, Ann, the Kaska language teacher and an elder herself, began to address the preschoolers directly, transforming their role in the event from passive observers to active participants. She accomplished this transformation by using some of the already-familiar Kaska classroom routines.

(3.5) Interaction at AHS between elders and students

20. Ann: Okay, enzį' dú yā?
       Okay, what's your name?

21. Flora: [sɛdni du:ya]

22. Ann: Say Flora gúye'.

23. Flora: Hunh?

24. Ann: I'm asking you what's your name, say Flora gúye'.

25. Flora: Flora [guya].

26. Ann: //mhm//

27. Rose: //mhm//

28. Ann: Neni hį́?
       And you?

29. Barb: Barb gúye'.

30. Ann: Etie.
       Good.

31.   Neni hį́? Enzį' dúyā?
       And you? What's your name?

32. Lisa: [???]

33. Ann: Lisa gúye'?

34.   Eszį' Ann gúye'. Dedi Elder Rose lāt'ā.
       My name is Ann. This is Elder Rose there.

35.   Say, say, [???].

36.   Say essū.
       Say grandma.

37. Flora: [Isu:]

38. Ann: Mhm, it means your grandma.

39. Lisa: [???]

40. Ann: Oh, good

41. Mrs. Rose, she sews, she's sewing beadwork, nēnehtsek.
   She's sewing.

42. Say nēnehtsek.

43. Flora: Nēnehtsek.
   She's sewing.

44. Ann: Ooh, lāne etie.
   Ooh, very good.

45. Neni hį? Say nēnehtsek.
   And you? Say she's sewing.

46. Lisa: unh, unh, unh

The children become distracted here. The exchange then resumes in the same manner:

55. Ann: Okay, say tāk'ātl.

56. Flora: [Ka:t'a:tɛl]

57. Ann: Means needle, you sew with needle

58. Tāk'ātl éh nēnehtsek.
   With a needle she's sewing.

59. With a needle she's sewing.

60. Tāk'ātl éh nēnehtsek, (???), kē'enhdi'.
   With a needle she's sewing (???), you say it like that.

61. Tāk'ātl.
   Needle.

62. Flora: [ta:k'a:tɛl]

63. Ann: Nēnehtsek, hadi.
   She's sewing, hurry.

64. Okay, kula. Mussi say.
   Okay, done. Thank you say.

With some embellishment, this style of interaction parallels that found in the public schools. For children, conversations in or emphasizing Kaska revolved around the identification of objects (or images) and repetition of adult utterances. Linguistically, children seldom, if ever, deviated from this routine. This lack of deviation suggests that children were learning to respond appropriately, to be competent students, but that they were not necessarily learning to speak Kaska. If so, the Kaska practices they were learning through these routines differed from the language practices of the language instructor and other elders when engaged in conversation.

To illustrate this difference, we can examine an exchange that took place between adult participants at a Kaska House of Language workshop. The morning had been spent documenting the Kaska language, including the various dialects represented by the participants, and developing literacy skills. The reward for our devoted attention, and attendance, that morning was the opportunity to scrape hair off a moose hide that afternoon. While such a task would require diligence, strength, and a sense of smell impervious to the unique fragrance emanating from the soaked hide, they also offered an occasion to mingle and chat with each other—ideally in Kaska. In the exchange below, the three women were critiquing a new federal law requiring the registration of guns and stipulating that they be carried unloaded with ammunition a designated distance from the firearm. (Eloise and Louise were elders; Cynthia was a younger woman.)

(3.6) Interaction between adults

1. Eloise: Géhdi la déndia.
   They say that you know.

2. Cynthia: Yeah, kēhgéhdi lā. ((agreeing))
   Yeah, they do say that.

3. Eloise: Already. únē élē they gonna take it away from us.
   guns already

4. Cynthia: I dēsgúh how you gonna sharpen it? (I) tell you.
   ((switch to talking about knife being used for shaving))

5. Louise: What that? Na'.
   Here.

(:08)

6. Eloise: Két'ē yéh dene ké(ge)díhts'ēh lā, Ī-i aghá' good.
   Like that with (hair) people sew, so with hair (it's) good,

7.   You see you gotta learn, one old man in Liard they
           say he get mean, you got to learn, you know, you
           gotta learn, you know, one guy from Pelly he act like
           (crazy man), what do you call that one, that big fat
           guy lā?

8. Louise: You mean that uh, uh—

9. Eloise: He tells anybody at meeting, "I want one wife, I want
              one."

10. Cynthia: (Dene Man) ?

11. Louise: //Yeah//

12. Eloise: //Yes// (Dene Man)

13. Louise: This one he tell me "how bony you are."
              I told him, "I don't want my belly. káhdácho," I tell him.
                                                        that big
              "Ené, what d'you say? what d'you say?"
              Auntie
              ((Other women laughing))
              Gee, number one crazy ol' man lāyédéssīn-ī.
                                                        I said about him.
              "Ets'égéts'į́', "Gee, I like this ets'égé'," éhdī.
              About the white lady, "Gee, I like this white lady," he said.

14. Eloise: Ezés kundzuhtl'ų́-hí (???).
              The hide, let's tie it up again (???).

15. Louise: Gukó, gét'ē dene āsādi kǫ' gúdét'in, azás téne'ōn a'seni.
              That's like our home, at home alone there are lots of skins there.

16. Eloise: (???)

17. Louise: Hǫ, kéndiyélí teyeli dechené' téne'ōn 'ah élé tēhtsįh.
              *Yes, he scrapes drum frames (and) there are even lots of snowshoes
              (there) that he made.*

Note that the exchange between these women is not formulaic like the
classroom exchanges between adults and children. The women seamlessly
shift conversational focus between discussing firearm restrictions to attending to the task at hand. Similar to learner-directed classroom exchanges,
the switches between English and Kaska exemplified by this exchange illustrate the nondisjunctive nature of these switches; they did not interrupt the
flow of conversation. The disjuncture appears between the interactional
style used by Kaska speakers with adults and the interactional style used
by Kaska speakers with learners. Constrained both by educational conventions and by social norms governing adult–child interactions, adults
conversed with preschool children in a highly routinized, grammatically

simplified style of Kaska. This same style of Kaska language interaction was not limited to preschool contexts.

Learning Kaska: Language, School, and Literacy

Tory rises early, at the sound of his alarm clock, and runs into his parents' room to check on his mother's state of wakefulness. Tory's mother tosses on a robe, quickly rouses the rest of the children, and heads toward the kitchen where a breakfast of Corn Pops and Fruit Loops will attract the children's attention. She hauls the cereal bowls down from the cupboard so the children don't have to climb on the counters to get them and then goes down the hall to check on their progress.

Tory is dressed and ready and off to the kitchen to stem his hunger pangs. His siblings are still attempting to dress themselves. He pours his cereal of choice, grabs the milk from the fridge, and plops down at the kitchen table with the cereal box for a good read. Soon his three siblings follow and the table is full. After reading up on the latest toy promotion on the back of the cereal box, Tory rinses out his cereal bowl and heads back to his room to gather up his school papers. In the meantime, his siblings all finish eating, and the youngest one plops down on the couch to enjoy early morning cartoons. Joining his youngest sibling in the living room, Tory sits down on the floor and tries to finish his math homework, while attempting discreetly to ask his mother questions until she realizes that he hasn't finished. She informs him that he will have to start his homework as soon as he arrives home after school, no playing. He frowns a little, puts away his papers and begins to put on his snow pants, boots, and parka for the frosty wait at the bus stop.

The entire morning is filled with English-centered images: the cereal box promoting the toy or movie du jour, the homework instructing the child in English to add and subtract, his mother's voice warning him of the consequences of not finishing his homework. The calendar on the wall is in English; the morning cartoons that his preschool sibling has decided to watch are in English; his mother's warnings for them to be quiet so as not to wake their father are all in hushes and English phrases. The bus driver is a monolingual English speaker, and Tory's siblings grumble their displeasure at the morning in English.

At 8:30 a.m. the doors open to let the students in from the freezing cold. Greeting them is a sign welcoming them to Johnson Elementary in English,

French, and Kaska. Kaska drums are displayed in a case below the sign. Over the stage in the gymnasium hangs the text of the Canadian anthem, with French and Kaska translations beside the English text. Further down the hallway are photos from a Kaska language and culture workshop decorating the wall and a map of the official aboriginal languages of the Yukon Territory. The children scatter to their individual classrooms, designated by grade. Outside of each room are hall-length benches with coathooks above and murals of children's artwork above those. One section displays children's descriptions of autumn in French, an assignment for the French class. They dump their coats and boots in their own personal space and head into their classrooms. Attendance is taken and the school day commences.

For Libby, Kaska class meets at 10:30 a.m. The class is a combined class of kindergartners and first graders. They file in and sit down in chairs arranged in a half circle facing a chalkboard and Mrs. Albert's adult-sized chair. Mrs. Albert, the Kaska language teacher, sits in front of them. To the left of her is a calendar with the month written in Kaska. On the far wall across from where she is sitting is a bulletin board. The left side has cards hung, each with a child's name on it; the middle section is blank, waiting for the next project; and the right side displays the children's artwork. Pictures of culturally appropriate objects decorate the classroom more than do Kaska words.

Mrs. Albert begins the lesson by going around the classroom of twenty and asking each child, "Enzí dū yā?" To which each child responds, "Eszí' (own name) gúyē." After each child takes a turn, Mrs. Albert directs the children's attention to some flash cards. The theme for this month is weather. Also depicted on the flash cards are two activities, fishing and berry picking, and words related to those activities. Mrs. Albert holds up a flash card (a simple sketch in black and white, produced by the Yukon Native Language Centre) and provides a Kaska phrase. The children in chorus repeat her utterance, but with varying degrees of phonological accuracy.

(3.7) Flash-card utterances
   a. nédādákhay   autumn   (lit., it's blowing)
   b. chǫ' nédetl'ít   rain is falling
   c. ā́ gúlīn   it's foggy
   d. ihts'ī néts'i'   wind it's windy
   e. k'os gúlīn   it's cloudy
   f. sā gúlīn   it's sunny
   g. gédéni   woman
   h. dene   man
   i. łūge   fish

j. gēs	salmon
k. dene tēhmíl detl'ų́	the man is setting a fishnet
l. gédéni dzídze nēbé'.	the woman is picking berries
m. eschul	rosehip(s)
n. dzídze	berries
o. gedā	moose

Following this exercise, Mrs. Albert presents two novel sentences for the students to repeat. Although all are still in a row facing Mrs. Albert, the chorus of voices begins to dwindle:

(3.2.2) Mrs. Albert's exercise
a. Mrs. Albert tēhmíl desetl'ūn.
   Mrs. Albert net has already set (something).
b. Mrs. Albert elígé' lūge sedlúh.
   Mrs. Albert one fish caught.

Fortunately, the activity shifts to the calendar. Mrs. Albert chooses one student—today it's Libby—to identify the day's date on the weather calendar, find the picture that represents the current weather conditions, and describe those conditions in Kaska. Libby produces the descriptive utterance "chǫ' nédetl'ít" (it's raining) and then places the picture of rain on the appropriate date. As Libby does this, some of the students begin to grow restless, prompting Mrs. Albert to order one particularly agitated student to behave: "Entl'á' kah senda'!" (Sit on your bum).

During the last ten minutes of class, Libby and the other students color pictures of a woman, a man, some berries, a cow moose, and a moose calf. Just before 11:00 a.m., they are all told to line up at the door, with greetings of "Engánustán-sį́" (I will see you$_{singular}$) and "Nehgánustán-sį́ (I will see you$_{plural}$) and go back to their kindergarten classroom. For Mrs. Albert, the rest of the day is filled with a steady stream of elementary students and the repetition of this same lesson in each class, beginning with a class of six third- and fourth-graders at 11:00, five second-graders at 11:30, broken up by an hour-long lunch, and then finishing with a 1:00 class of twenty kindergartners and a 1:30 class of five third- and fourth-graders.

Once Kaska class was over, the presence of the Kaska language within the school environment diminished to little or none. Even within the classroom, as is discernible from the description above, its presence was muted. From the students' chattering while they colored lesson-related pictures to requests for the hall pass, English conversations quickly replaced the opening ten minutes of Kaska language instruction. Teachers also had few opportunities within the classroom to engage in conversation in Kaska, whereas in other contexts, such as AHS or the workshops, adults who spoke or understood Kaska were usually present.

Instructionally, the lessons and techniques promoted yet constrained Kaska language learning. Socially, the opening organizational arrangement of the classroom maintained Kaska participatory conventions for children and youth (see Adele's statement on p. 63, lines 9–10) and tacitly reinforced practices of respect. The use of directives and adult-controlled interaction also adhered to Kaska social conventions. Linguistically, the flash-card drills and conventional dyadic routines encouraged language production while at the same time discouraging language development. Most of the students reported mastering the vocabulary introduced in kindergarten and first grade classes by the end of first grade. In simple picture-pointing tasks using the same flash cards, AHS students between the ages of two and five years old were able to identify the correct picture in relation to the word or phrase uttered. This result suggested that many of the elementary school students of Kaska ancestry knew this vocabulary even before entering the public school. On some occasions, Dene students produced Kaska utterances, ranging from a single lexical item to an entire phrase. On one of my volunteer days at the elementary school, I asked about a second-grader's absence. In response, another second-grader informed me that "Enid Whitehorse ts'į dahyā" (Enid had gone to Whitehorse). Given the unassessed competence of many of the students, the endless repetition of these same words and phrases eventually became tiresome for many of the students, such that by second or third grade, class sizes had dropped to five or six students, predominantly of Dene heritage. Explaining another student's choice to switch from the Kaska language class to the French one, one fourth-grader remarked, "He's not coming anymore because he's taking French, which he says gives him [a] better education, prepares him better for high school." She pointed out that in the French class students learned "new things" every year. The decline in enrollment and students' own statements reflect a sociolinguistic disjuncture in institutionalized instructional practices, especially between French, a "western" language with a well-established tradition of literacy, and Kaska language classes, an aboriginal language with emergent literacy practices.

In the classroom, Kaska language practices were mediated not only by the setting itself, an environment where English predominated, but by institutionalized conventions for aboriginal language instruction, reflected

Table 3.1. Time schedule by grade

Typical time allotments	
Grade	Time allotment
K	15 minutes
1–2	15 minutes
3–4	20 minutes
5–6	20 minutes
7 and up	20–30 minutes

in the recommendations of the aboriginal language teachers' curriculum guidebook entitled *Teaching Yukon Native Languages* (Bunn et al. 2003). For example, while noting that native language programs were a "valuable component of school curriculum," the guidebook recommended that native language classes be "short, yet frequent . . . , ideally held every school day," summed up as shown in table 3.1 (Bunn et al. 2003:N-7). The guidebook also advised aboriginal language teachers to switch to English when students were unresponsive, inattentive, or misbehaving. While switching to English seems intuitive, there is no evidence to suggest that the use of Kaska would be ineffective. Given that Kaska directives have been a successful linguistic device for maintaining control or redirecting attention in other situations (see above), and that the Kaska language teachers are fluent first-language speakers, the solution to inattention or misconduct is not necessarily to resort to English.

In contrast to aboriginal language instruction, French language programming in the Yukon Territory was more diverse, more developed, and better funded, with clear results. To illustrate, YTG announced in 2005 that more funding would be provided by the territorial government in support of language and literacy programming; $72,000 would be set aside to hire two full-time equivalent aboriginal language teachers, while $185,000 would be allocated for the late French immersion program in one elementary school (YTG 2005).[5] The French language program already had teachers and programs in every public school, from second-language classes to immersion programs, and one Francophone school. Even though French is an official federal language, the disparity between the financial support and resources allocated to second-language programming for French and that of territorially recognized aboriginal languages has been significant. Furthermore, the First Nations population was and is greater than the Francophone population, and the Yukon government recognizes equally French, English, and eight aboriginal languages (Harnum 1998). This economic privileging of French by the territorial government is somewhat surprising, given the territorial language policy and the fact that the aboriginal population is much larger than the Francophone population.[6] As a result, aboriginal language programs have been understaffed, underdeveloped, and underfunded. This predicament reinforced as well the emphasis on orality over that of literacy, because of the lack of funding to support the development and production of language curriculum materials, along with additional teacher training.

The focus of Kaska language curriculum in elementary education was on speaking rather than on reading or writing. The curriculum guidebook explicitly stated this in their introductory note on literacy (Bunn et al. 2003:N-8, my emphasis): "In school programs, . . . we have been emphasizing oral language teaching methods. Hearing and speaking are the first and most important steps in language acquisition. The introduction of written work will be taking place, *if at all*, in the higher grades only." Even at the high school level, literacy was deemphasized. Additionally, this section of the guidebook continues by noting that "[s]ome excellent materials *for adults* have been published" (Bunn et al. 2003: N-8, my emphasis), reinforcing the age-graded compartmentalization of literacy; reading and writing were for adults only.

Several explanations contribute to this seemingly unintuitive approach to aboriginal language literacy. The first is ideological; some community members of aboriginal descent expressed the attitude that their heritage languages should be taught orally, because in the past orality was the primary method used for acquiring linguistic and cultural knowledge. This sentiment filtered through several Yukon government publications: "Many times when I am teaching a lesson, a student will often ask me how to spell a word. . . . I could spell it but our methods stress mostly oral instruction" (quoted in Tlen 1986:36). It was also echoed in the conversations I had with some Dene people. As one of the First Nations women I spoke with noted, "Our language is an oral language; it should be taught that way."[7] While this sentiment discourages aboriginal language literacy among younger generations, literacy and documentation is a central part of the government-supported aboriginal language programs in the Yukon Territory, as reflected by the Web site for the Yukon Native Language Centre (YNLC):

Today the Centre staff is actively teaching, documenting, and promoting Yukon Native languages:

. . .

- YNLC *develops teaching and learning materials* for all the Yukon aboriginal languages. These include a curriculum guide, language lesson booklets and tapes, dictionaries and reference materials, and most recently a range of interactive computer materials such as Talking Books and a CD ROM devoted to Southern Tutchone place names and geography.

- YNLC works with First Nations Elders *to document* Yukon native traditions, oral history, personal names, and place names. YNLC also assists First Nations and other organizations with translations, transcriptions, and signage. (YNLC n.d.a; emphasis mine)

The Yukon Native Language Centre also trains and certifies aboriginal language teachers through the Native Language Teacher Training Program, which stresses literacy, and training native language speakers to write their languages has been a primary goal. Again literacy is being constructed as an appropriate practice or pursuit for those (First Nations) individuals who already speak an aboriginal language. During my fieldwork, YNLC-directed weeklong literacy workshops were commonplace. I never had the opportunity to participate in one of these workshops, because at that time only certified aboriginal language teachers and students in the Native Language Teacher Training Program were allowed to attend. All of this is to point out that people were not generally opposed to aboriginal language literacy; they were simply in support of refraining from teaching literacy skills to young students.

While a part of the pedagogical approach of the Centre and other public institutions, underemphasizing literacy skills in the school curriculum also had a practical side. Several of the aboriginal language teachers were uncomfortable writing their heritage languages. While not necessarily overtly proclaimed, their inhibitions underscored the statements of enthusiasm and encouragement they afforded me and other linguists. The teachers and elders with whom I worked encouraged me to learn how to read and write Kaska and frequently praised my writing skills; I had no inhibitions. Reinforcing my newly found expertise, elders and other adults would often ask me for the "correct" spelling of particular Kaska words, frequently words that had never been written down, documented, or standardized. (In return, they taught me to speak and understand Kaska.) So, even though the Centre devoted much time to training teachers to read and write their own aboriginal languages—one of their final projects being the creation of a booklet in their own language with an accompanying tape and textual translation into English, many teachers remained ill at ease with writing, preferring to teach their students through oral practice rather than written word. Their unease also indexes the recent emergence of aboriginal language literacy; very few words have been written down, and most speakers, including teachers, hesitate to participate in the written standardization of their aboriginal languages. Thus, the ideological proclivity to promote orality over literacy gained further reinforcement through the personal preferences of teachers, underscored by the fairly recent emergence of the systematization of writing Kaska.

The dichotomization of language practices along an oral–literate axis highlights several disjunctures. First, a disjuncture in practice between aboriginal language students and their teachers appeared; some students would like to have learned how to write the language, yet the teachers were uncomfortable with doing so. This disjuncture was aggravated by the strength and success of the French language curriculum. Another level of disjuncture emerged in relation to the historical differences between Kaska and French, between aboriginal educational conventions and "western" ones, and between "local" and "institutional" educational practices. This difference has led some community members to suggest that aboriginal language classes do not belong in public schools and to argue for an educational alternative as a way to resolve this disjuncture. A third sociolinguistic disjuncture arose in relation to the social conventions and the ideologization of learning. Emphasizing the acquisition of knowledge through narrative and observation rather than explicit instruction, assessment, and feedback, the experiences and conceptualization of learning of these elder aboriginal language teachers contradicted those of their training and the institution. The sociolinguistic distinction being maintained through the tacit awareness of these disjunctures was ultimately an aboriginal–"western" distinction, a covert mapping of western practices onto western languages, and nontransferable to aboriginal languages. While western and aboriginal conventions may be ideologically incongruous for some older generations, it would seem that the younger generations were beginning to reshape and dissolve this discontinuity.

One final disjuncture to be illustrated pertains to the different Kaska styles of speaking that are mediated by pragmatic and institutional conventions. The style of Kaska performed in school settings between aboriginal language teachers and students was becoming the style of Kaska performed between adults and children.

Kaska Interrupted: Language in the Home

The emergence and distinctiveness of a school variety of Kaska had been conditioned by several factors, such as the historical events and colonizing practices leading up to current linguistic discontinuities, the institutional goals and practices intended to encourage the revitalization of the Kaska language, and the interaction of social theories and linguistic practices within the community itself. As illustrated above, language practices in the Kaska language classrooms were influenced by the institutional context, the training of the Kaska language teachers, the audience, their competence as students, and the Kaska language curriculum, among other factors. The convergence of such factors within the public school had given rise to a style of Kaska that was different from the style of Kaska spoken among adults, and especially by elders. That this school-based style was being reinforced outside of the classroom was surprising.

School was not the only place where Kaska was spoken. Children and adolescents overheard Kaska conversations while watching television at home, while driving to Whitehorse for the weekend bingo game, and while roasting marshmallows at camp out in the bush. These conversations covered a range of topics and were performed in a range of genres, introducing novices to a vast array of linguistic knowledge not necessarily available to them in the school setting. On the other hand, these noninstitutional spaces continued to be dominated by English—Regis Philbin on television asking viewers if they want to be millionaires, the disc jockey on the radio prattling on about the Juno Awards and telling Mary to call George, who needs a ride to Whitehorse this weekend, and parents and peers out at camp switching between English and Kaska while chatting about jobs, children, and Friday night bingo, with an occasional query directed in Kaska to younger participants.

Evening: A Home Setting

Arriving home after school, George, a preteen, tosses his coat, bag, and boots by the door, grabs a microwaveable snack and juice box from the kitchen, and then plops in front of the television to watch cartoons. When his grandma arrives, they turn the channel to *Wheel of Fortune*, followed by Canadian Alex Trebek's game show, *Jeopardy*. Tonight George's grandma plays bingo, so they don't also watch *Who Wants to Be a Millionaire* on television. Instead, George's grandma drops him off at his cousin's house to play video games. Other than the occasional mumbled exclamation, very little conversation takes place between the two cousins. After bingo, George's grandma picks him up and takes him home. He stays up watching television for a bit and then heads off to bed, a twin located across the room from his grandparents' king. His grandparents' voices, a mix of Kaska and English, and the low rumble of the television set lull him to sleep.

Children's rooms tended to have few, if any, wall decorations. Some had plush toy animals, toy vehicles, dolls, books, dress-up items, and the like, but most children did not have a room full of toys and books. The local library loaned out both books and toys; children seemed to prefer the toys. Some families borrowed books, while others did not. In most of the homes I visited, books did not occupy much space, in children's rooms or elsewhere. According to some of the parents I spoke with, only a few parents read to their children at night. Bikes, skidoos, and computers played a much more prominent role in Dene children's lives. Although children and youth enjoyed the outdoors year-round, when indoors most preferred to play video games, watch satellite television, surf the Internet, or rent movies. Linguistically, all of these forms of entertainment were dominated by English. The potential exceptions were outdoor activities and activities involving elders. During these activities, children had the opportunity to listen to conversations in Kaska and to respond in Kaska themselves when addressed, but they predominantly spoke English.

In the home, Kaska language practices were not as strictly compartmentalized or regimented as they were in school settings. This freedom provided language learners with opportunities to practice Kaska. For example, children developed games involving Kaska words. One "game" simply emulated the teaching practices of the Kaska language classroom at school. Older children would ask younger children to identify objects in Kaska. When the younger child failed to do so, the older one supplied the appropriate Kaska word. Another "game" described to me by Trent, Mrs. Albert's grandson, who was ten years old at the time, involved using the Kaska language to establish peer control. I overheard this game one summer evening as I was walking over to Trent's aunt's home. A group of five children between the ages of nine and twelve years old were wandering around Two Mile and Two and One-Half Mile, boisterously laughing and teasing one another. Within this group, one youth appeared to be in charge, directing the course of their wandering. Another boy was attempting to challenge his authority, not physically but linguistically, using Kaska. According to Trent, each youth would take turns uttering a Kaska word or phrase, to which the others would respond by translating it into English. If none of the youth could translate the utterance, then the child to produce the uninterpretable Kaska phrase would become the leader. Elsewhere as well, children and youth frequently produced Kaska words and phrases. Young boys teasing their primary caregivers, often their fathers or grandfathers, would "order" them to behave, saying "Esséndli'" (Leave me alone), "Tsíni" (Be quiet), "Āná'" (Go away), or "Kulā" (Enough). Children and youth also code-mixed, replacing Kaska nouns with English ones. Remarking on their children's or grandchildren's utterances, adults would say "he knows the easy words" or "she knows the simple words," indicating the less morphologically complex word forms, and usually not verb words.

At a glance, this linguistic competence appears to be a cause for celebration, but is it really indicative of linguistic, and cultural, revitalization? Perhaps. At the very least, the language practices of the school were beginning to "bleed," or seep, into conversational domains beyond the school, especially simple question/answer dyads and translation pairs. Directives were being used, though not in ways paralleling the school context. This increase in use suggests that school efforts were having some net positive effect on Kaska language practices. They encouraged Kaska language use among children and adolescents and increased contexts for use.

Along with the institutional encouragement, most, if not all, Dene families were involved in some aspect of Kaska language revitalization. Every family had at least one (usually female) relative involved in a Kaska language project—as a consultant, teacher, teacher's aide, student, or translator. Some Dene families also had a copy of the Kaska language tapes produced by YNLC, which mirrored the routines and vocabulary emphasized in the school curriculum, and all children attended Kaska language classes their first year of elementary school. On several occasions across different families, I observed people invoking these as evidence of children's knowledge of Kaska and as a form of inclusion and accommodation. However, while the contexts of use expanded, few of these practices revealed an equivalent increase in grammatical complexity by language learners in relation to their ages or grades.

The interactional excerpt presented below illustrates this pattern. It also reveals the impact and role of the tape recorder. As noted in the preface, tape recorders were instruments to be used for educational purposes only; any other recording would be inappropriate. This meant that tape (and video) recordings were considered public, intended for distribution, and that the knowledge contained in the recordings should be disseminated or at least should facilitate dissemination. This conceptualization of recording and recordings also defined the recordable object as that which was communal, which meant that private or personal conversations were unsuitable objects for documentation. Again, the ideologization of media is an important consideration or factor in language revitalization. In the following excerpt, however, the recorded conversation leading up to the focal event was permissible, and it illustrates one way in which Kaska filtered into and out of interactions beyond the school classroom.

Two other potentially complicating factors in the following conversation are that one of the interlocutors was a Kaska language teacher and that I was present. While this might suggest that the resulting interaction is more indicative of the professional roles of these individuals than of the ways in which educational routines are shifting into everyday routines, the overall point remains: institutional practices are becoming part of (and could replace) everyday Kaska conversational routines. Given that the few remaining fluent and physically capable speakers are most often the people being recruited to teach in the schools, it is not surprising that the routines that compose a portion of their training have begun to infiltrate their interactional routines outside of the classroom. Additionally, this training creates a venue in which it is appropriate to converse with and encourage interaction from children. Otherwise, as the opening segment suggests, children and adolescents are expected to attend to adult conversations rather than to participate in them.

From Eht'út to Tl'ūł: Practicing Kaska in the Bush

It had been a long week in May, volunteering at AHS, visiting with people in the evenings, typing up verb charts, and attending a Kaska language workshop, all of which was punctuated by a funeral in Ross River that Saturday. Many of us were ready to escape the hectic urban lifestyle of Watson Lake and head out to the bush. It seemed like Mrs. Albert was always ready for such an escape. It seemingly takes Mrs. Albert only a matter of minutes to pack up everyone's belongings and food for a bush excursion. Extra blankets and bedding, bags of food, a duffle bag with clothes were all thrown into the bed of her pickup, and away we went. The ride down Campbell Highway, a primarily dirt road with touches of washboard, was always refreshing. Watching for moose, or grouse, or wolves while traveling gave additional meaning to these voyages. (If not the first question upon arrival somewhere, it was always the second one: did you see anything? The day before on our drive to Ross River, we spotted three moose, two black bear, three foxes, one beaver, and plenty of grouse and rabbits.) It was dusk when we headed out, making it difficult to spot anything that wasn't directly in the headlights. To pass the time, Mrs. Albert's grandson, Trent, began quizzing me: how do you say white? (dek'āle) lake? (men) mountain? (hés), and a litany of body-part and emotion vocabulary. I think I passed. Mrs. Albert's son, George, informed me that "coffee sedli' endān"—I was drinking cold coffee. The quiz had taken longer than I'd realized.

Arriving at the cabin, we began unloading the few items we had brought, including my tape recorder, my notebook, and some toys. While Mrs. Albert prepared supper, I began recording. Along with myself, Mrs. Albert, her adult son George, and her grandson Trent were her adult daughter (Sharon) and Sharon's two sons (Kent and Payne), with Mr. Albert in the background. Trent (10;11 years old) was older than Kent (5;4 years old).[8] One aim of recording that evening was to discover the ways in which Kaska was being used conversationally in noninstitutional contexts.

The recording reveals how Kaska utterances are distributed across interlocutors. As expected, Mrs. Albert used Kaska the most throughout the interaction, then Sharon and I, followed by Trent and Kent. Mr. Albert, George, and Payne (the three oldest males) were quiet throughout most of the interaction and peripheral to most of the exchange.

(3.9.a) Interaction among family members at their camp

1. Mrs. Albert: Nā yéhdia?   ((to daughter))
   What did she say?

2. Trent: What microphone? That microphone.

3. Sharon: //Boys, you can't speak like that.//

4. Barb: //See how it works.//

5. Trent: Yeah.

6. Sharon: Use big knife.

7. Trent: Where's the knife, then?

8. Sharon: Your uncle's, that big one over there.

(:04)

9. Mrs. Albert: Where did I put that knife?

The recorded interaction began with Mrs. Albert asking her daughter about what I had said. I had just turned on the tape recorder and was showing it to Trent (lines 2, 4, 5). At the same time, Sharon was reprimanding the boys (line 3) and directing Trent to help his grandmother cut up the meat for supper (lines 6–8). In line 1, Mrs. Albert used Kaska to ask her daughter a question, and then switched to English when addressing everyone (line 9). When her grandson asked questions, he used English (lines 2, 7). Her daughter also used English here. However, note that all of the daughter's utterances were directed at the children (lines 3, 6, 8), and not to her mother (Mrs. Albert).

In this next section of interaction, the daughter tried to get the children to sit down and speak Kaska.

(3.9.b) Interaction at camp (continued)

10. Sharon: Kent, don't bother the dog please, Kent. Kent bring your car and come speak Kaska.

11. Kent: Wait.   ((pots banging))

(:12)

12. Sharon: Kent, Kent, tell them tell them to be quiet then, in Kaska.

13. Kent: Quiet.

14. Sharon: Kaska, //how do you say it—//

15. George: //laughing//

16. Sharon: How you say it in Kaska?

17. Mrs. Albert: Say tsíni.

18. Sharon: He, he knows.

19. George: Shh he tell him.   ((aside to Barb))

20. Barb: How would you tell him to leave you alone if he was bugging you?

21. Kent: What?

22. Sharon: Essendli' say.

23. Kent: Essendli'.

Here the daughter (Kent's mother, Sharon) attempted to elicit a Kaska expression from her son in two ways. First, she used English directive and question forms to initiate the interaction for prompting a Kaska response (lines 10, 12, 16). Second, she provided the form to be translated, in this case "be quiet" (line 12). When the child did not provide the expected response (line 13), the grandmother joined the interaction, using a directive utterance to supply the child with the form requested (line 17). (Note that Mrs. Albert's directive corresponds with English syntax, "Say X," rather than Kaska syntax, "X éhdi"). In line 22, a directive utterance was used again to elicit the requested Kaska form; this time it was supplied by Kent's mother (note here that the word order corresponds with Kaska syntax, "X say"). Again, all of the utterances directed at Kent were in English. Only the elicited token was given in Kaska.

Continuing with the same recording, the conversation returned to a discussion about knives and to the dog Rita, rummaging through the garbage.

(3.9.c) Interaction at camp (continued)

28. Trent: Do you know where the knife is?

29. Mrs. Albert: Bēs ké'éndî?
            The knife, do you know where it is?

30. Sharon: That dog's in that garbage, Mom.

31. Mrs. Albert: Ná'.   ((handing knife to Trent))
            Here.

32.   Look what he do.   ((about the dog))

33. Trent: I'm starting to //cut meat//

34. Mrs. Albert: //mm my// cup (???)?

35. Barb: Oh, one of them's up over there.

36. Mrs. Albert: Oh, over there, etīn yéhdi.
              it's located, she said.

37. Trent: Oh, I know where the knife is.

(:08)

38. Trent: Is this here the garbage?

39. Barb: This the garbage?   ((to Sharon))

40. Sharon: Mhm, have you already put it in here?

41. Mrs. Albert: Ní'é' degé'!   ((to Rita))
           (Rita), stop!

42. Trent: Get out, Rita!   ((to Rita))

In this section, the grandmother switched back and forth between Kaska and English. Her utterances directed at her grandson (Trent) were in Kaska (lines 29, 31, 36), as well as the scolding directed at the dog (line 41).

However, both lines 29 and 36 were translations of previous English utterances (lines 28, 35/36). As shown, the other participants spoke English throughout the interaction. In particular, the daughter conversed with her mother (Mrs. Albert) using English (line 30). The grandson also used English when talking to his grandmother and to the dog. Opportunities to speak Kaska with the grandmother were declined.

After chasing the dog from the cooking area and carrying the last items from the truck, the interaction became a series of attempts to elicit a Kaska utterance from the children. As a result of this transition, the same expressions practiced in Kaska language classes were used, expressions familiar to the children enrolled in these classes and familiar to the adults as a mode of instruction.

(3.9.d) Interaction at camp (continued)

50. Sharon: Enzį' dúyā, Kent?
                Your name, what is it, Kent?

51. Barb: It sounds funny, though, to ask him his name and
                then say that.

52. Mrs. Albert: Say eszį' Kent gúye.
                Say my name, it's Kent.

53. Kent: ((quietly)) Kent gúye.

54. Sharon: Neni hį̄?   ((to Trent))
                And yours?

(:03)

55. Mrs. Albert: Enzį' dúyā?   ((to Trent))
                Your name, what is it?

56. Trent: Kent gúye.

Kent continued to be a hesitant participant in the exchange, even when his grandmother prompted him with the exact response (line 52). Trent produced a Kaska utterance, but not in response to his aunt's or grandmother's questions (lines 54–55). Instead he supplied his cousin, Kent, with the response, *Kent is my name* (line 56), responding to the initial question, *What's your name?* (line 50) as well as imitating his grandmother's utterance and participant role (line 52). In other words, Trent, the older child, was asserting himself as an authority over Kent, the younger child. In contrast to the earlier sections of interaction, here the daughter used Kaska in her attempts to elicit a Kaska response from her son (line 50) and her nephew, Trent (line 54).

Continuing the attempt to elicit Kaska utterances from the children, Sharon and I resorted to holding up objects (toys from my bag intended for use with the AHS students) and asking Kent and Trent to name them. This last attempt proved more successful in engaging the children than the previous attempts, but only after much laughing over my pronunciation of the Kaska phrase for "What is this?"

(3.9.e) Interaction at camp (continued)
((Barb holding up a puppet.))

66. Mrs. Albert: Destl'ede kēt'ē.
It's like a squirrel.

67. Trent: A cat?

68. Barb: Destl'ede?
Squirrel?

69. Trent: Uh, it's a squirrel.

70. Barb: Here, let's see all the rest of the things that I have, those are for little kids, hey?   ((to Trent))

71. Sharon: Kent, come look.

(:04)

72. Barb: Yā et'ā?
What is it?

(:08)

73. Barb: How would you call this?   ((holding up doll for Trent))

74. Trent: Ge-, I called the other one this.
((to Mrs. Albert))

75. Mrs. Albert: Which one?

76. Barb: Hm? Trent, how would you call it?

77. Kent: Gédéni.   ((whispering))
Woman.

78. Mrs. Albert: Gédéni?
Woman?

79. Trent:	Yeah, gédéni. *Yeah, woman.*
80. Barb:	Gédéni, Kent, what'd you say?
81. Kent:	Gédéni.
82. Barb:	How about what she's holding?
83. Mrs. Albert:	Nā etóna? *What is she holding?*
84. Kent:	Nā etón ((repeating Mrs. Albert's utterance))
85. Barb:	Etóna?
86. Sharon:	Nā etóna, it means what what is she holding?
87. Barb:	Oh.
(:03)	
88. Mrs. Albert:	Eht'út etón, //eht'út// *She's holding a baby, baby.*
89. Kent:	// Eht'út// etón
90. Barb:	Ehhe' she has a //baby//
91. Mrs. Albert:	//baby//
92. Barb:	Okay, Kelvin, yā et'ā? ((holding up shoelaces)).
93. Sharon:	Tl'ūł. *String (shoelaces).*
94. Barb:	Ha', your mom beat ya,
95. Sharon:	Say that, say tl'ūł. ((to Kent))
96. Kent:	Tl'ūł.
97. Sharon:	Mhm.
98. Barb:	Mrs. Albert?
99. Mrs. Albert:	Henh?
100. Barb:	Yā et'ā, how would you call this? ((holding up toy))
101. Mrs. Albert:	Oh, we don't have nothin' for shovel.
102. Barb:	Shovel?

103. Mrs. Albert: Just say shovel. ((laughing))

104. Sharon, Barb: ((laughing))

105. Barb: How would you say I'm holding a shovel?

106. Mrs. Albert: Shovel estón.

107. Barb: Estón.

108. Kent: Estón.

During this exchange, Kent became more comfortable producing Kaska utterances, whether answering or reproducing an adult's utterance (lines 77, 81, 84, 89, 96, 108). Trent, on the other hand, refrained from speaking Kaska, eventually answering my first question with two English responses (lines 67, 69), the second a correction of the first. His one Kaska utterance was produced as a statement of agreement with Kent's initial response to a question (line 79). As before, Mrs. Albert and Sharon directed some of the children's responses as well as translating (both to and from Kaska). Tangential to this exchange was one between George and Mr. Albert (lines 109–113). Though brief, it revealed the now-common pattern of the son, George, speaking English with the parent, Mr. Albert, even though Mr. Albert was a Kaska-dominant speaker and had spoken Kaska continuously around his children, including George, throughout their childhood.

In this final part of the exchange, Trent switched roles from elicitee to elicitor in relation to Kent.

(3.9.f) Interaction at camp (continued)

114. Barb: Trent, yā et'ā??
                    Trent, what is it?

115. Trent: uh, de—

116. Adults: ((laughing at the toy))
                    ((Trent holds up a toy dog for Kent to identify))

117. Kent: Tlį'.
                    Dog.
                    ((Trent holds up a plastic fish for identification))

118. Trent: Łūge, łūge.   ((identifies the fish himself))
                    Fish, fish.

119. Kent: Łūge, I know that.
                    Fish,

120. Barb: What we didn't catch any of.
                 ((Trent holds up a plastic yellow duck))

121. Kent: Túde.
                 Duck.

122. Barb: Túde?
                 Duck?

123. Kent: Túde.
                 Duck.

124. Adults: [aːh]   ((sounds of approval))

125. Barb: Yā et'ā?   ((holding up plastic carrots))
                 What is it?

126. Trent: What is that?   ((translating B's utterance))

127. Mrs. Albert: Say essậ.   ((whispering to Kent))
                 I don't know.

128. Kent: s—essậ.
                 I don't know.

129. Mrs. Albert: Essậ //mean you don' know that//

130. Trent: //What is that?//   ((asking Kent))

131. Barb: //Essậ.//
                 I don't know.

132. Kent: // Essậ.//
                 I don't know.

133. Mrs. Albert: Essậ say.
                 I don't know,

134. Kent: Essậ.
                 I don't know.

135. Sharon: I don't know.   ((translating))

136. Mrs. Albert: He don' know.   ((to Barb))

137. Barb: Carrot sticks.

138. Sharon: Is it?

139. Barb: They're supposed to be, it was one of those
                 healthy little—

140. Sharon, Mrs. Albert: ((laughing))

141. Trent: What is them? What is that?

142. Barb: The carrots?

143. Trent: Carrots?

144. Barb: Carrot sticks.

145. Trent: Mm.

This section of exchange began with me asking Trent for the name of a toy. He deflected my question by picking up the object and showing it to Kent, who then identified the object in Kaska. By doing this, Trent transitioned into an elicitor role and took control of the interaction momentarily. For the next few turns (lines 115–130), he acted as both elicitor and elicitee by controlling the objects used for elicitation as well as responding by naming one of the objects himself. His dual role playing instigated a response from Kent who interpreted this duality as a correction for his lack of a response (line 119), an adult practice, as opposed to the child's practice of supplying the target response. Again, the grandmother prompted Kent when he did not respond to the question being asked (lines 127, 133). Both the grandmother and the daughter continued to provide translations as well (lines 129, 135).

These Kaska language routines—the simple directives, the translation pairs, and the vocabulary elicitations—create continuity between home and school contexts. In addition to creating continuity and indexical links across language revitalization contexts, the sociolinguistic experiences of these young (and not-so-young) language learners perpetuate a sociolinguistic distinctiveness in relation to particular speakers and social positions such that the linguistic differences appear as an index of status rather than simply as differences in grammatical competencies. This ideologization of the sociolinguistic landscape interacts with other social conventions, such as the ideologization of respect, taciturnity, and expertise, further reinforcing the hierarchization of Kaska language practices.

These routines are also commonly found in child-directed speech. Cross-culturally, child-directed speech is often different from adult-directed speech (Bavin 1995; Ochs 1988; Ochs and Schieffelin 1984; Rushforth 1985; Schieffelin 1990; Schieffelin and Ochs 1986a, b). Different interactional routines are used with young children, including elicited imitation routines (Demuth 1986; Gleason and Weintraub 1976; Greif and Gleason 1980; Heath 1986; Peters and Boggs 1986; Watson-Gegeo and Gegeo 1986). Illustrated above, such imitation routines were frequently used in the Kaska language classroom and elsewhere where the expression *"say X"* was a prominent formulaic phrase across these exchanges. Along with this phrase, other formulaic routines were incorporated into the language learning environment, from words elicited with flash cards to simple conversational routines requesting interactants' names or weather conditions. For Kaska, then, the style of speech directed toward children and adolescents differed from the style of speech directed toward adults. While not surprising cross-linguistically, the institutional maintenance of this distinction across several grades was surprising. Furthermore, rather than creating intertextual links between adult conversational styles and educational routines, the educational versions used in the schools were slipping into noninstitutional contexts and further reducing opportunities for acquiring or augmenting a fuller range of sociolinguistic conventions—minimizing in various ways the success of such language revitalization efforts and further exacerbating the linguistic discontinuity.

In an endangered language context, linguistic regimentation may have unintended consequences, both positive and negative. Positively, the institutional regimentation of Kaska facilitated interactions between adults and children, between speakers and nonspeakers. Negatively, the grammatical form of the regimentation provided minimal scaffolding for children's or learners' growing linguistic knowledge. Thus, the institutional regimentation of speech may result in increasing the discontinuity between speakers and learners rather than resolving this sociolinguistic disjuncture.

Disjuncture: Institutional Erasures and Interactional Recursions

This chapter has examined the interactional routines used with children across different contexts and different speakers. The interactional patterns presented here suggest the following for the children and adolescents being socialized in this Kaska language community. First, adults and elders speak Kaska in the presence of children. Impressionistically, at a low estimate, 10–25 percent of all conversations were in Kaska. This provides children with the opportunity to acquire some knowledge of the language. Child-directed speech also adds to and reinforces these opportunities and encourages adult–child interactions. Second, adult child-directed speech reveals that adults frequently frame Kaska responses with English, by either translating the Kaska utterance or providing the Kaska response using the English command "say X." This suggests that code-switching is an unremarkable, socially acceptable practice. Inserting an English word into a Kaska frame and vice versa is entirely appropriate. The acceptability of code-switching also suggests that when young language-acquiring speakers switch, the switch will most likely go unnoticed. This lack of awareness also means that people are unlikely to realize the degree of shift the Kaska language has undergone. Third, child-directed routines focus on the elicitation of a limited range of Kaska utterances (or words). This suggests that children are being socialized to speak Kaska in an institutionally regimented style. In sum, this chapter has highlighted some of the interactional differences between child-directed and adult-directed speech, the sociolinguistic similarities between school and home contexts, and the social conventions mediating adult–child interactions, resulting in the emergence and mitigation of various disjunctures.

We have also seen how the regimentation of language by institutions, elders, and adults created disjunctures, affecting language production and, ultimately, revitalization. For example, while children learned specific routines resulting in the production of a limited set of Kaska lexemes, these educational situations also discouraged linguistic or grammatical development due to the minimal variation of these routines in relation to academic progression: hence, a sociolinguistic disjuncture between the frequency and form of linguistic production. The erasure or, more exactly, nonrecognition of this disjuncture occurred due to the complementary distribution of the two styles and the pragmatic conventions affecting their usage. By institutionalizing a functional difference between speech styles (teaching versus conversation), the grammatical differences become inconsequential. For language revitalization, however, they remain significant. Another disjuncture emerged as the result of interactional recursions facilitated in part by the social conventions linking particular styles with particular interlocutors. The shifting of school routines into nonschool contexts exemplifies this process. Again, the contextual coherence of participant roles moderates the sociolinguistic disjuncture. Elinor Ochs and Bambi Schieffelin (1995:93) have pointed out that "cultural values attached to particular codes do impact the acquisition (or nonacquisition) of those codes." Not only does the valuation of a language impact its acquisition, so do the pragmatic conventions and institutional conditions, especially in relation to moments of disjuncture in linguistic practice. Conjoined, these factors have reinforced the overall linguistic disjuncture between speakers and nonspeakers, between adults and children, that defines the Kaska language as an endangered one. What children are actually acquiring or not acquiring requires further investigation.

Finally, this chapter has revealed a disjuncture between the effects and the goals (and values) of language revitalization through educational programming. The institutionalization of this indigenous language, while celebrating its value for Kaska speakers, First Nations citizens, and Yukoners generally, has further constrained the language's conversational and grammatical repertoire. Rather than enhancing children's acquisition and competence, such institutionalizing practices have begun to replace the diverse conversational and grammatical range of fluent speakers with simplified and topically constrained routines of the school environment. The regimentation of indigenous languages required of such institutional contexts is tacitly erasing the grammatical and interactional versatility of the Kaska language. This disjuncture not only reinforces the generationally and socially defined sociolinguistic shift, rather than reducing or reversing it, but in doing so, works against institutional efforts intended to revitalize the language. These institutional practices interrupt noninstitutional opportunities to speak Kaska by replacing these nonregimented moments with institutionalized routines.

Having mapped the patterning and distribution of Kaska utterances and phrases in everyday interaction across different contexts and participants, this chapter has shown that Kaska language endangerment and language revitalization are intimately connected to the regimenting practices of institutions. One of the central questions arising from this realization is, what other language revitalization practices are affecting these generationally mapped linguistic differences? The next chapter addresses this question in relation to aboriginal language documentation and aboriginal language media: how are these languages being represented, and who are the people involved in developing and in using these media?

Manufacturing Legitimate Languages

The book is called *The Invisible Culture* because communicative patterns lack the tangible visible quality of houses, clothing, and tools, so that it is less easy to recognize their existence as culturally distinct phenomena. The purpose of this book is *to render that invisible culture visible* through description of its nature in the Warm Springs community and reconstruction of its impact in the classroom." (Philips 1983:12)

Educational contexts are prime sites for analyzing the construction of authority in relation to language and circulating (language) ideologies and discourses that support these constructions. Many previous studies have focused on the role the matrix, or dominant, legitimized language plays in these and other institutional settings (see Bourdieu 1977; Errington 1998; Fabian 1986; Heller and Martin-Jones 2001; Jaffe 1999; Kroskrity 2000; Milroy and Milroy 1985; Philips 1983; Rafael 1992; Scollon and Scollon 1981; Wortham and Rymes 2003), and specifically on how the dominant cultural institutions use language to produce, maintain, and assert their authority. These acts of domination are not limited to the promotion of the dominant language (and culture); they also *permeate* the ways in which minority languages are incorporated into dominant institutional frameworks, redefining linguistic practices, positions of linguistic authority, and corresponding indigenous or extant theories (or ideologies) of language.

Such institutional dominance is exemplified in Susan Philips's book about Warm Springs Indians (1983). She revealed the tacit interactional practices that led to miscommunication (or communicative disjunctures) between Warm Springs residents, especially students, and nonresident teachers, analyzed in relation to their different histories of socialization. Similarly, Carole Edelsky's work (1996) on Spanish–English bilingual classrooms some years ago highlighted the asymmetrical relationship between Spanish and English, such that even on "Spanish Days" the invisibly ubiquitous presence of English continued to infiltrate Spanish events. Obviously such "invisibility" infiltrates all social life, including indigenous language practices and projects of revitalization.

Language revitalization and preservation efforts in North America provide a clear example of such "invisible" permeations and some of the consequences that the institutionalization or *regimentation* of indigenous languages can have on indigenous language revitalization because of the materiality of these endeavors. The goal of this chapter is to examine the ways in which institutional practices, especially English language practices, disrupted Kaska language activities within and beyond the classroom, illustrating that those practices intended to raise the status of Kaska (and other aboriginal Yukon languages), in part by incorporating it into an institutionalized setting or bureaucratic event, inadvertently maintained its subordination. I focus on three aspects of this institutionalization: (1) participant roles, especially "expert" roles, such as "community-external" advisors; (2) linguistic representation circulated in language materials, bureaucratic reports, and maps developed by various people in different programs around the Yukon; and (3) the underlying theoretical preconceptions endorsed by these programs. Combined, this discourse reinforces the dominant state's hegemony, not only by indexically reflecting its dominion over indigenous, marginalized populations through government-controlled required education, but also by absorbing indigenous practices into the state's repertoire, under the guise of multiculturalism and multilingualism. However, I conclude by arguing that the practices of teaching and documentation should not be abandoned; theories can be changed, texts modified, and practices reconstructed to mediate these "invisible" hegemonic intrusions.

Sites for Linguistic Expertise

The technologies and associated practices used for language revitalization and preservation are embedded in institutional contexts that mediate and are mediated by ideologies of aboriginal, or "lesser-used," languages, as pointed out by Patrick Eisenlohr (2004b). Additionally, the predominant sites for linguistic manufacture—language revitalization and preservation being acts of manufacture—are embedded in an institutional framework that precedes the context of revitalization,[1] which provides the resources and support necessary for linguistic manufacture in the form of funding, documentation, curriculum, and training. Linguistic training at the university level can provide undergraduate and graduate students with skills useful for the documentation of endangered languages and can contribute to the maintenance of linguistically oriented programs within such institutions (see Adley-SantaMaria 1997; Charles 2005; Johns and Mazurkewich 2001; McCarty et al. 2001; McCarty et al. 2005; McCarty, Watahomigie, and Yamamoto 2001; Morgan 2005; Sims 2005; see also Hinton 2001b). The training itself has several dimensions, from the field methodologies to the theoretical and ideological assumptions that underlie the design and presentation of linguistic information. For language revitalization, such assumptions surface in dictionaries, grammars, lesson books, and other educational materials. When linguists are involved in a language revitalization project, the textual productions (if there are any) will most likely reflect this training; including their experiences with other textual traditions (see de Reuse 1997; Speas 2009). Such materials can also indirectly accentuate the dominant language's status and encourage dominant language intrusions. I address this below in the section that discusses language materials designed for Kaska language revitalization and education.

University training is recognized implicitly and explicitly by the state as certification for revitalization work. In doing so, it recognizes and thus legitimates the authority of those people who are products of dominant language establishments and tacitly invalidates those who are not. In the Yukon, one example of such linguistic validation appeared in the form of paid positions for language revitalization. There were three primary positions recognized by the territorial government, labeled linguist, Elder, and aboriginal language teacher. Elder was defined by Canada pension rules; teachers were certified by the Yukon College through the YNLC Language Teacher Training Program; linguist was a less formalized position but was similar to the government's understanding of consultant. These three roles or positions materialized as a direct result of the territory's commitment to aboriginal language revitalization, which began in the 1970s. In government documents, the expertise of elders and "professional linguists" or "specialists" was foregrounded, as evidenced in the passage below from an ALS program assessment report. Under the section "Factors involved in language programs and services," it was noted that

> professional linguists and language planners; research; and government policies and funding have been highlighted as important factors

to facilitate community-based language retention. . . . There is some evidence that successful language retention requires the presence of specialists/institutions in areas such as linguistic research; coordination and planning; and providing technical assistance to community-based programs. The most successful situations have been those in which specialists: respond to community priorities for research; work collaboratively with Aboriginal speakers and language workers, preferably training an Aboriginal linguistic worker on the job; and return results in an accessible and useful form to the community. (Leslie Gardner and Associates 1997:21, 22)

The necessity of professional linguistic expertise predictably appeared in project proposals as well, especially those proposals developed for Yukon First Nations by ALS. The following excerpt is from a proposal written by the then-director of ALS, requesting partial funding for a series of Kaska language workshops. In answer to one of the questions on the ALCIP (Aboriginal Languages Community Initiatives Program) project proposal form ("Do you have people in mind to work on this project?"), the Kaska House of Language project identified the following people:

Jim Morgan, Kaska linguist and Native Language Consultant for the Department of Education, will be assigned to this project as a part of his duties. Liza Dolittle, Interpreter, ALS, will also be assigned to work on the project. We will assign Maggie Crane to work on this project, to coordinate the actual training weeks and to maintain contact with the various people involved in the steering committee. Kaska elders have been approached to act as resource people for both the language content and the design of the project. Barbara Meek, doctoral student in linguistics and anthropology, will also provide assistance to the project.

All of these people fit into the institutional framework for language manufacture. Also, under "Project Overview," a section entitled "Faculty" listed the following personnel: Elders, Interpreter, Linguist, and Visiting faculty.

As suggested by the "Faculty" heading in project proposals, institutionally sanctioned expertise also spilled over into terminology used to talk about elders. The following is another excerpt from the proposal referred to above: "Elders will be key 'professors' in this pilot project. They will be involved in the 'content' part of the training, providing expertise in the Kaska language and culture, as well as the 'process' part of the training, providing guidance as to instructional approaches, evaluation, and student support." In this quote older Kaska people are metaphorically referred to as "professors," a term that indexes an institutionally sanctioned position, which then accords to the position of "elder" some degree of institutional authority. Elders' authority, or expertise, however, was limited to "the Kaska language and culture" in this example and elsewhere in bureaucratic rhetoric (see Meek 2002).

So, what about the expert position of linguist? These positions were typically held by outside, or community-external (Hinton 2002), experts believed to be able to document and write any language. As noted above, their expertise was recognized by the federal and territorial governments. Through this institutional (community-external) validation, linguists' credibility had become equally recognized by bridging organizations such as the Council of Yukon First Nations and community-internal institutions such as individual First Nations governments. Linguists working in the Yukon had developed the orthographies for the various Yukon languages, standardized the spelling for these indigenous languages, and founded the Yukon Native Language Centre and the Yukon Native Language Teacher Training Program. Currently, they coordinate and teach literacy workshops, among other things.

Linguists' expertise was recognized and naturalized among non-institutional, community-internal experts as well, through word of mouth and performances at public events, such as language workshops. For example, the women I worked with often praised me in the community, commenting on how well I was learning Kaska and how easily I wrote and pronounced the language. Often, people who were comfortable trying to write their own language often called on me to "correct" what they had written. Even in conversation, positive support for and encouragement of linguists' knowledge about aboriginal language was found. In the conversational excerpt below, a passing reflection on Jim Morgan's Kaska competence transpired. The conversation was recorded at the AHS in Upper Liard, in January 1999. Two elders, Ann and Rose, were sitting at a table waiting for some children to sit down for a beading demonstration. Amy was one of the teachers at the AHS and was the granddaughter of Rose. Amy understood Kaska but did not speak the language. I was sitting at the table, across from Rose next to Ann. The topic of conversation was beading but then switched to a discussion of Jim.

1. Amy: Yeah, I was wondering who is that, and

2.   I think I asked somebody I said I seen him.

3.   A non-native person speak Kaska language really good

4. Ann: Mezi
    his name

5. Amy: Is that over? ((to Rose about her sewing))

6. Ann: Mezį den(e) dāyāl gehdī la.
    They say his name is the man who continuously walks.

7.   It means he's always traveling.

8.   Kola eszį that one denehdí.
    He always said that that one was his name.

This portion of conversation illustrates the point made above, the positive evaluation and credibility of linguists (Amy's statement, line 1). Later in the conversation, the topic switched to homemade language tapes. Many families have borrowed this "tool of the linguistic trade," in their personal efforts to revitalize the Kaska language. In the excerpt below, the elders discussed Fred, Rose's grandson, who was attending college outside of Watson Lake at the time.

((23–39: talking about Rose's grandchildren))

40. Rose: "I got Auntie's tape," he say.

41. Ann: Oh, that Fred.

42. Rose: Mhm, "dedu ebéh łéndesjāde' łą́ nedests'ek esdēz-sį," éhdi.
    Mhm, "This summer when I come back, I'll really be able to understand you," he said.

43. Ann: Ham, yéndi-am?
    Yes, did you say?

44. Rose: Ham, "kulā, łą́ gutie," yéssīn.
    Yes, "That's really good," I said to him.

This second excerpt exemplifies the almost taken-for-granted nature of tape recordings in language preservation and revitalization efforts. These recordings often served as surrogates for aboriginal language experts (here elders), reinforcing the expertise both of elders and of linguists who utilized this technology.

   Both of these excerpts also illustrate people's everyday experiences with the Kaska language, where elders were the ones displaying their knowledge of the language by speaking it while other interlocutors spoke English. How this reinforces the expert status of elders is discussed in chapter 1. But this conversational practice also reinforces the expertise of linguists. Younger (non-elder) adults often downplayed or disavowed their own knowledge, making statements like the following: "I need to brush up on my Kaska—I'm fairly fluent. I can understand but I don't speak. I have no one to talk to except my parents. They speak Kaska and I speak English. . . . I need to brush up on my Kaska if I want to substitute in the schools." Such sentiments were echoed in adults' comments that researchers should interview elders and local linguists if they wanted to learn about Kaska history or acquire the language.[2] What such discourse and patterns of linguistic practice reveal is that linguists and elders were equally valued as linguistic authorities on Kaska. Ironically, then, a project aimed at reinforcing and expanding community-wide Kaska production and overall use through the language's explicit manufacture indirectly contributed to its increasingly limited and declining use by younger adults, adolescents, and children.

Through its recognition of community-external experts, and the metaphoric transfer of such legitimation to community-internal experts, and by specifying these individuals as the participants who crucially deserve payment, the dominant culture defined who was and was not a linguistic authority and qualified "manufacturer" of Kaska. This economic validation was reflected in such comments from people as, "We need dollars for teaching kids [Kaska]—it's work. Elders need to get paid when they work with young people," and "We need encouragement from Chief and Council to keep doing it [teaching Kaska]. It will cost some dollars to keep elders involved in teaching the language." Such arguments further widened the chasm between the generations, especially regarding children's and young adults' use of English. As we will see in the next chapter, community-external constructions of linguistic authority were being reinforced by community-internal language practices and concurrent ideologies of authority, which subsequently reproduced the government's discourse about aboriginal languages within the community setting. What the government had found to be "true" in its studies contributed to Kaska people's concepts of linguistic expertise in their own community. Similarly, the social positions of authority that linguists inhabited community-internally also ratified them as legitimate producers of aboriginal language materials.

Linguistic Manufacture: Texts and Lessons

As part of linguistic training, student-linguists are socialized into representing indigenous languages in particular ways, ways dictated by the discipline of linguistics. Since a common strategy in the revaluation of marginalized languages has been to manufacture them in ways similar to that of dominant languages, which has been done successfully in some cases (see, for example, McLaughlin 1992), students trained in such technologies would be ideal candidates for producing materials that build such parallelisms. For example, while Jim Morgan and I were trained as linguists and anthropologists at two different U.S. universities (I was at Arizona, he was at Indiana), we had similar ideas and approaches to language revitalization and the documentation of aboriginal languages. We had both read Keren Rice's (1989) *A Grammar of Slave*, which informed our conceptualization of Kaska grammar to a great extent. We differed in that I was more familiar with Southern Athabaskan structure, having formally studied and analyzed various Navajo and Apache dialects, whereas Jim was a fluent speaker of Slave and had been living and working in the Yukon much longer than I. Despite these differences, the commonalities in our training led us to produce materials and technologies for aboriginal language revitalization that met each other's expectations. The organization of aboriginal language texts, such as noun dictionaries and simple language lessons, was also predictable and matches that found elsewhere for other aboriginal or indigenous languages (such as Navajo [Platero 2001]; Nahuatl [Meek and Messing 2007]; Hupa [Bennett 1997]). Their appearance and structure resonate with academically sanctioned textual traditions.

Aboriginal languages are also manufactured according to pedagogical technologies. In the Yukon, current text-based lessons are modeled after earlier lessons developed in the 1970s by the YNLC. They maintain the practices associated with the educational models of that decade, rather than more contemporary pedagogical methods and theories, such as TPR (total physical response [Asher 1977]), child immersion through language nests (for Maori, see Fleres 1989; Harrison and Papa 2005; King 2001; for Hawaiian, see Kapono 1994; Warner 2001), and adult immersion through master–apprentice programs (Hinton 2002). As a result, the aboriginal language curriculum appears antiquated, especially in juxtaposition to both English and French language curricula in the Yukon Territory. This disjuncture with nonaboriginal language programs suggests that language revitalization efforts in the Yukon could benefit from the expertise of people trained in contemporary educational practices, along with people trained in linguistics and anthropology. The dilemma, however, is that in many of these cases it is difficult enough to find any individual to work on language revitalization, let alone one with such an interdisciplinary background.

This discussion of textualization shows that the professional manufacture of marginalized languages often reaffirms, rather than disengages with, the dominant language and culture. The next section examines this dominance in the textual materials produced for aboriginal language revitalization in the Yukon Territory. The materials are organized into three categories: language lessons, maps and surveys, and slogans. The first group of materials is geared toward language learners. These are materials that we would expect to "disrupt" the linguistic hierarchy as part of their promotion of the aboriginal language. The second set of materials is aimed at a general audience, from Yukon citizens to tourists and Web-browsing individuals. While attempting to change people's attitudes toward aboriginal languages by emphasizing multiculturalism, they present a simplified image of the sociolinguistic landscape. As part of this image, they also exclude any use of an aboriginal language in their narratives. The final illustration depicting Yukon citizens as a multicultural whole addresses an international audience and provides us with an explicit language ideology. As with the other materials, this final representation in its appeal for global interpretability continues to background aboriginal languages.

Aboriginal Language Materials: Storybooks and Language Lessons

As illustrated throughout chapter 3, text, texts, and textual production are not prominent in any Kaska language domain, whether language learning environments, First Nations government buildings, or family homes. In elementary school, Kaska writing exercises did not become part of the curriculum until grades three and four. Even then, writing played a marginal role in the students' education. The classroom was amazingly devoid of Kaska text (and English text as well) in contrast to the other classrooms, including the French language classroom, and the hallways of the school, all of which were covered with students' essays—some in English, some in French—and student artwork with titles or headings in English. Even a recent mural (fig. 4.1) celebrating traditional Kaska narratives presented the title of the narrative ("The Girl and the Mammoth"), the narrator ("as told by Mida Donnessy"), the illustrator ("drawn by Dennis Lutz"), and the painters ("painted by the students of Johnson Elementary School"), all in English. The lack of Kaska text in these examples, or its framing by the dominant Canadian languages, in conjunction with an emphasis on textual production, reflect both an ideological disjuncture between oral practices and literacy (see chap. 3) and a sociolinguistic disjuncture between the revaluation of the Kaska language and its representational marginalization.

The bell rang and the kids stampeded into their classrooms, having dumped their backpacks, puffy winter coats, and thickly treaded boots on the hooks and beneath benches lining the hallways outside their classroom door and

Figure 4.1. This school mural illustrates the positive valuing of Kaska traditions by dominant institutions through their incorporation into public institutional spaces, as shown here. Photo by the author.

throwing all into disarray. The teachers had quietly shuffled into their classrooms prior to this raucous, chaotic shift. Having deposited her lunch in the teachers' lounge, Mrs. Ann Albert, who was not quite a "kerchief elder," waited calmly in her classroom for the arrival of the kindergartners. She had aligned their chairs in a row in front of one of the chalkboards, their desks arranged as tables behind them. Mrs. Albert's own desk was in the corner by the windows, a heavy, steel-framed object that held grade books, lesson plans, and other teaching paraphernalia, along with her beadwork, a pair of moccasins, and some snacks fit for all, including those with diabetes. The bulletin boards were plainly decorated with wavy cardboard borders outlining sheets of colored paper—one yellow, another blue, and another white. On display were the pièces de résistance, the students' assignments. The most eye-catching was the one with the giant brown moose (surrounded by pages of text describing his encounter with a hunter, Kedā Kah Ejedéhya'). On another wall was a shelf lined with photocopied exercises, books, various versions of the YNLC curriculum guide with accompanying flash cards neatly collected in a blue binder, the two-volume Kaska noun dictionary, the Kaska narratives volume, which included a tale or two recounted by Mrs. Albert's husband, and an unremarkable, thin, blue 8×12 paperback—another Kaska noun dictionary produced by the students and teachers at the elementary school. This book was the one Mrs. Albert turned to when searching for words and checking spelling conventions, the text she knew most intimately, having helped with its development and in which some of her former students had illustrations.

The bulletin board at the front of the classroom displayed a calendar, a regular feature in the aboriginal language classroom no matter what the grade. Chalk littered the trays underneath the chalkboards even though the boards were seldom used, and miscellaneous games, one of which was bingo, lay scattered in the corner. The plan for this morning was simple; five minutes of greeting and introduction, five minutes of calendar, and five to ten minutes of flash cards (including review). The flash cards were plain, black-and-white drawings created at the YNLC, available for purchase, along with the curriculum guide. No words accompanied these drawings, and few teachers considered writing the words on the chalkboard, as the students responded automatically to these stimuli. The remainder of the time would be spent coloring one or two pictures—reproductions of the flash cards—as further review.

Typical of many aboriginal language classrooms at that time, the educational materials available for native language teachers were somewhat limited: a handful of storybooks with accompanying software for use with older students, language lesson templates found in the Yukon Native Language Teachers curriculum guide emphasizing orality over literacy in the classroom, a noun dictionary or two, and pages of drawings for coloring. While many communities debate whether or not literacy should play a role in their own efforts at language revitalization, including the Kaska language community, one of the arguments presented in opposition to literacy and textual production appeals to historical practice, to oral acquisition as being a more organic, traditional approach to learning aboriginal languages than "modern" text practices. One of the difficulties in creating useful educational texts is the invasive presence of English and the underlying English-oriented pedagogical styles informing these materials. The following genres of texts serve to illustrate these difficulties.

The first samples are storybooks narrated by aboriginal language teacher trainees as part of their training and then produced and published through the Yukon Native Language Centre. These "computer storybooks" were meant to enhance or complement language instruction in the schools.

The story pamphlets had accompanying software so that children could listen to the stories on a computer by themselves. There were four story topics: moose hunt, drying fish, at home, and camping. Teachers composed these stories "in their own words" by looking at the pictures provided by YNLC and then translated their stories into English. According to YNLC's Web site, this was done so that "the story is not translated from English. This avoids awkward or forced native language translation and ensures that the content will reflect native culture." This suggests that these stories were more "authentic" or culturally infused (cf. Hinton and Ahlers 1999). Even though the student teachers to a great extent created the stories themselves, the YNLC linguists (non-native) edited the texts, checking the spelling of the aboriginal words and the accuracy of the English translations.

The storybook used by the teachers in Watson Lake, and reflected on the bulletin board with the moose drawing, was a story about a man going hunting for a moose. On the front cover of this booklet, the only Kaska language text presented was the title, which was accompanied by an English translation underneath. Place names (Watson Lake, Yukon), author's name, identification of the publisher, and the language of the text ("Kaska Language") were all in English.[3] In contrast, the title character's name (Tsílát) was not translated into an English one.[4] Several of the subsequent pages within the booklet were also in English: the inside cover of the storybook; the copyright page, which provides publication information, sponsor information, and information on additional language materials for purchase; and the biographical page, which briefly sketched the author's occupational and educational background. In particular, the biographical page informed the reader that the author had worked in the public school as a Kaska language instructor for over fifteen years, and that her training was through the YNLC. The last statement on this page, noting that the author "continues to participate in Kaska Literacy offered by the Yukon Native Language Centre," was particularly interesting, because it omitted any reference to local Kaska language efforts that also emphasized literacy, events in which the author of this booklet had participated. This omission highlights the government-funded institution's role in aboriginal language events and suggests that the Centre's methods and literacy approach were the appropriate or "correct" ones for aboriginal language preservation and revitalization.

In contrast to the English-focused exterior, the body of the text was written in Kaska, with no English. The translation into English (because, of course, there was one) appeared at the end of the booklet, keyed by page number. The translation was represented sententially, where English phrases appeared beneath corresponding Kaska phrases. Unlike linguistic representations in grammars, scholarly articles, and some dictionaries, no word-by-word gloss was provided, nor was there a morpheme-by-morpheme one. Following the story's translation into English, the back cover of the booklet returned to English-only text, providing the publisher's contact information, the ISBN number, and the sponsor's name (Yukon Native Language Centre) in large, bold letters.[5] Even though the Kaska language predominated within the story itself, the story or narrative representation of Kaska was submerged entirely in a sea of English, indexing the authority of English and the dominance of Canadian-English institutions.

The convenience and utility of these storybooks were also limited. During my research, I had only one opportunity to observe students interacting with the software that accompanied them. On that occasion, students assembled in the computer lab to listen to the story. The lab was a reassigned classroom with plenty of desks and one computer per desk. A screen at the front of the room facilitated demonstrations. Totaling ten students from Mrs. Albert's and Mrs. Simon's classes, these fourth-graders had attended Kaska language classes since kindergarten. As a language learner myself, I found the software much more engaging than the booklets alone, largely due to the audio component and opportunities for self-assessment; the students appeared less enthralled. While some of them interacted with the software, applying their knowledge of Kaska and exercising their Kaska literacy skills, several students entertained themselves with other activities found on the computers. For the most part, the teachers remained on the periphery of this educational activity.

These next samples are from two different, but related, texts for Kaska language education. The first is a page from a language lesson book published by the YNLC and coproduced with the teacher trainees in YNLC's teacher training program, as with the computer storybooks above. These booklets were distributed by YNLC and came with tapes. The intended consumer was anyone interested in learning an aboriginal language, including adults and older adolescents. These lessons also reflected the curriculum used in the public schools. Ideally, these materials presented an opportunity for parents in the Yukon to learn with their children and reinforce their children's lessons. However, very few parents, if any, actually had copies of these booklets. Those that did seldom cracked them open, preferring to verbally engage their children rather than textually (for a comparative study of textual and narrative practices, see Heath 1983, 1986). Here the colloquial verb forms, _dé'_ and _ná'_, along with objects associated with hunting, are the focus of the lesson (fig. 4.2). Most of the children with whom I worked knew these expressions before entering school. While more elabo-

Passing Objects

1. Hand me the axe.   Tsį̄ɫ dé'.

2. Here, take it.   Ná'.

3. Hand me the knife.   Bēs dé'.

4. Here, take it.   Ná'.

Bush Objects

1. Hand me the knife.   Bēs dé'!

2. Hand me the axe.   Tsį̄ɫ dé'!

3. Hand me the gun.   Ūnē dé'!

4. Hand me the bullets.   Ēdetĕ' dé'!

5. Hand me the big knife.   Bēs cho' dé'!

6. Hand me the small knife. Bēs zǭze dé'!

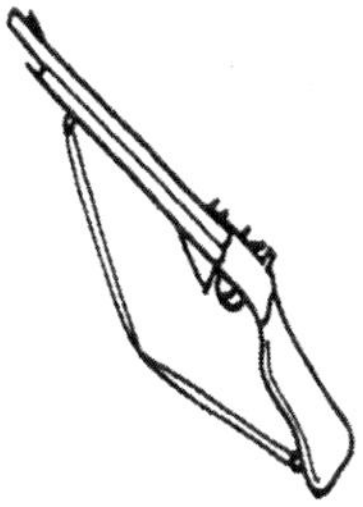

Figure 4.2. Page from *Kaska Language Lessons: Watson Lake Dialect* (Mercier and Wolftail 1994:9). Reproduced with permission of the Yukon Native Language Centre.

rate or grammatically complex verb words (or verb phrases) associated with these English translations exist (such as the handling verb forms, *esyén'á, esyénká, esyénlé, esyénhtéh*, or *esyénhtsūs*), these early lessons focus on abbreviated expressions, reinforcing the use of generic routines and deemphasizing the overall grammar and vocabulary of the Kaska language. Additionally, the entire lesson is framed by English: English headers, English section headings, translations, title pages, and so forth. English text surrounds the Kaska text, highlighting yet minimizing, or muting, the orthographic presence and ideological position of the aboriginal language. The textual layout reflects an institutional format presumed by its designers. It is a format that fails to interrupt the dominance of English.

The second textual example appeared in the picture noun dictionary mentioned above. Produced community-internally by educators and students at Watson Lake's elementary school, the intended audiences were the students, parents, and teachers at the elementary school. As noted above, the Kaska language teacher with whom I worked most closely frequently used this text rather than the ones provided by the government, which were the YNLC-produced curriculum guide and accompanying language lesson books. Again, though, we see institutional "shadows" (Irvine 1996) in the overall layout of the dictionary. For example, in the page below a textual style similar to the booklet page above was used to organize the Kaska language text—section headings are in English, and English translations precede Kaska phrases (fig. 4.3) (Burns, Darling, and Magun 1997:39).While English remains central to this text, reflecting to some extent the text's institutional affiliation, the arrangement of topics and the categorization of words and phrases differ from those produced elsewhere. For example, the YNLC language lessons contain weather terms such as "rain," "wind," and "snow." The local dictionary expands on this topic, including terms for the sky, celestial objects and events, terms for the location of the sun and the arrangement of stars into constellations, and Kaska words for fog, dawn, and lightning. Most significantly, this dictionary does not borrow directly from some matrix language text or other institutional resource. It is not a direct translation of some English book. This originality minimizes the indexical links to the matrix language. One option for further reducing the presence of English could be through the illustrations. Since illustrations are provided, as with the oral flash-card exercises, it is perhaps not entirely necessary to accompany the Kaska phrases with English glosses.

To some extent, these two texts are not comparable, in that one of them is intended to be a language lesson, and the other a word repository for children. However, they are similar in that both stress noun forms.

WEATHER/SKY

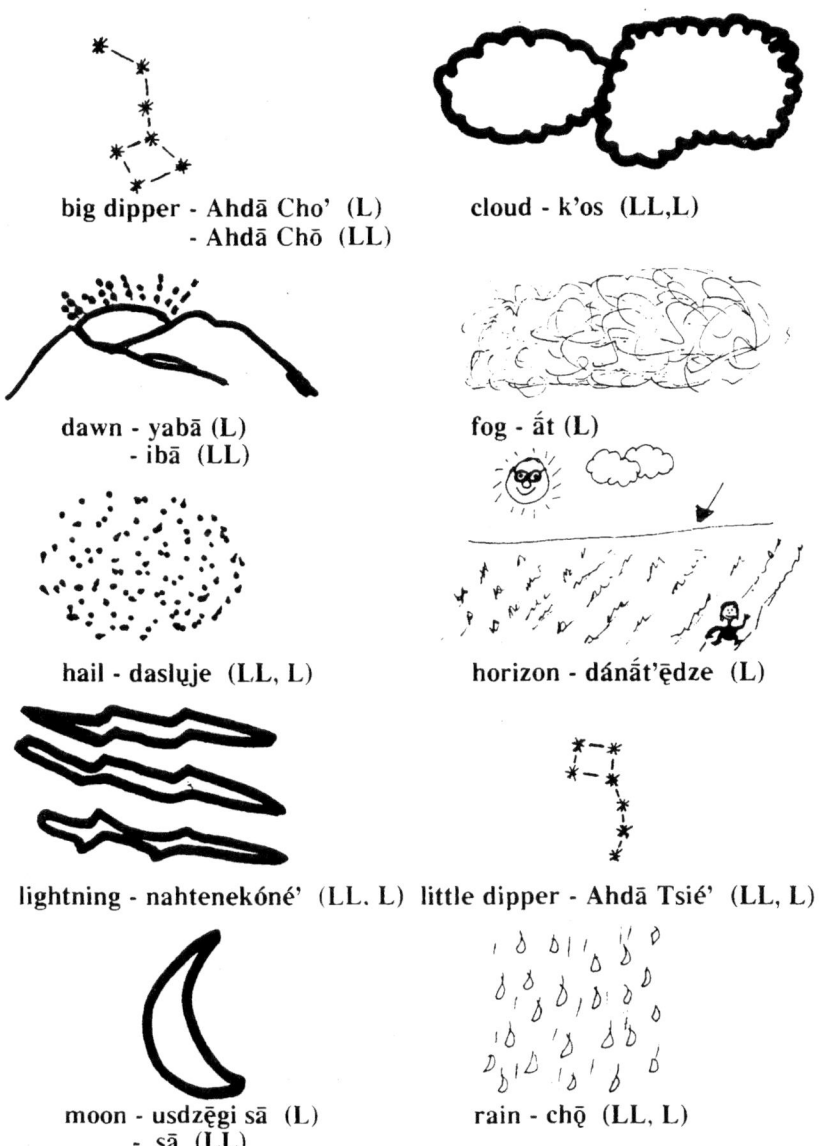

big dipper - Ahdā Cho' (L)
            - Ahdā Chō (LL)

cloud - k'os (LL,L)

dawn - yabā (L)
       - ibā (LL)

fog - át (L)

hail - dasluje (LL, L)

horizon - dánát'edze (L)

lightning - nahtenekóné' (LL. L)

little dipper - Ahdā Tsié' (LL, L)

moon - usdzēgi sā (L)
       - sā (LL)

rain - chǫ (LL, L)

Figure 4.3. Page from the locally produced booklet *Kaska Picture Dictionary* (Department of Education, Liard River First Nation 1997:39). Reproduced with permission of the Department of Education, Liard River First Nation.

While expected of the noun dictionary, the emphasis on nouns in the language lessons hinders the overall goal of Kaska language revitalization—to pass on the social and linguistic knowledge of preceding generations. The lessons focus primarily on nouns and states of being presented in minimal word phrases ("*Bēs déʼ*" [Hand me the knife], "*Ūnē déʼ*" [Hand me the gun]). All words on the page are in English, except for the target indigenous phrase, and the English translations precede their indigenous language correspondents—all in the same font size.

While the aboriginal language stands out against this backdrop of English, it also remains visually minimized within these instructional texts. This textual minimalism also pertains to the selection of terms (nouns, simple verb words) and their translations, glossing the aboriginal terms and phrases in a word-to-word or word-to-phrase style, with no morphological analysis (the exception being the December lesson on possessives [Mercier and Wolftail 1994:24]). This practice promotes an oversimplification of Kaska grammar by erasing the morphological complexity of the aboriginal language forms, especially poignant given the complexity of Athabaskan verb morphology (cf. de Reuse 1997). As a technique for developing literacy practices, these simplified linguistic images offer an accommodating introduction; as a technique for revitalizing speaking practices, these images portray the language as communicatively impoverished (and thus not appealing for learners who already have some linguistic competence). Constrained perhaps by a desire to appeal to a broad audience, such materials are disjunctive in relation to the goals of language revitalization because of their generic representations.

Another way in which English presided over these interactions was through the various educational dialogues used to promote language use, such as the routine for introducing oneself that ceremoniously marked the beginning of each Kaska class in the elementary school. A common routine in preschool, elementary school, and other Kaska language situations, this routine also appeared in the language lesson book; a Kaska version is pictured in figure 4.4 (Mercier and Wolftail 1994:6). This lesson reflects the template guiding this routine. While this may be a common practice in some settings (like the first day of class in a discussion section or seminar, perhaps, where everyone goes around introducing themselves), this was not a conventional practice among these students or adults. Most everyone was somehow related to each other, and so everyone already knew each other—eliminating the need for introductions. Also, in formal settings where introductions would be made, the routine for doing so was usually by having someone else perform the introduction rather than introducing

Names

1. What is your name?

Enzí' dúgúyā ?
Enzį' dúgúyā ?

2. My name is Ann.

Eszí' Ann gúye'.
Eszį' Ann gúye.

3. What is his/her name?

Mezí' dúgúyā ?

4. His/her name is Pat.

Mezí' Pat gúye'.
Mezí' Pat gúyc.

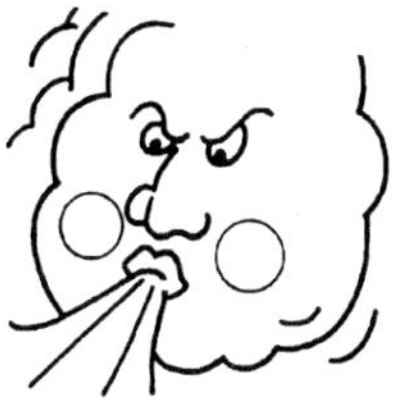

Weather

1. It is fall time.

Nédādáhhay.

2. It is getting cold.

Gúsdlī gudadī́ł.

3. It is snowing.

Zas nédetl'ī́t.

Figure 4.4. Page from the *Kaska Language Lessons: Watson Lake Dialect* (Mercier and Wolftail 1994:6) illustrating textually the routine used to begin each Kaska language class period from kindergarten through grade 5. Reproduced with permission of the Yukon Native Language Centre.

yourself. (This was how I was introduced and how others were introduced to me if I didn't already know who they were, following Dene politeness routines [Basso 1990; Goulet 1998].) This educational routine, in its directness, is awkward and unconventional, interrupting Dene interactional conventions and socializing students to use Kaska in a way that they probably never would.

These instructional routines were often scripted, taken from either the YNLC language lessons books or the curriculum guidebook. And while the students often never saw these lesson books or the guidebook, these texts dictated the teachers' practices and educational activities. Students did, however, see, as flash cards, the illustrations that accompany these texts (and additional ones provided by YNLC), such as the one in figure 4.5 of a Hudson's Bay blanket.

Such routines and artifacts reduce aboriginal languages to a compilation of nouns and token phrases, emphasizing the referential aspect of language while downplaying all other indexical dimensions, and thereby diminishing their sustainability as complex systems of and for communication. Additionally, the framing of the aboriginal language within the dominant language—by word order in translation or within dominant-language book covers and section titles or through elicitation using dominant-language commands—can be iconic of its subordination. For Kaska, the linguistic representations being institutionally manufactured semiotically textualized the predominant English-speaking Canadian regime (cf. Irvine and Gal 2000). This reinforces precisely the hierarchy that these language projects attempt to interrupt.[6]

Graphic Representations of Endangered Languages

Within the realm of state-run institutions, such as universities, government programs, and grant agencies, distinct institutional rhetorics have developed, which are manifested predictably in certain kinds of products, such as reports, evaluations, assessments, and plans (see chap. 5). Linguists, anthropologists, and other community-external experts involved in language revitalization must also produce some tangible document that conforms to the rhetorics of their discipline. Sometimes this conformity means that the final product (whether written or employing other media) must be intelligible and of interest to a wider public, a public composed of more than just First Nations or tribal Nations citizens (cf. Hill 1999). Other times this conformity encourages language experts to focus on the production of dictionaries and grammars (Hinton 2003), which are not always

Figure 4.5. This flash card of a blanket exemplifies the style of images used to teach aboriginal languages in the public schools. Reproduced with permission of the Yukon Native Language Centre.

useful to the aboriginal public (Hinton and Weigel 2002; Rice and Saxon 2002; see also Frawley, Hill, and Munro 2002; Kroskrity 2002). But overall, the existence of institutional and disciplinary rhetorics constraining expert discourse means that institutions, such as universities and government-funded centers, have been more invested in language standardization and the manufacture of materials than in the production of speakers—the ultimate goal of language revitalization efforts (Zepeda 2005).

Such standardized materials mediate the "practical and discursive" ideological reformulations that "(re)shape linguistic and social structures" (Gal and Woolard 2001:2), changing how minority language speech communities interpret and evaluate their own sociolinguistic fields. In this chapter, my goal has been to show how the institutional construction of linguistic authority authorizes particular individuals to develop materials and methods for the revitalization and preservation of aboriginal languages, and how such materials and methods, in this case aboriginal language texts, resonate with the institutional ideologies from which they emerge. One result is that these texts may alienate the people who are most needed for aboriginal language revitalization. To combat such alienation, many, if not all, language activists recommend engaging in a dialogue with endangered-language communities in the development of language materials and educational practices for aboriginal languages (for example, Dementi-Leonard and Gilmore 1999; Hinton 2002; Hinton and Ahlers 1999). Such collaboration reflects in part a cross-disciplinary move toward recognizing the agency of indigenous peoples in the production of their own media (Mahon 2000:475). The next linguistic representations manifest such ideological conditions, exhibited in part by the unmarked dimensions of the sociolinguistic landscape.

Mapping Language

Language lessons and books were not the only materials produced as part of the Yukon's language preservation and revitalization efforts. Maps and statistical diagrams were also an important part of these efforts. These images in particular were the ones that appealed to bureaucrats and non–First Nations people; they made sense within the dominant institutional rhetoric.

The map in figure 4.6 produced by the Yukon Native Language Centre and found on its Web site, is the map I encountered the most during my fieldwork. Aboriginal Language Services distributed these maps to their employees, to First Nations governments, to tourists who happened upon their office, and to eager scholars (especially one scholar whose apartment walls would have remained bare except for the generosity of her friends and colleagues at ALS who gave her a poster-size copy of this map).

The origins of the Yukon Native Languages map are to be found in nineteenth-century anthropology and colonial administrative practices, when the goal was to "civilize" and deterritorialize indigenous populations. John Wesley Powell, working under the authority of the U.S. Bureau of Ethnology, presented the seminal map of "Linguistic Stocks of American

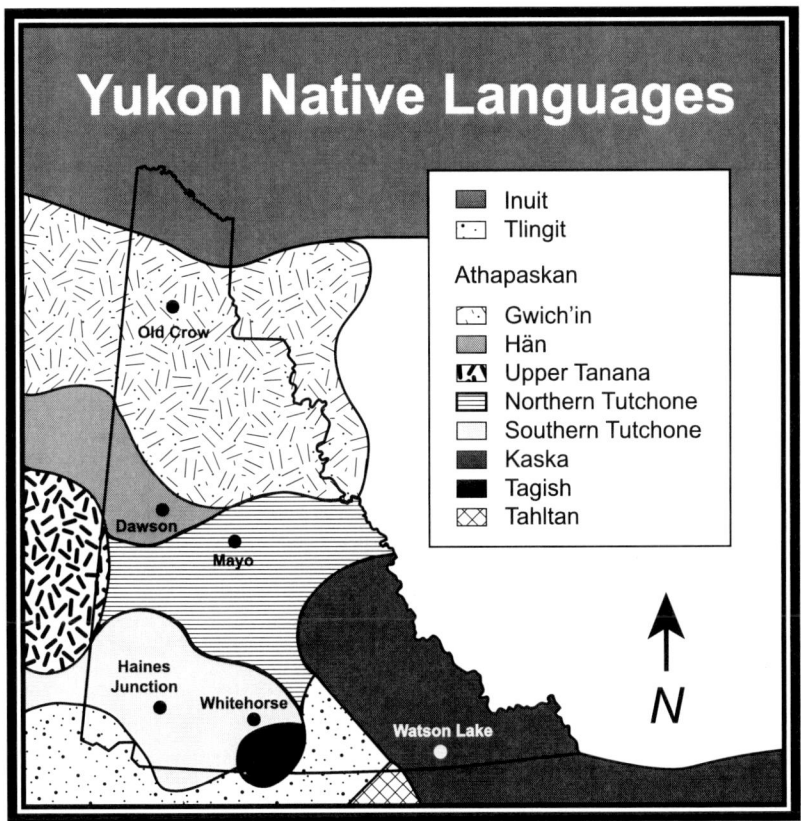

Figure 4.6. Yukon Native Language Centre map illustrating the way in which languages, peoples, and territories have been popularly and bureaucratically conceptualized and represented. It provides a more detailed visual representation of the aboriginal language scenario and the degrees of relatedness across aboriginal languages spoken in the Yukon Territory. Reproduced with permission of the Yukon Native Language Centre.

Indians North of Mexico" (Powell [1891] 1991). A map of language families, it represented the first major synthesis of scattered linguistic data from this continent. Interestingly, color-coding was used to distinguish the language families. Also, reflecting the ethnological association of language and environment, Powell's map paralleled the "culture areas" of North America. With further research in the twentieth century, a refined picture emerged of the individual languages comprising these families. By the time the Smithsonian Institution published its series *Handbook of North American Indians,* black-and-white, line drawing maps indicating the "tribal territories" associated with these languages were in circulation. Volume 6 of this series, *The Subarctic* (Helm 1981), maps the Athabaskan languages of the Yukon and Alaska. The Alaska Native Language Center's 1982 map follows this plotting, reviving Powell's use of color coding and extending coverage into the neighboring Yukon Territory. This is the map from which the standard Yukon Native Languages map derives. Color on these maps also indicates the relatedness of the languages; on each, Inuit is marked in blue, while the closely related Athabaskan languages are shades of red and yellow. From the time of Powell, such maps have been issued as reconstructions of territorial boundaries between ethnolinguistic groups at the time of contact.

Yet the cartographic representation focuses more on languages and their linguistic relatedness than on the people—the speakers, the semi-speakers, and the passive users of these languages. The sociolinguistic landscape depicted in this map locates each indigenous language, and the bodies that speak or are ancestrally affiliated with these languages, within a particular, bounded area and in a very static, atemporal way. There are no dates given here. The map depicts an ethnographic present before Europeans arrived, populated by aboriginals locked into the environmentally determined subsistence pattern typifying their culture area. Furthermore, as scholars have noted for areas other than North America (see Haugen 1966; Irvine and Gal 2000, for example), such depictions erase much of the sociolinguistic diversity present. In this case, they render invisible the multilingual reality of people living in the Yukon, especially their competence in and use of English.

At the same time, the language of entextualization, English, remains dominant yet "invisible." The map uses English throughout, even though it is a map about aboriginal languages. Granted, English is the language read by most and is probably the most effective code for sharing this information with a global audience, but there are ways to incorporate aboriginal languages (see Nunavut's Web site, http://www.gov.nu.ca/, for example), ways that might be accomplished more easily on a Web site than on paper.

Throughout these bureaucratic text-artifacts, First Nation peoples move in and out of focus in relation to the languages that they speak. Most clearly embodied in these materials are the native languages of the Yukon and, by extension, their most expert speakers, those who lived in the past. Invisible are the speakers of American Indian English varieties and the passive users of aboriginal languages. With respect to language revitalization, these materials representationally simplify the sociolinguistic landscape even in their historical and linguistic dimensionality.

Iconizing Linguistic Identity

The textual semiotics of aboriginal languages becomes further simplified in the government design used to increase awareness and promote support for these languages. In contrast to the language lessons and language maps above, this textual example immerses the English text in a sea of aboriginal languages (fig. 4.7). The graphic artwork was originally commissioned for the Voices of the Talking Circle conference in 1991. Whitehorse artist George Poulin created the design with traditional Athabaskan imagery on the left side, and Tlingit cultural symbols on the right. The faces from each culture represent dialogue, collaboration, and the sharing of spiritual knowledge, and are encompassed within the pan-Indian circle

Figure 4.7. The Aboriginal Language Services logo captures succinctly the overall conceptual framework used to promote, unite, and revitalize aboriginal language use in the Yukon Territory. Reprinted with permission of the Yukon Territorial Government, Aboriginal Language Services.

motif signaling unity (ALS 1991b). The theme of that 1991 language conference was "We Are Our Language," and when it became the slogan of ALS, it was added to George Poulin's original text-free circle design to create the ALS logo (Leslie Gardner and Associates 1993). Around 1994, a series of posters was produced that featured Yukon First Nations elders' photos and phrases in the eight languages, such as "We are happy when you try to speak your language." The phrase "We Are Our Language" was then translated into the eight languages and arranged around the circle logo for inclusion on the posters and other signage. Over the years, the logo has been used extensively by both ALS and YNLC, appearing on stickers, T-shirts, canvas bags, and several, if not all, ALS reports and publications, and YNLC's language map.

Looking at the logo, we can see that the most prominent text is the English slogan, displayed in large, bold font in the center of the circle. Moving out from the center is Poulin's artwork, and beyond this are the phrases indexing the eight recognized aboriginal languages of the Yukon Territory. This arrangement is superficially similar to the linguistic arrangement in the language lessons and equally iconic of the subordinate status of aboriginal languages. First, the most prominent phrase is in English. Second, the aboriginal language phrases are in a smaller font and are set at the periphery. Third, all of these phrases are glosses or derivatives of the highlighted English phrase. Rather than disrupting English's dominance, this logo centralizes English in its representation, sending the message that while individual communities should recognize and celebrate their own aboriginal languages and identities, the language that unites the Yukon is English.

Along with this general representational hierarchization, there are several other semiotic processes at work within this one image, resulting in the reproduction of several dimensions of social difference. First, the phrase "We Are Our Language" reinforces the "one language, one people" concept. This is a process that Irvine and Gal (2000) have identified as "iconicization," and in this case it depicts "our" language as an essential or natural characteristic of "our" identity. This denies the ubiquity of English and any corresponding bilingualism, multilingualism, or dialect differences of this varied sociolinguistic landscape. Second, this process of iconization differentiates the aboriginal population according to their ancestral languages and not their politically recognized First Nations, which are not always congruent with language groups. The orthographic representation itself also reinforces this linguistic essentialism; each language has its own unique orthography, distinguishable by a handful of language-specific orthographic symbols. The isomorphism of the maps is reproduced in the orthographies.

Next, through the semiotic process of erasure, the logo renders invisible the fair speakers, the poor speakers, and the nonspeakers by excluding them from the linguistically essentialized "we" of aboriginal identity. In the context of language revitalization, this slogan more tacitly implies that the loss of an aboriginal language by a First Nations person is accompanied by a loss of aboriginal identity, a sentiment expressed in many of the discourses surrounding language revitalization (see chap. 5).

Disjuncture: Linguistic Stratification, Graphic Erasure

Throughout these materials and routines, the aboriginal languages have been visually surrounded, and subordinated, by English. The many dialects spoken, aboriginal or otherwise, are backgrounded or erased in language lessons, and the predominant language routines socialize students into one "correct" (legitimate) variety, perhaps at the expense of their own. The languages themselves are represented as being purely and simply referential, presenting aboriginal forms in basic word-to-word or phrase-to-word correspondences and erasing all other meaningful aspects. These examples have illustrated the ways in which dominant institutional approaches can intrude on indigenous language efforts, and, in cases like Kaska, how the aboriginal language can become tied to institutionally recognized positions of authority and institutionally recognized procedures for maintaining, preserving, and re-creating endangered languages. An unintended consequence of this framing can be, and in this case has been, the increased stratification of the sociolinguistic field and the further marginalization of potential speakers. During the first few decades of language revitalization projects in the Yukon, only a select few were actually encouraged to speak, write, and therefore maintain the aboriginal language. People who did not inhabit any of the legitimate positions of linguistic authority were being indirectly discouraged from speaking the language and were most definitely *not* sanctioned to teach and pass on the language to novices. This constraint has applied to most of the aboriginal community, including those learners who will subsequently determine the fate of the language.

Furthermore, in relation to recent discussions of "publics" and "public sphere" (Gal and Woolard 2001), the language materials produced by university-trained linguists, materials which then serve as models for the production of more materials, acquire legitimacy not only through authorship (and "the institutional locations from which their proponents speak" and write (ibid.:3–4; see also Silverstein [1981] 2001), but also through their connection with other language materials. As Gal and Woolard have noted, "images of linguistic phenomena gain credibility when they create ties with other arguments about aspects of aesthetic or moral life" (Gal and Woolard 2001:3). Indigenous languages in the Yukon acquire legitimacy through written form because of the high valuation attached to literacy beyond the Kaska language community (see also Gal 1989).

Realizing the interconnectedness of language manufacture and the production and conceptualization of (linguistic) authority becomes important for understanding a subordinate language's current status and possible future, as has been pointed out by several researchers (for example, see Fishman 1991, 2001; Krauss 1998). How linguistic authority is constructed and conceptualized can impinge upon the vitality of a language and the willingness of an entire community to use their heritage language. Generally, researchers have assumed that revaluing heritage languages and their speakers will always have a positive effect on revitalization efforts. But in the case of Kaska, the opposite appears to be true. The goal of trying to re-create Kaska as a legitimate, revitalized language has led to the emergence of specialized roles marked by linguistic expertise, thus restricting the production of Kaska to those select few—in particular, university-trained linguists and bureaucrats—who are authorized to manufacture it.

Finally, not only do these revitalization practices suppress nonregimented language varieties and play into the overall subordination of these languages (even in contexts where they are intended to predominate), but they exacerbate issues of ethnicity and authenticity through the iconization of language and the erasure of linguistic diversity and complexity. On the one hand, raising the visibility of these languages through maps and charts and government logos increases nonaboriginal people's sociolinguistic awareness. On the other hand, the impracticality of representing both the sociolinguistic and grammatical complexities of these language varieties, and so the erasure of these subtle and not-so-subtle differences, decreases aboriginal people's sociolinguistic awareness and can unintentionally create a linguistic hierarchy that privileges certain dialects over other ones. This dilemma then creates tension between people who are differentially invested in the project of language revitalization, most notably between language revivalists and 16–35-year-old people of aboriginal descent. However, images in and of themselves may not be meaningful to the viewer, as with the Hudson's Bay blanket flash card in figure 4.5. These images are mediated by discourses that guide our interpretations. The next chapter addresses this issue, analyzing the various ways in which aboriginal peoples' discourses and government rhetoric have been mutually constitutive and contradicting in relation to the representation and ideologization of language revitalization for the Yukon Territory; what are the discourses circulating in the Yukon that render such images interpretable? Are there any ideological differences across the various groups of people involved in aboriginal language preservation and revitalization in the Yukon, and in Watson Lake in particular?

"We Are Our Language"

The Political Discourses of Language Endangerment

> [T]hose who seek to defend a threatened linguistic capital . . . are obliged to wage a total struggle. One cannot save the value of a competence unless one saves the market, in other words, the whole set of political and social conditions of production of the producers/consumers. (Bourdieu 1991:57)

It was the middle of a snowy Yukon winter, near the shortest day of the year. The thermostat recorded a temperature of −50 degrees outside, and if it weren't for the snow reflecting the illuminated night sky, it would be pitch black. As I wrote out verb paradigms for Kaska, the radio news broadcast reported that another First Nations person was stabbed to death (by accidentally falling on a knife repeatedly), another guy froze to death on his way home from a friend's, and elders throughout the Yukon were being hospitalized for pneumonia. Suddenly my obsession with documenting and analyzing Kaska grammar seemed even more urgent and yet not urgent at all in the face of these tragedies. Even more absurd was the thought of myself standing in front of a council of elders and telling them that their language was dying, that there were only a few speakers left, and that "we" needed to document more of the language before it vanished. The absurdity, however, was in the imagined rhetoric, not the goal of preservation and revitalization.

Against such depressed, and occasionally violent, social backdrops, language issues would appear to be of less importance and urgency than other community concerns. Statements like "There is only one speaker of Tagish left" or "The Kaska language is dying" may not have as much force in social situations where it is not just the language that is dying. As Bourdieu suggests in the quote above, however, these statements work to "save" the conditions of production underlying the sociolinguistic marketplace. One of these conditions is the discourse surrounding language. Endangered or otherwise, one avenue for changing a sociolinguistic environment is by changing the discourse surrounding the linguistic situation. For language endangerment, this entails diversifying the discourse of endangerment, to create, or expand, the linguistic marketplace.

Indigenous language issues also emerge as an opportunity to address a variety of social problems (such as addiction, illiteracy, and poverty), while providing people with an opportunity to reclaim their own heritage or to celebrate its persistence. Such language projects, however, require institutional resources and are therefore constrained by the political contexts within which they are formulated. The discourses of language advocacy, a dimension of these projects, often reflect these institutional constraints. In separate articles on language endangerment rhetoric, Jane H. Hill and Leanne Hinton identified two different categories of discourse: "expert rhetoric" and "community-internal" discourse (Hill 2002; Hinton 2002). Within these categories, a variety of discursive themes, from ecological metaphors and the depiction of language as the heritage of humanity, to the role of language in the construction of an identity, have been deployed, where the goal, as Hill has pointed out, has been in part to "establish new markets, not only in the extended sense advanced by Bourdieu (1982), but in the narrow sense of providing salaried positions for speakers of endangered languages" (Hill 2002:124).

These expert ways of talking about language, however, do not always map directly onto community-internal or local discourses about language circulating among the people whose languages are shifting out of use. One reason, then, that reversing sociolinguistic changes may be such a daunting, seemingly insurmountable task, pertains to the mismatches, or disjunctures, between expert and community-internal rhetoric, as well as corresponding conceptualizations of language. That is, different people have different understandings of endangerment, of success, of what it means to "save" a language, and methods appropriate to the task (see Nevins 2004 on Apache; England 2003 on Mayan; see also Whiteley 2003). The goal of this chapter is to reveal some of the ways in which institutional, expert discourse and community-internal discourses about language dialogically inform, oppose, or disengage with each other across different contexts, resulting in different degrees of disjuncture. There are three genres of discourse that I examine: community-external or expert rhetoric, local community-internal discourse, and global community-internal discourse. The data illustrating these genres come from government documents, meetings, and interviews.

Beginning with the discursive themes of community-external advocacy, or "expert rhetorics," followed by an analysis of themes found within local community-internal discourse, I reveal a disjuncture between the discourses of these two communities, which is understandable in relation to the different social and political contexts that motivate these two discourse communities. Complicating this picture is the fact that the Yukon government has attempted to create a unified aboriginal language ideology in dialogue with the fourteen Yukon First Nations (Meek 2009). This means that the "expert rhetoric" has been influenced or blended with other discursive themes and conceptions of language expressed by First Nations citizens, producing an emerging multivocalic, syncretic Yukon (meta)discourse about aboriginal language. While this may imply that disjunctures can be minimized, an analysis of pedagogical materials and practices shows that the discursive and ideological disjunctures remain intact, in spite of everyone's best intentions.

Linguistic Expertise and the Fight to Save the World's "Dying" Languages

Several scholars have begun to enumerate the various discursive strategies or themes employed by language advocates (Dorian 2002; England 2002; Errington 2003; Fishman 2002; Hill 2002; Hinton 2002; Maurer 2003; Whiteley 2003). In 2002 the *Journal of Linguistic Anthropology* published an issue on language endangerment, inviting commentaries from several well-known linguistic experts on the focal article written by Jane H. Hill about "expert rhetorics." Many in the academic commentary elaborated upon the discursive themes that Hill identified. However, in contrast to these "expert" themes, Leanne Hinton pointed out several different themes that she associated with the rhetoric of "community-internal" advocacy, discursive themes found in the statements of indigenous people. While many of these themes may be deployed by different advocates, all of these themes are marketable to or interpretable by the general public. The question is whether or not these same themes are invoked at events across different discourse communities, from government-run conferences and media to personal narratives. This would help answer the question Jane H. Hill posed (2002:119): do members of communities who are custodians of endangered languages borrow from global, "expert" discourse in formulating their advocacy, or do they prefer to use quite different discourses?

According to Hill, there are three prominent themes found in the discourse of language "experts," those "community-external" advocates such as linguists, bureaucrats, and other public spokespersons (Hill 2002:120). These themes are: (1) enumeration: documenting the number of remaining speakers, (2) universal ownership: identifying all people as (equally) invested in and responsible for the world's languages, and (3) hyperbolic valorization: expressing the inestimable worth of endangered languages. Often these occur in publications and other media that are intended to raise their audiences' awareness of language endangerment and to promote support for threatened languages, financial or otherwise. Such media, especially government reports, also are written to justify past expenditures and to secure future funding. Since conducting formal language assessments is often a contested task (ALS 2004a; Nevins 2004), government reports in particular serve as evidence of the success or failure of these language ventures. All three of these themes can be found in the government discourse about endangered aboriginal languages in the Yukon Territory, Canada.

Enumeration: Pie Charts, Bar Graphs, and Counting Bodies

The first theme, enumeration, while pervasive across the literature on endangered languages, also appears in typological analyses of languages (Nichols 1992), accounts of changes in the "status" of languages (Ammon and Hellinger 1992), and areal descriptions of language and language use (Edwards 1998; Smalley 1994). It also appears more broadly, in media such as the *New York Times*, *Scientific American*, the *New Yorker*, and *Nature*, where it is readily understood by consumers of numbers. Two discursive devices typify this theme. The one device uses prose, portraying language change through evocative statements about language death and loss. The second device depicts such change through statistical diagrams, such as bar charts and graphs, which representationally quantify speaking bodies. These diagrams are often, if not always, accompanied by the first device of enumerative discourse: statements highlighting the significant aspects of the statistical image. In the Yukon, the rhetoric of enumeration guided the 1990 field study *A Profile of Aboriginal Languages* (ALS 1991a), the statistics from which are reproduced in evaluation reports and proposals, and printed on posters sent out to the communities. The enumerative rhetoric is also central in the 2003 fluency assessment undertaken by ALS and the Yukon Bureau of Statistics (ALS 2004b).

The example here (see fig. 5.1) is one of these widely distributed images from the first study. While those who design and compose these materials are certainly aware of the problems with counting speakers and assessing fluency (ALS 1991a:x; ALS 2004a, 2004b; see also Cook 1998; Lieberson 1980; Rickford 1987), this discursive device has remained a central part of such indigenous language media. This graphic form in particular has been used to represent the status of each of the eight territorially recognized indigenous languages, as well as the status of all of them together. The one shown in figure 5.1 is for the latter. The statistical narrative begins with a pie chart that identifies four categories of speakers: non-speakers, poor, fair, and good-to-excellent. This chart shows that the majority of aboriginal people still speak and understand to varying degrees some aboriginal language, an atypical indigenous language situation. Redirecting this narrative, the bar graphs then foreground two of the four categories of speakers, "good to excellent" speakers and "non-speakers," thus emphasizing a dichotomy indicative of language shift while at the same time backgrounding "poor" and "fair" speakers. Furthermore, the bars highlight a nonspeaking aboriginal language population aged sixteen to thirty-five years. When read from top to bottom, these diagrams present a narrative about competence and loss, locating the endangerment (and death) of aboriginal languages in the Yukon in the speaking, or as it were, the nonspeaking bodies of 16–35-year-olds. Although this narrative initially begins by leading the reader to believe that aboriginal languages in the Yukon Territory may not be as endangered as indigenous languages elsewhere, the final image adjusts this impression by targeting the subgroup where the language shift has been most severe.

While such enumerative illustrations are used to portray indigenous or aboriginal languages as endangered, not all consumers interpret these media in this way. During one of my visits to a high school classroom, a student, who was within the targeted age range, perused the charts for the Kaska language and commented that rather than indicating language death, these charts showed that language use would increase with age. Elsewhere I have argued that this interpretation reflects a dominant Kaska language ideology that associates speaking Kaska with particular positions of authority, especially that of elder (Meek 2007). In government documents, however, such alternate interpretations become muted by the accompanying enumerative text that socializes the reader into the interpretation that such illustrations are intended to document, as well as a corresponding conceptualization of aboriginal or indigenous language as endangered. Enumerative statements in any context reinforce an understanding of language shift that emphasizes the disappearance of the linguistic object, the indigenous language.

From Universal Ownership to the Yukon Model

According to Hill (2002), revitalization discourse often claims that language groups, and sometimes outside publics, "own" language and are

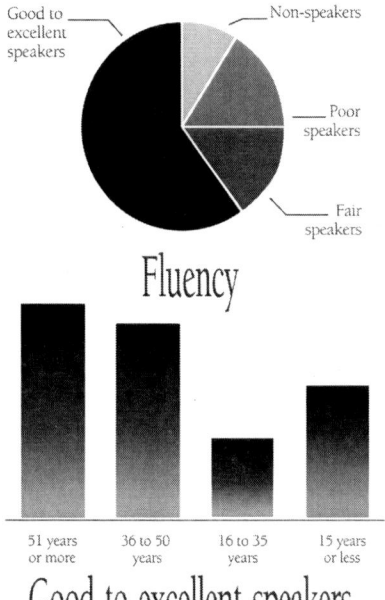

Fluency

Good to excellent speakers

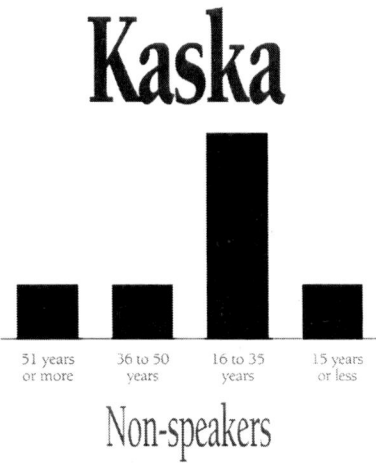

Kaska

Non-speakers

Figure 5.1. Chart exemplifying representational
styles used initially by the territorial government to
motivate people to speak and to support aboriginal
language revitalization by visually depicting aboriginal language loss in a severely contrastive manner.
Reproduced with permission of the Yukon Territorial
Government, Aboriginal Language Services.

responsible for it (see also Errington 2003). In the Yukon the theme of ownership is prominent in the foundational documents of ALS, which, as discussed in chapter 1, emerged during the finalization of land claims settlement in the Yukon and the time of formal recognition of the territory's aboriginal languages through the Yukon Languages Act (1988). This first statement describes the "Yukon Model." This model refers to the approach taken by the Yukon Territorial Government in first developing ALS, which, inspired by the principles of self-determination being negotiated for the Umbrella Final Agreement, stressed aboriginal community partnership with government to design programs that would "be supportive and facilitative of Aboriginal people's self-determined language objectives, directions, and choice of activities" (Leslie Gardner and Associates 1997:1). The statement itself is reproduced exactly in several ALS texts:

> The Yukon model for Aboriginal language preservation, development, maintenance and renewal was based on the fundamental principle that *the people are the proper stewards of their languages. . . . Because the people own the language,* the intent of the program model was to engage the people in a culturally respectful way. The cultural tradition was to provide a context for the rational program development which was to reflect Aboriginal values and orientation of Yukon First Nations. (Leslie Gardner and Associates 1993:12; my emphasis)

The rhetoric of ownership was infused into the discourse at least as early as the 1991 *Voices of the Talking Circle* conference, when Tony Penikett, then premier of the Yukon government and chief land claims negotiator through the 1980s, stated: "Your languages are your property. They belong to you as people, as individuals, families and the community" (ALS 1991b:27). This rhetoric follows the logic of land claims in that it conceptualizes language as inherently aboriginal but dispossessed during assimilation. However, during the development of programming, this discursive theme was transformed, relating ownership to the process of language revitalization, as opposed to the possession of a linguistic object, aboriginal languages. Again, it was the rhetoric of self-determination that guided the rhetoric of aboriginal responsibility in revitalization. Within the section "What Lessons Were Learned" is the statement that

> [r]eaffirmation of the strong sense of ownership of language renewal, "If someone else is working on preserving our language without our participation it is not benefiting us at all." (ALS 2004a:37)

The objectives of the Agreement (Canada–Yukon Cooperation Agreement for Aboriginal Languages 1998–2003): 1. To foster the maintenance, revitalization, growth and protection of the aboriginal languages of the Yukon, 2. To enable Yukon Aboriginal communities *to assume increased ownership of their Aboriginal language responsibilities.* (ALS 2004a:23; emphasis mine)

In the most recent assessment report on the state of the Yukon's aboriginal languages, the theme of ownership moves in a new direction. Returning to the idea of language as possession, it now expands ownership of that possession to all Yukoners, native and non-native alike.

> The threat of losing any one of the eight Yukon First Nation languages *should be of concern to every Yukon person,* both First Nation and non–First Nation, as the impact will affect the present generation and the generations to come. (ALS 2004b:133; emphasis mine)

> If even one language is lost Yukoners will either directly or indirectly experience it, . . . and the Yukon will become less culturally and linguistically diverse. (ALS 2004b:133)[1]

With the contentious and politically divisive period of land claims over, government discourse in the Yukon turned for inspiration to broader Canadian themes, most notably diversity. In expanding the ownership of and responsibility for Yukon aboriginal languages to all Yukoners, the revitalization discourse projects an imagined community, a new multicultural Yukon public that is a microcosm of multicultural Canada.

Hyperbolic Valorization

The third expert theme identified by Hill is that of "hyperbolic valorization." These are statements about the worth or value of endangered languages (Hill 2002:123–125). In the Yukon, they are sprinkled throughout the various government reports and documents pertaining to the territory's aboriginal languages. The two examples below are from the most recent language status report produced by the Yukon government.

> It is with the fluent speaking Kaska population that the main supply of wealth exists in terms of knowledge about the Kaska culture, heritage and language. (ALS 2004b:58)

> This means that almost 25 percent of the Kaska population is in a position in which they are able to contribute to maintaining the Kaska respondents' most valuable resources, which essentially is the Kaska language, as their language provides access to their authentic culture and to their unique and distinct heritage. (ALS 2004b:63)

Similar valorizing statements also appear on expert Web sites. These next two examples are from the Yukon Native Language Centre's Web site.

> The Yukon Native Language Centre promotes an awareness of the richness and beauty of Yukon First Nations Languages and an appreciation of the fundamental role they play in the transmission of culture and values from one generation to another. . . .
>
> The Yukon Native Language Centre recognizes *the intrinsic positive value of First Nations Languages* in contemporary education for both native and non-native students at all levels, from pre-school to adult education. (YNLC n.d.c; emphasis mine)

All of these valorizing statements proclaim the inherent worth of the Yukon's aboriginal languages. And, like the "ownership" statements, they construct these languages as invaluable to all people, "both native and non-native students at all levels, from pre-school to adult education." They also describe aboriginal languages as fundamental to the transmission of "authentic" culture, "unique" heritage, values, and indigenous knowledge. Such statements are used also in the 1996 *Report of the Royal Commission on Aboriginal Peoples* in relation to the importance of preserving Canada's own unique heritage and multicultural state.

In sum, such expert rhetorics address their publics in a way that decontextualizes the status and fate of indigenous languages, reformulating the changing sociolinguistic fields or environments into a global issue. While raising global awareness of language extinction, these rhetorics represent indigenous languages as objects—of study, of value, and of endangerment. Such discourse objectifies and compartmentalizes endangered languages in ways that often contrast with the local discourses circulating among people who speak or historically spoke these languages.

Local Discourses of Language Endangerment

Within indigenous communities, more specialized discursive themes emerge. Part of this is due to the fact that different communities have different language needs and are at different stages of language shift (Fishman 1991). A review of published government language meetings in the Yukon shows that different First Nations (and language groups) emphasize different aspects of language endangerment—different goals, approaches, and concerns. Here I focus on statements made by various Kaska First Nations people and compare them to the more generalized expert rhetoric discussed above. The statements are taken from interviews, small group discussions, and meetings that focused on or led to talk about the Kaska language. Within this local discourse, two themes predominate: "language as socializing practice" and "language as history."

The first theme, "language as socializing practice," may appear similar to the above bureaucratic stance, because the statements below relate identity to language. However, in these cases, the discourse emphasizes sociocultural knowledge, historical narratives, and past cultural practices as aspects of realizing an identity, knowledge that elders and other "tradition bearers" remember. Returning to the interview with three elderly women in chapter 1, this sentiment was reiterated over and over by many different elders and adults.

> Martha: Dene cho' dę gudeji yagháde dene meyudíha.
> I guts'įh how many years yagháde dene gudíha long time ago, eh?
>
> *Elders tell stories so that a person can learn.*
> *From this, so that many years from now people will have knowledge from*
> *long time ago, eh?*

In particular the statement "Dene cho' dę gudejī yagháde dene meyudíha (Elders tell stories so that a person can learn)" emphasized the pedagogical, socializing dimension of these interactions. For this elder, language, aboriginal or otherwise, served as a tool for instruction, important for understanding the past and the present. As such, language is established as the means for acquiring historical knowledge, knowledge around which identity revolves. Thus, knowing one's language becomes central to understanding one's history and, subsequently, one's identity.

A significant dimension of this knowledge is the conceptualization and practice of respect, articulated most clearly in people's discourses about á'i. From chapter 1, this next passage illustrates this concern and remarks on the need for recording and writing their discussion down, so that children and others "may learn from it."

> Martha: Yeah, á'i gēhdia i kḗt'ē yédé ghạ gudēhdéh. Ts'édāne
> meyēgudíhi dega, k'úk kah megēgun(e)gets dega lēdī,
> k'úk kah megēgudíhi-gedai, yéhdī léhdī. Á'i yāgíhdia á'i? Á'i
> gíhdī yédé ghạ gudendéh dé kola etie.
>
> *Yeah, á'i they call it that, like that, so let's talk about it so that children*
> *can learn about it, and she ((Barb)) can write it down, so that if they see*
> *it on paper, they can learn what somebody says X means. So, á'i, what*
> *do they mean by á'i?*

Again, these elders recounted in several ways the primary reason for recording such discussions, so that present and future generations of children can avoid "hard times" resulting from broken taboos and being disrespectful. These two excerpts from the discussion in chapter 1 highlight this reasoning.

> Beatrice: That's for kids growing up (so) they know
> and (when) they go in the bush,
> if they (get) hard time,
> something gonna help them.

> Beatrice: It really hard.
> These days nobody sayin' (this).
> Kids they got good time ((laugh))

> Adele: "No," they say.
> I think they need to learn it, eh?
> They need to know these things, you know?

Additionally, there is an emphasis on language, language as an activity or "verb" (Maurer 2003), such that acts of talking, saying, or telling lead to the acquisition of knowledge. This contrasts with strategies like enumeration, which quantify language by focusing on speaking bodies.

On other occasions, such as during Elders' Days at the Aboriginal Head Start Centre, elders frequently reminded children to act respectfully, demonstrated by sitting quietly and listening. The role of elders and adults as educators was also emphasized.

> Adele: The only, the only time we would uh maybe speak up was
> when they ask us questions, but often they would, the Elders
> would just come and tell stories and we'd listen. . . . We don't
> disobey, ya know, somebody tell you you gotta do something,
> we do it, even /???/ everywhere. We say, kids, they have to
> learn how to be respectful to everything, you can't pull flow-
> ers (and) when somebody talk to you gotta listen. Ya hear?
> You listen to your grandma when she talks to you? (to three-
> year-old child). . . . When you grow up that's how you got to
> teach your kids, you gonna have kids when you grow up?

Elders focused on oral instruction, reminding the students that as adults, they should teach their children this way—through talking. Here language, whether English or Kaska, as talk becomes the primary means for establishing continuity across generations. Throughout all of these statements, "information" or cultural knowledge was intertwined with language, and language became a pedagogical tool for the preservation of certain (gender-appropriate) kinds of knowledge. Additionally, a sense of historical loss and the need for persistence became mapped onto the discourse of language loss. This mapping also occurred during a First Nations' language planning meeting.

> We need to teach them (the children) the Dene k'eh . . . We need to tell our kids how we grew up a long time ago. . . . Kids are trained different in school. They don't know their names, their tribes if they don't have the language. . . . We need to tell stories, and then they (the children) will understand. I still remember my grandparents' stories. (Elder [female], FN language planning meeting, 5/11/98)

> I would teach the language, about the long time ago ways, about ways of making a living. (Elder [female], FN language planning meeting, 5/11/98)

Elders were not the only advocates encouraging a connection between language and history. An administrator also articulated this connection in her statement at this First Nations language planning meeting: "Concerns about language are being expressed in community meetings. As elders are passing away, *the history and the language is passing away with them*" (May 11, 1998, emphasis mine). These sentiments were articulated by local language advocates addressing their own First Nation, their children, and their grandchildren. This theme of "language as history" links language with cultural knowledge, knowledge about appropriate ways to be and to interact with the world around. In addition to these public and semipublic events, statements from interviews about reasons to learn Kaska reiterated these themes.

> It's my history, my family's history and culture.

> To better understand history from a Kaska point of view.

> To bring back memories, traditional lifestyle.

> To learn more about history and culture, and relate to elders.

> To know the stories that have been passed on for generations, stories of different areas.

As part of a language survey, these statements were produced by individuals ranging in age from mid-twenties to over sixty. Many of them spoke Kaska themselves or had parents or grandparents who spoke Kaska.

The theme of "language as history" naturally ties into the other pervasive theme of "language as socializing activity," ideas about appropriate interaction, in that both themes emphasize different aspects of sociocultural knowledge. Furthermore, language change within First Nations communities was discussed almost entirely in terms of knowledge and the changed sociocultural circumstances of aboriginal language use in contrast to grammatical or interactional changes. The primary concern for the Kaska language community was the disappearance of knowledge, a change affected in part by language shift. In contrast, the dominant concern articulated in the expert rhetorics focuses on numbers of speakers and numbers of remaining indigenous languages.

Interestingly, the historical theme transcended these local discourses and appeared in, or even motivated, some of the texts produced by both community-external and community-internal advocates. One textual example that connects language and history is the book *Dene Gudeji: Kaska Narratives* (1999), compiled and edited by Patrick Moore, with support from the Kaska Tribal Council. Within this book are numerous historical narratives and legends, all providing historical details that can be found nowhere else in print. These texts inform the reader about the Kaska language, prehistory, and history, both family-specific and group-related (see also Moore 2002; Moore and Hennessy 2006). Another example from elsewhere in the Yukon is the Vuntut Gwich'in oral history project. "The project involved filming and recording Elders on the land. Vital traditional knowledge was recorded in the Gwich'in language. The recordings were transcribed and incorporated into an extensive database that provides access to information gathered on languages and traditional knowledge. The database also details research projects related to the Gwich'in people and their land" (from ALS 2004a:22). A more general concern with history is reflected in the television series *Haa Shagoon*, a Yukon program that shares the narratives of elders. Though not necessarily about discourses of language endangerment, this historical theme also pervades contemporary native North American anthropological research, as in Julie Cruikshank's *Life Lived like a Story* (1990) and David Dinwoodie's *Reserve Memories* (2002) (see also Anderson 1998; Collins 1998b, 2003; Kroskrity 1993).

Convergence and Divergence across "Internal" and "External" Discourses

While recent research on language endangerment rhetoric has juxtaposed the "external" with the "internal" (Dorian 2002; England 2002; Errington 2003; Fishman 2002; Hill 2002; Hinton 2002; Whiteley 2003), the language endangerment discourses found in the Yukon are not as transparently distinct. Because of the Yukon model itself, a model developed by the government in consultation with the First Nations, the external and the internal are polyvocal discourses echoing each other's words. This is shown below with thematically similar samples of discourse from different events, bureaucratic and local. There are two additional themes that surface across these advocacy events: "language as biological" (cf. England 2002) and "language as embodied," a merging of the themes identified by Hinton as "language as healing," "language as carrier of culture and worldview" and "language as key to identity" (Hinton 2002:152).

Language as Biological

The "language as biological" theme represents language as a living organism, where indigenous languages can be discussed in terms of health or well-being. This theme similarly objectifies language as the above expert themes do, but the materiality of language in this case assumes a degree of agency, expressed through terms such as "aggression" and "weakness" (emphasis mine in all):

> on their journey *to breathing life back into their languages to make them strong and everlasting once again* (ALS 2004b:3)

> (languages are being replaced by) *stronger and more aggressive languages* like Chinese, English, and Spanish languages (ALS 2004b:8)

> stages of language health (borrowed from Fishman 1991, ALS 2004b:19)

> As long as the English language continues to replace the Kaska language as the mother tongue, *the language will continue to weaken and the degrees of danger, in terms of becoming an extinct language, will only increase and intensify.* (ALS 2004b:60)

> *We would hate to see our language being buried*—are we going to do anything? (Administrator, local language planning meeting, 5/11/1998)

This last statement further extends the theme, imagining languages as decaying bodies that will eventually require burial. All of these examples portray language as alienable and separate from speaking human bodies.

Language as Embodied

The second theme, "language as embodied," works with and transforms the "language as biological" theme, reintroducing the social life of language. This theme represents language as an activity or process rather than as a state of being. In the following statements, this is shown in relation to language's role in community well-being (Hinton 2002:152). In such cases, language serves as an index or a gauge of a group's or population's overall health. This is exemplified by the following statements.

> We need to speak the language to feel good, and to keep a positive image. (Administrator, local language planning meeting, 5/11/1998)

> There is a shared recognition that *learning and speaking one's Aboriginal language contributes to the solution of problems facing Aboriginal communities.* And that you can't separate a peoples [sic] language from their culture. (ALS 2004a:38; emphasis mine)

This can apply to individuals as well, emanating from concerns about younger generations and issues of respect and responsibility. "One of the social effects of this loss of knowledge is seen in the many young people who are lost. Language is really important to maintain identity, but it is hard to do" (administrator, local language planning meeting, 5/11/1998). In other words, language is important for establishing, maintaining, and reproducing an indigenous identity. Cultural knowledge acquired through language enables people to know who they are, a requirement for personal well-being. The rallying slogan for aboriginal language revitalization in the Yukon Territory succinctly sums up this idea, claiming "We Are Our Language."

Along with identity, the most pervasive dimension of "language as embodied" is that of language and culture (see Hinton 2002; Whiteley 2003). Hinton's theme of "language as carrier of culture," a theme she equates with community-internal discourse, appears in both personal and bureaucratic statements. Excerpts from a recent government report and a past language conference illustrate the ubiquitous presence of this theme.

> Culture and language are one. (ALS 2004b:27)

> Being that the main purpose of language is to provide a method of communicating in a world in which it was created from, *the culture and the heritage should be learned alongside that of the language.* (ALS 2004b:27; emphasis mine)

> All of the languages of the Yukon have their base in a strongly oral culture . . . they [the elders] weren't only talking about language, they were talking about culture. (Tlingit woman, quoted in ALS 1991b:20)

> By doing this [preserving aboriginal languages], we bring alive our cultural heritage, our self-identity, and most important our self-dignity and sense of value of ourselves as a people. (Gwich'in elder, ALS 1991b:26)

Vibrant evolving cultures are the crucibles of languages. (ALS
1991b:29)

In these last examples, language and culture become intertwined, a discursive move that has been noted elsewhere for other languages (see Basso 1990; Collins 1998a; Whiteley 2003). This underscores the theme in personal commentaries that emphasize grounding language in daily life and sociohistorical narratives, all of which suggest that language can be learned only in context, in "culture." This conceptualization contrasts sharply with the decontextualized image of language found in expert rhetorics.

Opportunities for Change

A further question remains: in what ways do disjunctures persist between "internal" and "external" approaches to language revitalization, given the heteroglossic creation of a territory-wide language ideology and program? One difference perhaps is that for educators, bureaucrats, and those who work within national institutions, language is conceptualized as isolatable, as distinct from other domains of life (see Haugen 1972; Maurer 2003, Mühlhäusler 1992, 1996, 2002; Silverstein 1979, 1998). For the Yukon's First Nations people, and Kaska elders in particular, language was praxis, signifying action not isolatable from other domains of life. In many examples throughout this book we see language as part of the process of passing on knowledge to novices; language's primary purpose—as talk, as narrative, as interaction—was socialization. The conventional use of the phrases "dene k'eh" or "Indian way" to refer to aboriginal language, along with any other aboriginal practice, underscores this ideological emphasis on the embeddedness of language in social life. Similar observations have been made by other researchers working with different American Indian communities (for example, Nevins 2004; Philips 1983; Scollon and Scollon 1979). Such differences are magnified by these institutional settings. Thus, while there is superficial similarity in language revitalization rhetoric between the internal and external, there remain unarticulated differences that perpetuate an ideological disjuncture that then allows people to continue to talk past one another.

An arena within which ideological disjunctures become equally pronounced is, of course, policy making, which plays a significant role in language preservation and revitalization efforts. While some policies may only "create a space" for minority languages, and others provide financial support for the development of materials and training of teachers, language policies have become a central aspect of minority language research and a site for the circulation of the discourses analyzed above. In Suzanne Romaine's article on the ways in which language policy can impact language endangerment (2002), she examined then-current research on language policy around the world. Throughout her review, she highlighted various points of disconnect, or disjuncture, between state or national policies and the minority languages these policies were intended to recognize and support. She argued that there is no direct causal connection between policy and language, but that the relationship between the two is complex and variable. Part of this complexity and variability is found in the ideological differences subsumed by the discourses used by policy makers, experts, elders, and other language advocates. By attending to these discourses, disjunctures between the conceptualization of language and, by extension, the institutionalization of language are foregrounded, reinforcing Romaine's point that "[a]ny policy for language, especially in the system of education, has to take account of the attitude of those likely to be affected" (2002:20) Even in so doing, the attitudes of those who are affected may remain opaque, obscured by a shared rhetoric. Putting into practice the intentions underlying a language policy illustrates the real impact that such ideological disjunctures may have on a sociolinguistic landscape. One example of this impact can be seen in the history of aboriginal education in the Yukon and Canada. There, as in the U.S., indigenous groups supported the idea of education for their people. However, for the colonial regimes, "education" was incompatible with aboriginal culture, language, and identity. Contemporary aboriginal language revitalization projects face similar ideological disjunctures.

To mediate such disjunctures, First Nations are finding additional opportunities for reviving and sustaining their languages. Alongside the problematic aboriginal language classes in state-run institutions, the Kaska people have developed extracurricular activities to reinforce and revitalize their heritage language practices, and alternative language learning events, such as the Kaska House of Language workshops. These government-supported workshops incorporated more directly community ethics and knowledge, First Nations history and literature, and a multimodal learning experience. They were also better able to address local community concerns. The Kaska House of Language workshops and KTC's publication *Dene Gudeji* both realize this multifaceted goal. Developed outside of the territory's bureaucratic apparatus, the projects were better able (than the public schools) to emphasize the historical and narrative dimensions of language. Though not replicating exactly the educational experience of the community's elders, these projects succeeded in acknowledging both the grammatical elements and the social dimensions of aboriginal language practices, and hence were considered more successful than the state-controlled programs. This is not surprising, given that similar grassroots initiatives have flourished elsewhere, such as Australia (Lo Bianco and Rhydwen 2001), Cameroon (Gerbault 1997), Hawaii (Warner 2001; Wilson and Kamanā 2001), Ireland (Maguire 1991) and New Zealand (Benton and Benton 2001; King 2001).

Disjuncture: Ideological Snags in the Discursive Fabric

In this chapter I have illustrated the major themes in the discourse of language revitalization by both outside experts and their community-internal counterparts, discussed their divergence and convergence, and have remarked on some of the ways such discursive disjunctures can impinge upon language revitalization in practice. Part of the problem lies in the institutionalization of linguistic practice, in the focus on enumeration and the privileging of linguistic structure over the sociolinguistic dimensionality of endangered languages.

These disjunctures emerge, then, at the intersection of fundamentally different, though rhetorically similar, ideologies about language and the process of language revitalization. On the one hand, communities' discourses about language loss and revitalization, and cultural preservation more generally, depict language as a historical archive, and an integral, social practice, resulting in efforts to record, transcribe, and translate the knowledge of elders and to integrate their social knowledge into language projects, rather than to create or re-create more speakers. On the other hand, the government and expert rhetorics privilege a more biological and objectified conception of language, resulting in an emphasis on enumeration, structure, and assessment of verbal competence rather than a concern with social practice and knowledge. These ideological disjunctures then affect the ways in which the "health" of the linguistic environment is diagnosed, and, ultimately, the health, or success, of language revitalization. Elders attend to children's and adolescents' behaviors to gauge the well-being of their language; government officials attend to charts and graphs to evaluate that same well-being. To mediate such ideological influences requires vigilance, revisions, and an ongoing commitment to expanding and elaborating the educational opportunities and pedagogical techniques devised to facilitate (aboriginal) language education and revitalization. Simply put, language revitalization is a process that, like any other process,

Figure 5.2. A view of the backside of the welcome sign, thanking visitors as they leave. Photo by the author.

ebbs and flows, converges with and separates from other social practices, ideologies, and institutions, and ultimately should be changing, along with the sociolinguistic landscape it's intended to change. The aboriginal language rhetoric in the Yukon is changing; it is now time for the accompanying practices to follow suit.

From Revitalization to Socialization

Disjuncture and Beyond

> Any picking-out of interdiscursive links implies a gap, an exclusion
> of links with other chunks of discourse in the world. (Irvine 2005:76)

Having journeyed through various "gaps" in one deforested but regrow-
ing sociolinguistic landscape, where have we ended up? We have seen not
only that language revitalization is a tremendously political endeavor, as
has been pointed out by Michael Walsh (2005), but it is a significantly
social one in other respects as well. The fact that a student's utterance, such
as *kedā* (moose), may at the same time refer to a moose, index an important
part of daily life, and symbolically express the student's heritage indicates
that such linguistic acts are embedded in a sociolinguistic environment
where varied and fluid semiotic schematizations of language and practice
affect both the continuity and the transformation of such acts. Thus, while
a language revitalization project is an intentional transformation of linguistic practice within a sociolinguistic landscape, its trajectory is affected by
the social practices, ideologies, and moments of disjuncture involved in its
expression and aspiring expressiveness.

Language revitalization involves reestablishing past "[linguistic] forms
of connectivity across events" (Agha 2005:1), such as grammatical utterances
and narrative genres, as well as establishing new lexical items to refer to computers, video games, and pizza, and new linguistic forms that result from the
inclusion of linguistic features from a dominant language. To explore those

processes, the previous chapters examined the complicated and often contradictory practices, concepts, and contexts that mediate the ways in which people maintain and change an endangered sociolinguistic landscape when they undertake language revitalization projects.

Socializing Disjunctures

A main goal of this book has been to show that one of the dilemmas of redirecting change is the arbitrariness and reconciliation of disjuncture. Appealing to Giddens's (1984) notion of structuration, we might see an ongoing human project in the creation or re-creation of consistency, cohesion, or pattern, especially when patterns (or structures) appear to be missing, disrupted, or "broken." To recognize such disjunctures requires a person or persons first to "know" the patterns, to have certain expectations about and awareness of such configurations and practices (cf. Silverstein [1981] 2001). Language endangerment and revitalization are excellent arenas for the investigation of the range or limits of such awareness, especially in relation to recognition, and misrecognition, because the proliferation of research and discourse on endangered indigenous languages has brought many aspects of linguistic practice, and their (mis)recognition, to the fore. An ethnographically informed study of language revitalization entails an investigation of the appropriateness and effectiveness of various sociolinguistic practices (for speaking, reading, writing, performing, and so forth).

Furthermore, by investigating the many aspects of the social life of endangered languages, the everydayness of disjuncture becomes salient. Disjuncture is more than just an extreme condition resulting from colonization or political upheaval (Appadurai 1996). People encounter moments of disjuncture all day and every day. In consequential moments especially, such as the onstage or first-time encounters Goffman (1959) often described—moments like presenting oneself at a job interview, meeting the future in-laws, or presenting research to a tribal council—people are invested in presenting the right "face." Part of the work of the interaction is to discover what that means for the particular occasion, to identify other similar situations, and to extrapolate that knowledge across those situations. Through such extrapolations, this interactional work becomes habituated, so much so that our awareness of the work invested in the performance (of such interactions) is obscured, minimized, or perhaps erased. Practices of extrapolation, a dimension of intertextualization and interdiscursivity, erase moments of disjuncture.

Language socialization becomes relevant because socialization studies are concerned with the ways in which novices acquire these habituated practices through their own experiences, the (expert) discourse(s) explaining these practices, and the regulation of authority in relation to their socialization. Educational research, institutional or otherwise, also provides evidence of such social coalescence (and related problems). Thus, social reproduction, as language socialization, is about creating continuity: creating a sense of structure in the contingencies of the moment, a sense of structure in which meaningful interactions or movements can take place and accomplish real-time goals, from writing a dissertation to feeding a family, to revitalizing a language. When these taken-for-granted "bundlings" (coalescences of meaning and practice) are interrupted or ruptured, rather than simply extrapolated, awareness is achieved—and that awareness may even produce the impetus, or "instigation" (Keane 2003:418) to action. I turn now to a reframing of these chapters, considering Kaska language revitalization, in relation to such bundlings, as an interdiscursive project.

Intertextuality and Interdiscursivity in Kaska Language Revitalization[1]

Emerging from a history of domination and attempted erasure, the multivalent semiotic dimensions of Kaska language found renewed expression through changes in the political-economic situation for minority populations and minority languages in Canada. New developments in funding and institutional support, among other changes, facilitated the incorporation of aboriginal languages into dominant institutional settings and discourses through the employment of aboriginal peoples, a collaborative articulation of a territorial language ideology, and the development and inclusion of an aboriginal language curriculum in the public schools. State-run employment practices also underscored the practices and discourses of First Nations elders, especially those aspects that promoted the authority of elders; in Watson Lake, when I lived there, Kaska was becoming ideologically the language of elders. Their authority was reinforced further by the pragmatic conventions and socializing discourses articulated during Kaska language learning events, especially those involving children and adolescents. In particular, these socializing narratives delineated behavioral expectations for children's and adolescents' roles in interactions with adults, emphasizing the expression of respect through the performance of silence and stillness. These expectations coincided with institutional expectations in classrooms where children and adolescents were expected primarily to sit still and listen. In Kaska language classes, however, students were also encouraged to speak, albeit through classroom routines. On the one hand, these routines facilitated teacher–student interactions, and by extension adult-learner interactions, expanding the domains in which younger individuals were permitted to converse with adults and elders, even if the younger persons' linguistic competence in Kaska was limited. On the other hand, these routines did not sustain the further development of grammatical or communicative competence. The routines did not change over educational time; they began, moreover, to seep into noninstitutional domains of linguistic practice. In other words, the institutional "seepage" connected interdiscursively different language learning contexts.

With limited linguistic practice now found in more and more domains of talk, new intertextual connections were forged as the Kaska language found expression through various educational texts and promotional media, all of which were intended for an adult audience. While these expressions raised the visibility and prominence of the Kaska language and its speakers, Kaska's representation was muted by the visual dominance of English and the underarticulation of Kaska morphology and other expressive elements. For example, in the adult language lesson books and school curriculum guides, there are no history lessons, and no attempts to connect the language lessons with sociocultural knowledge. If an indigenous language, as a grammatical system or set of vocabulary items, were intended to serve only as an index of a Yukon Indian identity, and locally as a sign of status, then simply speaking an aboriginal language, knowing a grammar, or even knowing only tokens of a grammar would satisfy the Yukon's revitalization goals. In that case, the curriculum materials would suffice. However, if grammatical competence is *not* the primary endpoint, if the goal of language revitalization includes, instead, the acquisition of social and cultural knowledge through language, then these basic lessons have failed. The ideological disjuncture has transcended the discourse and ruptured into the actual activities intended to revitalize and change the current linguistic situation.

Still more mutations can be seen in the mapping and enumeration projects that located the Kaska language in a particular geographic space and bodily site: fluent elder speakers. At the level of the territorial government, the various discursive themes about aboriginal languages and Kaska in particular rendered only a partial image of the sociolinguistic landscape. For example, the Yukon government's slogan "We Are Our Language," while intended to communicate solidarity through the identification of a language and culture with a people, ideologically marked heritage speakers (elders) as core members of the "We" and erased those large numbers of First Nations people who do not speak an aboriginal language. Counter to such a monolithic representation is the actual linguistic diversity pervasive across most, if not all, communities. There is a mismatch between the actual ethnolinguistic identities that people enact locally and those imagined by governing agencies. Frequently the work of language revivalists and the agencies funding this work allow such linguistic diversity to fade into the background of their public, expert rhetorics (Hill 2002), creating the likelihood of disjuncture.

For Kaska, not only do such agency discourses and media construct language as crucial to identity, but the constructions undergo further elaboration locally, within First Nations communities. The bureaucratic practices, discourses, and representations of aboriginal language endangerment in the Yukon envision an iconic relation between aboriginal languages and First Nations, as if the one transparently stood for the other. They envision a similarly iconic relation between First Nations elders and aboriginal languages. Linguistic differences that are seen in terms of ethnic identity are thus more specifically delineated in terms of chronological age or maturity. This image has then undergone interpretation through a community-internal conception that emphasizes differentiation of status. As a result, adolescents construe bureaucratic depictions of Kaska language shift as a representation of social difference rather than a linguistic one; for them, Kaska speech was indexical of status, not linguistic competence.

These ideological links, underscored by Kaska language entextualizations, encouraged people to misrecognize or to overlook the language practices of younger generations, even when the practices were the misrecognizer's own. Meanwhile, the focus on elders' speech as authoritatively "Kaska" enhanced another distinction between elders' discourses and other generations' sentiments; elders perceived the current sociolinguistic environment as disrupted or discontinuous while younger generations perceived it as continuous. While both generations focused on speakers' Kaska practices, younger generations repaired the discontinuity in relation to the sociocultural conditions, both local and territorial, that mediated the role of elder. They interdiscursively projected an ideological link between the Kaska language and the social positioning of elders.

The Yukon Government and external language advocates also began to transform their ideologies and practices through the incorporation of aboriginal peoples into government and other dominant institutional arenas. This transformation took place, in part, through discursive work and the forging of intertextual links. The development of the Yukon slogan, "We Are Our Language," exemplifies this effort at constructing intertextual connections between government discourses depicting language as an integral part of identity, either in the form of property or essence, and First Nations' statements depicting language as a crucial dimension of cultural and historical preservation. Language revitalization becomes imperative because it is through these languages that First Nations people, and youth in particular, will be able to fully realize their aboriginal "identity," by learning the knowledge "archived" in these aboriginal languages. Similar sentiments can be found expressed by elders in other language shift environments (Bonner 2001; Cavanaugh 2004; Hill 1998; see also Wilce 2005). Again, such laments, eulogizing the language and knowledge of older generations and deploring their loss, make salient the generational differentiation and the linguistic discontinuity. What remains to be discovered is whether or not a younger generation, abandoning lament—and thus abandoning its particular discourse of disjuncture—will thereby impede or promote Kaska language revitalization, especially if "40 becomes the new 2," the new age for acquisition. And it also remains to be seen whether, in repairing that disjuncture, another one arises, an interdiscursive "rip" between speakers and emergent speakers, or between some language advocates and emergent speakers.

Given only the disjuncture between intra-community status (the elder as authority and archive) and ethnic "identity," if the ultimate achievement for language revitalization is the creation of new first language speakers, then revitalization of the Kaska language might fail. However, if a growth in the numbers of adult speakers results, then the potential for raising first language speakers improves. Although challenging, especially in an endangered language situation, disjunctures make salient opportunities for change, for creating or re-creating new intertextual, interdiscursive, and interactional connections and improving or building upon current practices. They emerge as potential indexes of gaps and tears in some intertextual "fabric," depending on the reader or the discussant or the observer and his or her own past experiences, with all that those experiences mean for presuppositions, expectations, and action (Irvine 2005; Silverstein 2005).

The interpretive challenge, especially in an endangered language situation, lies in discovering the ways in which people weave together different events or experiences in the on-going interpretation of new events and experiences that are mediated by social conventions ("types") and past events ("tokens"). Language revitalization involves the recovery of particular "types" and the reconstitution of linguistic events in relation to past "tokens," hence the critical role of elders in such projects. The institutionalization of language revitalization efforts aggravates the rupture between Dene elders' educational experiences and those of most Dene adults' and children's, because "the presupposing of a source that can be indexed" is not discernibly "focusing both sender and recipient upon the characteristics of the source"

(Silverstein 2005:9); the linguistic histories of elders are not indexically available to younger generations of language learners. To rephrase the concern for loss expressed through elders' narratives, what is at stake is a particular schematization of contrast, of likeness and difference, not necessarily a "language." It is not only or even most crucially the structure of a language that is shifting, but the salience of particular distinctions embedded within a particular sociolinguistic environment that is shifting. To understand language shift, language endangerment, and language revitalization requires future research to acknowledge and explore the materialization, maintenance, and transformation of such social, practical, and ideological differences. Thus, as language revitalization efforts attempt to halt some "gap" through the picking-out and re-chaining of interdiscursive links, new "gaps" will emerge on the sociolinguistic horizon.

Language Revitalization as Cultural Production

Moving from objects of "entextualization" to the production of these objects, language revitalization research can inform and be informed by the growing anthropological investigation of cultural producers, media, power, and representation. Mahon (2000:468, 472) points out that this scholarship "view[s] media and popular culture forms as both cultural product and social process and examine[s] the ways in which individuals and groups negotiate the constraints of the particular material conditions, discursive frameworks, and ideological assumptions in which they work." Mahon identifies a range of cultural institutions, from television producers and news media professionals to advertising agency executives and museum professionals; missing from the list are language professionals. Yet, recent linguistic anthropological scholarship fits well within this scholarly domain. By asking "who gets to define what counts as language" (Collins 2004:491; see also Briggs and Bauman 1999; Bauman and Briggs 2003; Collins 1998a, 1998b; Moore 1993; Nevins 2004), linguistic anthropologists working in native North America raise questions very similar to those raised by anthropologists exploring other forms of cultural production and media.

Recent research by linguistic anthropologists also reflects—and reflects on—the collaborative nature of many language preservation and revitalization projects, a collaboration between language professionals and endangered language communities. Contemporary ethnographic studies in native North America increasingly exhibit this trend in scholarship; there is a general upsurge in the investigation of collaborative ventures between institutions and tribal governments, between "external" and "internal" advocates, between "local" community members and "distant" professionals (for example, Biolsi and Zimmerman 1997; Clifford 2004; Cruikshank 1990, 1998; Erickson, Ward, and Wachendorf 2002; Evers and Toelken 2001; Field 1999, 2004; Nadasdy 2003; Whiteley 2003; see also Strong 2005). A recent article by Moore and Hennessy (2006), describing the ideological contestations surrounding the development of an on-line aboriginal language project (First Voices), illustrates both the growing attention to language technologies and the cooperative dimension of such projects (see also Eisenlohr 2004b; Kroskrity and Reynolds 2001; Miyashita and Moll 1999). But in all these collaborations, and commentaries on collaborations, who speaks for whom? Where do perspectives crucially differ? Where are the disjunctures, the repairs, and where do they lead? Recent scholarship has been addressing these concerns, but many fruitful questions remain to be pursued.

Some Final Thoughts

Gaps, disjunctures, and discontinuities are a part of life; they do not inevitably signal the loss or "death" of a language. Given that linguistic discontinuity is not necessarily linguistic death, how then do we conceptualize language revitalization and success? Christine Sims (2005:104) writes that "language revitalization at its heart involves reestablishing traditional functions of language use in the context of everyday speaker interactions." Yet what is meant by "traditional"?

If "traditional" means "native," particular varieties of English spoken by American Indians and First Nations people can become objects of revitalization. While such "vernaculars are officially ignored, stigmatized in schools and derided by outsiders, they remain a ubiquitous linguistic means for socializing children, fashioning distinct identities, and, in general, giving voice to everyday life," including aesthetic domains such as native-authored literature and film (Collins 2004:494). They can also become the vehicles of a new kind of semiotic domination in which native people get to "play Indian" for native and non-native elites (cf. Graham 2002; Mannheim 1998).

"Traditional" might also refer to the grammar documented by some missionary in the late 1800s or some linguistic publication in the 1970s. If so, then second-language speakers who speak a different variety from the documented one would have only approximately revitalized the language. Particular conceptualizations of "traditional" also have implications for linguistic practice beyond speaking, such as the use of print and electronic media, of recordings, radio broadcasts, and television. Should people be allowed to develop only practices that hark back to precolonial days? Can "modern" practices be used to preserve or re-create a preconquest scenario? Can "modern Indians" even be "traditional"? Have we ever been "traditional"? If the troubling word "traditional" disappears, then language revitalization becomes the establishment of new language practices in everyday interactions.

As people involved in language revitalization projects begin to complicate their practices and critically evaluate old and new sites for maintaining, contesting, and transforming a sociolinguistic landscape, new ventures and new research will help us to walk even further with indigenous languages and to realize the revival or renewal of indigenous linguistic practices, the reconfiguration of the academy, and the empowerment of alternative views and approaches. It will be a challenging but rewarding journey.

Appendix A

List of Acronyms

The following is a list of acronyms used throughout the book:

AHS	Aboriginal Head Start program
ALS	Aboriginal Language Services
CBC	Canadian Broadcasting Corporation
CYFN	Council of Yukon First Nations
HBC	Hudson's Bay Company
KTC	Kaska Tribal Council
LFN	Liard First Nation
RCMP	Royal Canadian Mounted Police
YNLC	Yukon Native Language Centre
YTG	Yukon Territorial Government

Appendix B

Transcription Notation

This is a list of the transcription symbols and descriptions of what they represent (see Sacks, Schegloff, and Jefferson 1974; see also Duranti 1994).

:	Colons separate speakers from their utterances
//	Double slashes indicate points of overlap
-	Hyphens indicate abrupt interruptions
(word)	Words in parentheses indicate a best guess at the spoken material
?	Question marks within parentheses or between slashes represent uncertain or unintelligible material
(:00)	Numbers between parentheses mark length of pause
(( ))	Material within double parentheses provides extralinguistic or contextual information or additional description.
italics	Italicized words are English glosses.

For child participants in interviews, X;Y indicates the children's ages, where X is years of age, and Y is months.

Notes

Preface

1. The four prominent spelling conventions for this language family are: Athabaskan, Athapaskan, Athapascan, and Athabascan. For consistency in this ethnography, "Athabaskan" is used. Another term used to refer to people and language is "Kaska," which is most frequently used to refer to the language, and sometimes to people who identify as "Kaska." I also use the Kaska term "Dene" to refer to people who identify as Kaska.

2. Some speakers of Mountain Slavey and Tahltan also live in the Yukon, but these languages are not necessarily considered indigenous to the area (see Harnum 1998).

3. Krauss and Golla (1981) lump Sekani, Tahltan, and Kaska together as one language and claim that only a few hundred speakers of each remain (see also Cook 1998:131). Interestingly, the reported overall Kaska population is only 1,526 (Statistics Canada 1996). Given a few hundred remaining speakers, it is feasible that one-third of the population are fluent Kaska speakers. This suggests that Kaska may not be "moribund" (where "moribund" means that no children are learning the language), because some acquisition is still occurring.

4. None of the categories in the census correspond with any of the aboriginal languages indigenous to the Yukon. I assume that the 705 responses correspond with the Yukon languages.

5. Interestingly, the Department of Indian and Northern Affairs (DIAND) (1995) shows an increase in "Amerindian language as mother tongue" acquisition for all subcategories (Registered Indian On Reserve, Registered Indian Off Reserve, Inuit, and Métis), yet a decrease overall. Thus, the 16.9 percent reported must reflect responses from aboriginal individuals who are not registered.

6. DIAND (1995) reports that 0 percent of the non-aboriginal population first learned an Amerindian language. Adjusted numbers are the following: Carmacks 20.0, Mayo 15.0, Pelly Crossing 19.0, Old Crow 42.8, Carcross 16.7, Carcross Indian Settlement 14.3, Burwash Landing 37.5, Upper Liard 36.4,

Two Mile 45.0, Two and One-Half Mile 0.0 (25.0), Ross River 50.9, Lower Post 0.0, Good Hope Lake 13.3.

7. Based on data from the 1996 census, fifteen elders, aged 55 years old and up, resided in the Upper Liard–Two Mile–Two and One-Half Mile area; 125 individuals were between the ages of 25 and 54; thirty individuals were between the ages of 15 and 24; seventy-five individuals were between the ages of 0 and 14 (Statistics Canada 1996).

8. I recorded approximately eighty-nine hours of interaction, ranging from children's playtime at AHS and language games to grammatical elicitation in one-on-one interviews with elders and Kaska House of Language workshops. I had approval to work with and record nineteen children, twelve boys and seven girls, ranging in age from four months to twelve years old, with most between the ages of two and six years old. I interviewed three grandparent-parent-child triads, filling out a modified MacArthur Communicative Development Inventory for each one, and conducted semistructured interviews with fifteen adults focusing on their own language practices, attitudes, and sociolinguistic biographies.

9. This research was conducted with the support of the Kaska Tribal Council and was guided by prevailing standards of informed consent. However, in the intervening years, many Yukon First Nations, as with bands and tribes across North America, have adopted more stringent protocols for ethnographic and linguistic research in their communities. Now subsumed under the larger categories of Traditional Knowledge (TK) and Heritage Resources, the Kaska language and knowledge about it are considered material regulatable by KTC according to its internal policies and supporting legislation by the Yukon Territorial Government. These policies more clearly articulate the appropriateness of recording as well as specify who controls the data collected.

10. To disentangle referents, I will use "Kaska" to refer to the aboriginal language and "Dene" to refer to First Nations people who speak or are ancestrally affiliated with the Kaska language.

11. Similar to Eisenlohr's discussion of the linking of time and nationhood through language, and an ancestral language in particular (Eisenlohr 2004a), aboriginal languages in the Yukon Territory serve a similar purpose. Briefly, bureaucratic and public discourses about language and territory, a crucial dimension of land claims negotiations, focus on historical time ("empty, homogenous" [Eisenlohr 2004a:82]), while other First Nations narratives reflect a temporal simultaneity, recognizing the continued presence of ancestors and ancestral practices. For First Nations peoples in the Yukon, as with Hindu Mauritians, such disjunctures are negotiated semiotically.

Chapter 1

1. The average winter temperature for the Watson Lake area is −24.6 degrees Celsius, and the average summer temperature is 14.9 degrees Celsius, with

extreme high and low temperatures of 34.2 degrees Celsius and −58.9 degrees Celsius respectively (Bureau of Statistics 1997).

2. Lower Post is a community physically located in British Columbia but socially tied to Watson Lake. For example, Lower Post children attend high school in Watson Lake, and all residents buy their groceries in Watson Lake.

3. Lower Post has a band office located in the community center, which functions separately from Liard First Nation (LFN). Nationally, however, the Lower Post contingent is not recognized as independent or separate from LFN. Subsequently, Lower Post members are included in the LFN roster. Locally, Lower Post and Liard are viewed as separate First Nations. According to the federal government, though, there are only three Kaska First Nations; according to the Kaska bands and councils, there are four.

4. The term "band," or "Indian band," refers to those groups organized under the Indian Act, whereas "First Nations," like those in the Yukon, are organized under later treaties (like the Umbrella Final Agreement in the Yukon's case) that replace the Indian Act for those specific treaty signatories. However, informal use of the term "First Nation" has existed since the 1970s as an alternative to "Indian band." Yukon First Nation elders often use the older terminology, referring to themselves as "Indian" and their political unit as a "band."

5. In accordance with Internal Review Board protocols for the 1997–2000 research, personal names have been replaced with pseudonyms.

6. Classic ethnographic accounts portray indigenous Athabaskan communities in the Yukon, the Kaska included, as seminomadic hunter-gatherers (Cruikshank 1990; Honigmann 1981, 1954, 1949; McClellan 1975; Osgood 1971; see also Yerbury 1986). Within these communities, kinship practices were predominantly matrilineal, with matrilocal or neolocal residence, depending on the season or the event. The typical residential family unit was often the nuclear family but could include extended family members such as maternal grandparents or maternal sisters and their families. Historically, families moved around in the bush year-round and congregated in larger numbers in spring and early summer, while staying in small family units during the lean winter months. As mentioned above, many people had continued this pattern of movement, though to a lesser extent and for much shorter periods of time. Politically, the family group had a "headman," typically the oldest adult male, who held the position of authority. These patterns were consistent across the Northern Athabaskan bands (VanStone 1974; see also Helm 1981; Krech 1980; Rushforth 1991).

7. As mentioned above, the coastal Tlingit had a well-established trade operation and trading routes by the time the HBC arrived in the Yukon (see Coates 1991; Cruikshank 1990; McClellan 1975).

8. See 2006 census data: http://www12.statcan.gc.ca/census-recensement/2006/dp-pd/prof/92-594/details/page.cfm?Lang=E&Geo1=PR&Code1=60&Geo2=PR&Code2=01&Data=Count&SearchText=Yukon Territory&SearchType=Begins&SearchPR=01&B1=All&Custom=.

9. The Umbrella Final Agreement stipulates a 25 percent blood rule, but the public discourses emphasize descent over blood as the defining characteristic of membership. Additionally, each First Nation has the right to establish its own conceptualizations of membership, resulting in a much more complicated scenario of recognition and belonging than this chapter has space to detail.

10. In March 2007, Aboriginal Language Services had been incorporated into the Land Claims division of the Yukon government, and ALS employees were preparing for the devolution of the program to the individual First Nations. The Cooperation Agreement had been renewed for one year, providing $1.1 million for funding aboriginal language projects in 2007.

11. At the time of my fieldwork, the ages of individuals regularly employed by ALS ranged from forty years old to over fifty-five years old.

12. All of these jobs are related to teaching or using the Kaska language.

13. "This" refers to talking about cultural values, prohibitions (taboos), and the sharing of knowledge.

Chapter 2

1. For more comprehensive surveys of the field of language endangerment, see Hinton 2003; Mufwene 2004; Tsunoda 2005; Walsh 2005.

2. Contemporary scholarship on language endangerment and revitalization discusses how to assess (or "diagnose") at which stage of loss a language is, and ways to stop or reverse this linguistic deterioration (for examples, see Bradley and Bradley 2002; Crystal 2000; Fishman 1991, 2001; García 2003; Grenoble and Whaley 1998, 2006; Hinton 2002, 2003; Hinton and Hale 2001; Hornberger 1997; Janse and Tol 2000; Krauss 1998). Frequently, these appeals are in the name of biodiversity (Abley 2003; Dalby 2003; Maffi 2001; Nettle and Romaine 2000; see also Hale et al. 1992). Most recently, Grenoble and Whaley (2006) wrote a scholarly guidebook for how to determine whether language revitalization is an appropriate quest to embark on for a particular language community. This is a useful text for exploring the complexities and potential crises to be encountered when undertaking language revitalization. Focusing more on particular situations, Hinton and Hale (2001) also offer a range of approaches to language revitalization and revival grounded in examples of current language revitalization projects. Additionally, Hinton, Vera, and Steele (2002) provide a specific pedagogical approach and practical lessons for individuals interested in reviving their own language practices. Related to this research on language endangerment and revitalization is current research on language change and language evolution. This research is also concerned with identifying (grammatical) patterns of change and the "ecologies" surrounding these changes, whether they are linguistic, sociocultural, or some intricate combination (see for example, Clyne 2003; Mufwene 2001; Mühlhäusler 1996).

3. While my theorization of the phrase "sociolinguistic disjuncture" was inspired by Foucault's "principle of discontinuity" and Appadurai's macroformulation of

"disjuncture," the concept as it is used here does not rely on a modern–traditional dichotomy present in many discussions of modernity, globalization, and institutionalization; it attempts to interrupt this dichotomization of peoples, practices, and societies (cf. Latour 1993) by recognizing the multivocal and biographically complex compositionality of all peoples, aboriginal or otherwise, and the everydayness of disjuncture.

4. Interestingly, this is the way many pueblo groups maintain a power structure in society—by restricting the access of specialized ritual knowledge to only a few individuals. If language becomes theorized in this same way, the goals of language revitalization and retention will need to articulate with this conceptualization.

Chapter 3

1. There are a multitude of terms in use now to differentiate particular kinds of speech or varieties of language (see Eckert and Rickford 2001). I have chosen to discuss the variability in Kaska language patterns discussed in this chapter in terms of "style" rather than "register" because I want to emphasize the processual, semiotic, and emergent dimensions of the differences, for both novice and expert speakers, and the "principles of distinctiveness that may extend beyond the linguistic system to other aspects of comportment that are semiotically organized" (Irvine 2001:31–32; see also Mendoza-Denton 1999).

2. All Athabaskan languages have a closed lexical set of verb stems referred to as classificatory verbs. These verbs lexically mark semantic features that can correspond with or identify these same features in a related noun phrase. That is, these verbs can deictically reference subjects or objects based on physical features such as number, dimension, pliability, containment, etc. Across the language family, these verbs vary in the number of lexical roots and types of associated semantic features. These verbs are also differentiable based on movement. Categorizing the classificatory verbs this way, Davidson, Elford, and Hoijer (1963) identify four sets: neuter verbs (set A), verbs of handling (set B), verbs of partially controlled action (set C), and verbs of free movement (set D). The focus here is on set B, the handling verbs. These are the verbs used frequently in directives to children.

3. See Witherspoon (1977) on Navajo kin term k'eh; see also Field 1998a.

4. The director/teacher was a woman of Cree descent who spoke English with the children; while she knew Cree, she did not speak any Kaska.

5. This funding was in addition to the $6.75 million provided by the federal government (distributed over five years).

6. The 2001 Canadian census indicates that the aboriginal population in the Yukon Territory is approximately 6,540, while the Francophone population is roughly 975 (http://www12.statcan.ca/english/profil01/CP01/Details/Page .cfm?Lang=E&Geo1=CSD&Code1=6001009&Geo2=PR&Code2=60&Data= Count&SearchText=Whitehorse&SearchType=Begins&SearchPR=60&B1=

All&Custom=; September 11, 2006). The census also notes that almost twice as many people have American Indian heritage (6,370) as French (3,815) (http://www12.statcan.ca/english/census01/products/highlight/ETO/Table1 .cfm?Lang=E&T=501&GV=3&GID=6001; September 11, 2006).

7. This sentiment has been expressed by other indigenous people who are trying to revitalize, and reclaim, their heritage languages and is a matter of ongoing debate among educators and language activists who participate in language revitalization programs (Brandt 1982; Hinton 2001a; Hornberger 1997; McCarty 1998, 2002; Sims 2001). I return to this debate in chapter 4.

8. Trent is not one of the child participants in the AHS program.

Chapter 4

1. To emphasize the active, intentional construction of linguistic materials, and languages, for the purposes of revitalization/re-creation/preservation, and in opposition to organically acquired first languages, I use the term "language-linguistic manufacture," defined as the deliberate construction of language as it is linked to particular institutional or institutionalized sites and regimented positions of authority. Related to Bauman and Briggs's (1999; see also Bauman and Briggs 2003) conceptual varieties of "contextualization" and discussions of production, "manufacturing" is what happens when people engage in the preservation, revitalization, or re-creation of a language, another aspect of the pervasive process of "globalization."

2. However, not all elders are equally evaluated or valued in this regard. Some preference is given to those who speak particular dialects and have a particular family history. One family with whom I work has only recently begun to document their dialect. Previously, they had been overlooked, in part due to their linguistic heritage.

3. The language of the text is identified because each language teacher trainee translates this story into her or his own language and dialect. For instance, this story can be purchased online from YNLC in Gwich'in, Northern Tutchone, Kaska, Han, etc.—up to sixteen different translations.

4. The Kaska forms can deviate from Kaska orthographic conventions with respect to the marking of long vowels. Double vowels can be used in place of a bar over the lengthened vowel.

5. Throughout this short (thirteen-page) booklet, YNLC's logo appeared three times, with one additional reference to the Centre, making a total of four references. This was one way in which the Centre subtly promoted its authority over the production of textual materials in the Yukon's indigenous languages. The actual funds for producing and publishing these texts came from various government agencies and from funds intended for use by the First Nations themselves.

6. In contrast to the YNLC and ALS publications were noun dictionaries produced and financed locally. These texts displayed a range of styles and appealed to a range of audiences.

Chapter 5

1. This statement could also exemplify Errington's "structural diversity" theme, because it emphasizes the need to save languages to preserve structural diversity or knowledge about grammatical structures of language. Except for this statement, this theme appears to be missing from language endangerment rhetoric in the Yukon.

Chapter 6

1. Following Silverstein (2005), interdiscursivity is conceptualized as entailing intertextuality (cf. Briggs and Bauman 1992; Silverstein and Urban 1996).

References

Abley, Mark (2003). *Spoken Here: Travels among Threatened Languages.* New York: Houghton Mifflin.

Aboriginal Head Start (1998). Principles and guidelines. The Public Health Agency of Canada and Health Canada. http://www.phac-aspc .gc.ca/dca-dea/publications/pdf/ahs_princguide_e.pdf.

Aboriginal Head Start (2000). Aboriginal Head Start initiative: Children making a community whole: A review of Aboriginal Head Start in urban and northern communities. The Public Health Agency of Canada and Health Canada. http://www.phac-aspc.gc.ca/dca-dea/publication/ cmacw-eng.php.

Aboriginal Language Services (1991a). *A Profile of the Aboriginal Languages of the Yukon.* Whitehorse: Yukon Executive Council Office.

Aboriginal Language Services (1991b). *Voices of the Talking Circle.* Whitehorse: Yukon Executive Council Office.

Aboriginal Language Services (2004a). *Evaluation Report: Hope for the Future: A Call for Strategic Action: Five Year Report, 1998–2003.* Whitehorse: Yukon Executive Council Office.

Aboriginal Language Services (2004b). *Sharing the Gift of Language: Profile of Yukon First Nation Languages.* Whitehorse: Yukon Executive Council Office.

Adley-SantaMaria, Bernadette (1997). White Mountain Apache language: Issues in language shift, textbook development, and Native speaker– university collaboration. In *Teaching Indigenous Languages,* ed. Jon Reyhner, Pp. 129–143. Flagstaff: Center for Excellence in Education, Northern Arizona University.

Agha, Asif (2005). Introduction: Semiosis across encounters. *Journal of Linguistic Anthropology* 15(1):1–5.

Ahlers, Jocelyn (2006). Framing discourse. *Journal of Linguistic Anthropology* 16(1):58–75.

Ammon, Ulrich, and Marlis Hellinger (1992). *Status Change of Languages*. Berlin: Walter de Gruyter.

Anderson, Jeffrey (1998). Ethnolinguistic dimensions of Northern Arapaho language shift. *Anthropological Linguistics* 40(1):43–108.

Appadurai, Arjun (1996). *Modernity at Large: Cultural Dimensions of Globalization*. Minneapolis: University of Minnesota Press.

Asher, James J. (1977). *Learning Another Language through Actions: The Complete Teacher's Guidebook*. Los Gatos, CA: Sky Oaks Productions.

Axelrod, Melissa (2000). The semantics of classification in Koyukon Athabaskan. In *The Athabaskan Languages: Perspectives on a Native American Language Family*, ed. Theodore Fernald and Paul Platero, Pp. 9–27. New York: Oxford University Press.

Basso, Keith (1990). *Western Apache Language and Culture*. Tucson: University of Arizona Press.

Bauman, Richard, and Charles Briggs (2003). *Voices of Modernity: Language Ideologies and the Politics of Inequality*. Cambridge: Cambridge University Press.

Bavin, Edith L. (1995). Language acquisition in crosslinguistic perspective. *Annual Review of Anthropology* 24:373–396.

Bennett, Ruth, ed. (1997). It really works: Cultural communication proficiency. In *Teaching Indigenous Languages*, ed. Jon Reyhner, Pp. 158–205. Flagstaff: Center for Excellence in Education, Northern Arizona University.

Benton, Richard, and Nena Benton (2001). RLS in Aotearoa/New Zealand 1989–1999. In *Can Threatened Languages Be Saved?* ed. Joshua Fishman, Pp. 423–450. Clevedon, UK: Multilingual Matters.

Berkhofer, Robert (1978). *The White Man's Indian*. New York: Knopf.

Biolsi, Thomas, and Larry Zimmerman, eds. (1997). *Indians and Anthropologists: Vine Deloria Jr. and the Critique of Anthropology*. Tucson: University of Arizona Press.

Blair, Heather, and Shirley Fredeen (1995). Do not go gentle into that good night. Rage, rage against the dying of the light. *Anthropology and Education Quarterly* 26(1):27–49.

Blot, Richard K., ed. (2003). *Language and Social Identity*. Westport, CT: Praeger.

Bonner, Donna M. (2001). Garifuna children's language shame: Ethnic stereotypes, national affiliation, and transnational immigration as factors in language choice in southern Belize. *Language in Society* 30(1):81–96.

Bourdieu, Pierre (1977). *Outline of a Theory of Practice*. Cambridge: Cambridge University Press.

Bourdieu, Pierre (1991). *Language and Symbolic Power*. Cambridge: Harvard University Press.

Bradley, David, and Maya Bradley, eds. (2002). *Language Endangerment and Language Maintenance*. New York: RoutledgeCurzon.

Brandt, Elizabeth (1982). Native American attitudes toward literacy and recording in the Southwest. *Journal of the Linguistic Association of the Southwest* 4(2):185–95.

Briggs, Charles, and Richard Bauman (1992). Genre, intertextuality, and social power. *Journal of Linguistic Anthropology* 2(2):131–172.

Briggs, Charles, and Richard Bauman. (1999). "The foundation of all future researches": Franz Boas, Native American texts, and the construction of modernity. *American Quarterly* 51(3):479–528.

Bunn, Collyne, Doug Hitch, Jo-Anne Johnson, John Ritter, Gertie Tom, and Margaret Workman (2003). *Teaching Yukon Native Languages: A Guidebook for Native Language Instructors*. 2nd ed. Whitehorse: Yukon Native Language Centre.

Bureau of Statistics (1997). *Yukon Environmental Statistics*. Whitehorse: Yukon Territorial Government.

Burnaby, Barbara (1999). Policy on aboriginal languages in Canada: Notes on status planning. In *Theorizing the Americanist Tradition*, ed. Lisa Philips Valentine and Regna Darnell, Pp. 299–314. Toronto: University of Toronto Press.

Burns, Alison, Rhonda Darling, and Kathy Magun (1997). *Kaska Picture Dictionary*. Whitehorse: Department of Education/Curriculum Department.

Carter, Robin (1976). Chipewyan classificatory verbs. *International Journal of American Linguistics* 42(1):24–30.

Cassuto, Leonard (1997). *The Inhuman Race: The Racial Grotesque in American Literature and Culture*. New York: Columbia University Press.

Cavanaugh, Jillian (2004). Remembering and forgetting: Ideologies of language loss in a northern Italian town. *Journal of Linguistic Anthropology* 14(1):24–38.

Charles, Walkie (2005). "Qaneryaramta egmiucia": Continuing our language. *Anthropology and Education Quarterly* 36(1):107–111.

Charlie, Lena (1999). Lena Charlie interview. In *Dene Gudeji*, ed. Patrick Moore, Pp. 157–183. Whitehorse: Kaska Tribal Council.

Charlie, Mary (1999). Tés Ní'ā (Standing Cane Mountain). In *Dene Gudeji*, ed. Patrick Moore, Pp. 246–267. Whitehorse: Kaska Tribal Council.

Christian, Jane, and Peter Gardner (1977). *The Individual in Northern Dene Thought and Communication: A Study in Sharing and Diversity*. Mercury Series, 35. Ottawa: National Museums of Canada.

Clifford, James (2004). Looking several ways: Anthropology and native heritage in Alaska. *Current Anthropology* 45(1):5–29.

Clyne, Michael (2003). *Dynamics of Language Contact*. Cambridge: Cambridge University Press.

Coates, Ken S. (1991). *Best Left as Indians: Native-White Relations in the Yukon Territory, 1840–1973*. Montreal: McGill-Queen's University Press.

Collins, James (1998a). Our ideologies and theirs. In *Language Ideologies: Practice and Theory*, ed. Bambi Schieffelin, Kathryn Woolard and Paul V. Kroskrity, Pp. 256–270. New York: Oxford University Press.

Collins, James (1998b). *Understanding Tolowa Histories: Western Hegemonies and Native American Responses*. New York: Routledge.

Collins, James (2003). Reclaiming traditions, remaking community: Politics, language, and place among the Tolowa of Northwest California. In *Language and Social Identity*, ed. Richard K. Blot, Pp. 225–241. Westport, CT: Praeger.

Collins, James (2004). Language. In *A Companion to the Anthropology of American Indians*, ed. Thomas Biolsi, Pp. 490–505. Malden, MA: Blackwell.

Cook, Eung-do (1998). Aboriginal languages: History. In *Language in Canada*, ed. John Edwards, Pp. 125–143. Cambridge: Cambridge University Press.

Council for Yukon Indians (1977). *Together Today for Our Children Tomorrow: A Statement of Grievances and an Approach to Settlement by the Yukon Indian People*. Whitehorse: CYI.

Crawford, James (1991). *Bilingual Education: History, Politics, Theory, and Practice*. 2nd ed. Los Angeles: Bilingual Educational Services.

Cruikshank, Julie (1990). *Life Lived like a Story*. Omaha: University of Nebraska Press.

Cruikshank, Julie (1998). *The Social Life of Stories: Narrative and Knowledge in the Yukon Territory*. Lincoln: University of Nebraska Press.

Crystal, David (2000). *Language Death*. Cambridge: University of Cambridge Press.

Dalby, Andrew (2003). *Language in Danger*. New York: Columbia University Press.

Daniel, E. Valentine (2000). Mood, moment, and mind. In *Violence and Subjectivity*, ed. Veena Das, Arthur Kleinman, Mamphela Ramphele, and Pamela Reynolds, Pp. 333–366. Berkeley: University of California Press.

Davidson, William, L. W. Elford, and Harry Hoijer (1963). Athapaskan classificatory verbs. In *Studies in the Athapaskan Languages*, ed. Harry Hoijer, Pp. 30–41. University of California Papers in Linguistics 29. Berkeley: University of California Press.

Deloria, Philip (1998). *Playing Indian*. New Haven: Yale University Press.

Dementi-Leonard, Beth, and Perry Gilmore (1999). Language revitalization and identity in social context: A community-based Athabascan language preservation project in western interior Alaska. *Anthropology and Education Quarterly* 30(1):37–55.

Demuth, Katherine (1986). Prompting routines in the language socialization of Basotho children. In *Language Socialization across Cultures*, ed. Bambi Schieffelin and Elinor Ochs, Pp. 51–79. Cambridge: Cambridge University Press.

de Reuse, Willem J. (1997). Issues in language textbook development: The case of Western Apache. In *Teaching Indigenous Languages*, ed. Jon Reyhner, Pp. 116–128. Flagstaff: Center for Excellence in Education, Northern Arizona University.

DIAND (1995). *Highlights of Aboriginal Conditions 1986, 1991: Demographic, Social and Economic Characteristics*. Ottawa: Minister of Public Works and Government Services Canada. http://www.collectionscanada.gc.ca/webarchives/20071206053159/http://www.ainc-inac.gc.ca/pr/sts/hac/hilts_e.pdf.

Dinwoodie, David (2002). *Reserve Memories: The Power of the Past in a Chilcotin Community*. Lincoln· University of Nebraska Press.

Dorian, Nancy, ed. (1989). *Investigating Obsolescence: Studies in Language Contraction and Death*. Cambridge: Cambridge University Press.

Dorian, Nancy C. (2002). Commentary: Broadening the rhetorical and descriptive horizons in endangered-language linguistics. *Journal of Linguistic Anthropology* 12(2):134–140.

Drapeau, Lynn (1998). Aboriginal languages: Current status. In *Language in Canada*, ed. John Edwards, Pp. 144–159. Cambridge: Cambridge University Press.

Duranti, Alessandro (1994). *From Grammar to Politics*. Berkeley and Los Angeles: University of California Press.

Eckert, Penelope, and John R. Rickford, eds. (2001). *Style and Sociolinguistic Variation*. Cambridge: Cambridge University Press.

Edelsky, Carole (1996). *With Literacy and Justice for All: Rethinking the Social in Language and Education*. Bristol, PA: Taylor and Francis.

Edwards, John (1998). *Language in Canada*. Cambridge: Cambridge University Press.

Eisenlohr, Patrick (2004a). Temporalities of community: Ancestral language, pilgrimage, and diasporic belonging. *Journal of Linguistic Anthropology* 14(1):81–98.

Eisenlohr, Patrick (2004b). Language revitalization and new technologies: Cultures of electronic mediation and the refiguring of communities. *Annual Review of Anthropology* 33(1):21–45.

England, Nora C. (2002). Commentary: Further rhetorical concerns. *Journal of Linguistic Anthropology* 12(2):141–143.

England, Nora C. (2003). Mayan language revival and revitalization politics: Linguists and linguistic ideologies. *American Anthropologist* 105(4): 733–743.

Erickson, Patricia Pierce, H. Ward, and K. Wachendorf (2002). *Voices of a Thousand People: The Makah Cultural and Research Center*. Lincoln: University of Nebraska Press.

Errington, J. Joseph (1998). *Shifting Languages: Interaction and Identity in Javanese Indonesia*. Cambridge: Cambridge University Press.

Errington, J. Joseph (2003). Getting language rights: The rhetorics of language endangerment and loss. *American Anthropologist* 105(4):723–732.

Evers, Larry, and Barre Toelken, eds. (2001). *Native American Oral Traditions: Collaboration and Interpretation*. Salt Lake City: Utah State University Press.

Fabian, Johannes (1986). *Language and Colonial Power: The Appropriation of Swahili in the Former Belgian Congo, 1880–1938*. Berkeley and Los Angeles: University of California Press.

Fader, Ayala (2007). Reclaiming sacred sparks: Linguistic syncretism and gendered language shift among Hasidic Jews in New York. *Journal of Linguistic Anthropology* 17(1):1–22.

Ferguson, Charles (1964). Baby talk in six languages. In *Sociolinguistic Perspectives: Papers on Language in Society, 1959–1994*, ed. Thom Huebner, Pp. 103–114. New York: Oxford University Press.

Ferguson, Charles (1971). Absence of copula and the notion of simplicity: A study of normal speech, baby talk, foreigner talk, and pidgins. In *Pidginization and Creolization of Languages*, ed. Dell Hymes, Pp. 141–150. Cambridge: Cambridge University Press.

Field, Les W. (1999). Complicity and collaborations: Anthropologists and the "unacknowledged tribes" of California. *Current Anthropology* 40(2): 193–209.

Field, Les W. (2004). Beyond "applied" anthropology. In *A Companion to the Anthropology of American Indians*, ed. Thomas Biolsi, Pp. 472–489. Malden, MA: Blackwell.

Field, Margaret (1998a). Maintenance of indigenous ways of speaking despite language shift: Language socialization in a Navajo preschool. PhD diss., University of California, Santa Barbara.

Field, Margaret (1998b). Politeness and indirection in Navajo directives. *Journal of Southwest Linguistics* 17(2):23–34.

Field, Margaret (2001). Triadic directives in Navajo language socialization. *Language in Society* 30(2):249–263.

Fishman, Joshua (1991). *Reversing Language Shift: Theoretical and Empirical Foundations of Assistance to Threatened Languages.* Clevedon, UK: Multilingual Matters.

Fishman, Joshua (2001). *Can Threatened Languages Be Saved? Reversing Language Shift, Revisited: A 21st Century Perspective.* Clevedon, UK: Multilingual Matters.

Fishman, Joshua (2002). Commentary: What a difference 40 years make! *Journal of Linguistic Anthropology* 12(2):144–149.

Fleres, Augie 1989. Te Kohanga Reo: A Maori language renewal program. *Canadian Journal of Native Education* 16(2):78–88.

Foley, William A. (1988). Language birth: The process of pidginization and creolization. In *Linguistics: The Cambridge Survey.* Vol. 4, *The Sociocultural Context,* ed. Frederick Newmeyer, Pp. 162–183. Cambridge: Cambridge University Press.

Foucault, Michel ([1968] 1972). *The Archaeology of Knowledge.* New York: Pantheon.

Frawley, William, Kenneth C. Hill, and Pamela Munro, eds. (2002). *Making Dictionaries: Preserving Indigenous Languages of the Americas.* Berkeley and Los Angeles: University of California Press.

Gal, Susan (1979). *Language Shift: Social Determinants of Language Change in Bilingual Austria.* New York: Academic Press.

Gal, Susan (1989). Language and political economy. *Annual Review of Anthropology* 18:345–67.

Gal, Susan, and Judith T. Irvine (1995). The boundaries of language and disciplines: How ideologies construct differences. *Social Research* 62(4): 967–1001.

Gal, Susan, and Kathryn Woolard, eds. (2001). *Languages and Publics: The Making of Authority.* Manchester, UK: St. Jerome Publishing.

García, MaryEllen (2003). Recent research on language maintenance. *Annual Review of Applied Linguistics* 23:22–43.

Garrett, Paul B. (2000). Language socialization, convergence and shift in St. Lucia, West Indies. PhD diss., New York University.

Garrett, Paul B., and Patricia Baquedano-López (2002). Language socialization: Reproduction and continuity, transformation and change. *Annual Review of Anthropology* 31:339–361.

Garroutte, Eva Marie (2003). *Real Indians: Identity and the Survival of Native America.* Berkeley and Los Angeles: University of California Press.

Gerbault, Jeannine (1997). Pedagogical aspects of vernacular literacy. In *Vernacular Literacy: A Re-evaluation,* ed. Andrée Tabouret-Keller, Robert B. Le Page, Penelope Gardner-Chloros, and Gabrielle Varro, Pp. 142–185. Oxford: Oxford University Press.

Giddens, Anthony (1984). *The Constitution of Society*. Berkeley: University of California Press.

Gleason, Jean Berko, and Sandra Weintraub (1976). The acquisition of routines in child language. *Language in Society* 5(2):129–136.

Goffman, Erving (1959). *The Presentation of Self in Everyday Life*. New York: Anchor Books.

Goulet, Jean-Guy A. (1998). *Ways of Knowing: Experience, Knowledge, and Power among the Dene Tha*. Lincoln: University of Nebraska Press.

Goulet, Linda, Marjorie Dressyman-Lavallee, and Yvonne McCleod (2001). Early childhood education for aboriginal children: Opening petals. In *Aboriginal Education in Canada: A Study in Decolonization*, ed. K. P. Binda with Sharilyn Calliou, Pp. 137–153. Mississauga, ON: Canadian Educators' Press.

Graham, Laura (2002). How should an Indian speak? Amazonian Indians and the symbolic politics of language in the global public sphere. In *Indigenous Movements, Self-Representation and the State in Latin America*, ed. Kay Warren and Jean Jackson, Pp. 181–228. Austin: University of Texas Press.

Greif, Esther Blank, and Jean Berko Gleason (1980). Hi, thanks, and goodbye: More routine information. *Language in Society* 9(2):159–166.

Grenoble, Lenore A., and Lindsay J. Whaley (1998). *Endangered Languages: Current Issues and Future Prospects*. Cambridge: Cambridge University Press.

Grenoble, Lenore A., and Lindsay J. Whaley (2006). *Saving Languages: An Introduction to Language Revitalization*. Cambridge: Cambridge University Press.

Hale, Kenneth (1998). On endangered languages and the importance of linguistic diversity. In *Endangered Languages*, ed. Lenore A. Grenoble and Lindsay J. Whaley, Pp. 192–233. Cambridge: Cambridge University Press.

Hale, Kenneth, Michael Krauss, Lucille J. Watahomigie, Akira Y. Yamamoto, Colette Craig, LaVerne M. Jeanne, and Nora C. England (1992). Endangered languages. *Language* 68(1):1–42.

Hanks, William F. (1999). Indexicality. *Journal of Linguistic Anthropology* 9(1–2):124–126.

Harnum, Betty (1998). Language in the Northwest Territories and the Yukon Territory. In *Language in Canada*, ed. John Edwards, Pp. 470–482. Cambridge: Cambridge University Press.

Harrison, Barbara, and Rahui Papa (2005). The development of an indigenous knowledge program in a New Zealand Maori-language immersion school. *Anthropology and Education Quarterly* 36(1):57–72.

Haugen, Einar (1966). Dialect, language, nation. *American Anthropologist* 68(4):922–935.

Haugen, Einar (1972). *The Ecology of Language: Essays by Einar Haugen.* Stanford, CA: Stanford University Press.

Heath, Shirley Brice (1983). *Ways with Words: Language, Life and Work in Communities and in Classrooms.* Cambridge: Cambridge University Press.

Heath, Shirley Brice (1986). What no bedtime story means: Narrative skills at home and school. In *Language Socialization across Cultures,* ed. Bambi Schieffelin and Elinor Ochs, Pp. 97–124. Cambridge: Cambridge University Press.

Heller, Monica, and Marilyn Martin-Jones, eds. (2001). *Voices of Authority.* Westport, CT: Ablex.

Helm, June, ed. (1981). *The Handbook of North American Indians.* Vol. 6, *The Subarctic.* Washington, DC: Smithsonian Institution.

Hill, Jane H. (1985). The grammar of consciousness and the consciousness of grammar. *American Ethnologist* 12(4):725–737.

Hill, Jane H. (1993). Structure and practice in language shift. In *Progression and Regression in Language: Sociocultural, Neuropsychological and Linguistic Perspectives,* ed. Kenneth Hyltenstam and Åke Viberg, Pp. 68–93. Cambridge: Cambridge University Press.

Hill, Jane H. (1998). "Today there is no respect": Nostalgia, "respect," and oppositional discourse in Mexicano (Nahuatl) language ideology. In *Language Ideologies,* ed. Bambi Schieffelin, Kathryn Woolard, and Paul Kroskrity, Pp. 68–86. New York: Oxford University Press.

Hill, Jane H. (1999). The meaning of writing and text in a changing Americanist tradition. In *Theorizing the Americanist Tradition,* ed. Lisa Philips Valentine and Regna Darnell, Pp. 181–194. Toronto: University of Toronto Press.

Hill, Jane H. (2002). "Expert rhetorics" in advocacy for endangered languages: Who is listening and what do they hear? *Journal of Linguistic Anthropology* 12(2):119–133.

Hill, Jane H., and Ken Hill (1986). *Speaking Mexicano.* Tucson: University of Arizona Press.

Hinton, Leanne (2001a). New writing systems. In Hinton and Hale 2001, Pp. 239–250.

Hinton, Leanne (2001b). Training people to teach their language. In Hinton and Hale 2001, Pp. 349–350.

Hinton, Leanne (2002). Internal and external language advocacy: Comments on Jane Hill's "'Expert rhetoric' in advocacy for endangered languages: Who is listening and what do they hear?" *Journal of Linguistic Anthropology* 12(2):150–156.

Hinton, Leanne (2003). Language revitalization. *Annual Review of Applied Linguistics* 23:44–57.

Hinton, Leanne, and Jocelyn Ahlers (1999). The issue of "authenticity" in California language restoration. *Anthropology and Education Quarterly* 30(1):56–67.

Hinton, Leanne, and Ken Hale, eds. (2001). *The Green Book of Language Revitalization in Practice.* New York: Academic Press.

Hinton, Leanne, Matt Vera, and Nancy Steele (2002). *How to Keep Your Language Alive: A Commonsense Approach to One-on-One Language Learning.* Berkeley: Heyday Books.

Hinton, Leanne, and William F. Weigel (2002). A dictionary for whom? Tensions between academic and nonacademic functions of bilingual dictionaries. In *Making Dictionaries: Preserving Indigenous Languages of the Americas,* ed. William Frawley, Kenneth C. Hill, and Pamela Munro, Pp. 155–170. Berkeley and Los Angeles: University of California Press.

Hoijer, Harry (1945). Classificatory verbs in Apachean languages. *International Journal of American Linguistics* 11(1):13–23.

Honigmann, John J. (1949). *Culture and Ethos of Kaska Society.* Yale University Publications in Anthropology, 40. New Haven: Yale University Press.

Honigmann, John J. (1954). *The Kaska Indians: An Ethnographic Reconstruction.* Yale University Publications in Anthropology, 51. New Haven: Yale University Press.

Honigmann, John J. (1981). Kaska. In *The Handbook of North American Indians.* Vol. 6, *The Subarctic,* ed. June Helm, Pp. 442–450. Washington, DC: Smithsonian Institution.

Hornberger, Nancy H. (1997). *Indigenous Literacies in the Americas: Language Planning from the Bottom Up.* Berlin: Mouton de Gruyter.

House, Deborah (2002). *Language Shift among the Navajos: Identity Politics and Cultural Continuity.* Tucson: University of Arizona Press.

Howe, Nina (2000). Early childhood care and education in Canada: An overview and future directions. In *Early Childhood Care and Education in Canada,* ed. Larry Prochner and Nina Howe, Pp. 293–314. Vancouver: University of British Columbia Press.

Irvine, Judith T. (1996). Shadow conversations: The indeterminacy of participant roles. In *Natural Histories of Discourse,* ed. Michael Silverstein and Greg Urban, Pp. 131–159. Chicago: University of Chicago Press.

Irvine, Judith T. (2001). "Style" as distinctiveness: The culture and ideology of linguistic differentiation. In *Style and Sociolinguistic Variation,* ed. Penelope Eckert and John R. Rickford, Pp. 21–43. Cambridge: Cambridge University Press.

Irvine, Judith T. (2005). Commentary: Knots and tears in the interdiscursive fabric. *Journal of Linguistic Anthropology* 15(1):72–80.

Irvine, Judith T., and Susan Gal (2000). Language ideology and linguistic differentiation. In *Regimes of Language: Ideologies, Politics, and Identities*, ed. Paul V. Kroskrity, Pp. 35–83. Santa Fe: School of American Research Press.

Jaffe, Alexandra (1999). *Ideologies in Action: Language Politics on Corsica*. Berlin: Walter de Gruyter.

Janse, Mark, and Sijmen Tol (2000). *Language Death and Language Maintenance: Theoretical, Practical and Descriptive Approaches*. Amsterdam: John Benjamins.

Johns, Alana, and Irene Mazurkewich (2001). The role of the university in the training of native language teachers. In Hinton and Hale 2001, Pp. 355–366.

Johnston, Basil H. (1989). *Indian School Days*. Norman: University of Oklahoma Press.

Kantor, Rebecca, Peggy M. Elgas, and David E. Fernie (1989). First the look and then the sound: Creating conversations at Circle Time. *Early Childhood Research Quarterly* 4(4):433–448.

Kapono, Eric (1994). Hawaiian language revitalization and immersion education. *International Journal of the Sociology of Language* 112:121–135.

Keane, Webb (1997). Religious language. *Annual Review of Anthropology* 26:47–71.

Keane, Webb (2003). Semiotics and the social analysis of material things. *Language and Communication* 23(3):409–425.

King, Jeanette (2001). Te Kōhanga Reo: Māori language revitalization. In Hinton and Hale 2001, Pp. 119–128.

Krauss, Michael (1992). The world's languages in crisis. *Language* 68(1):4–10.

Krauss, Michael (1996). Status of Native American language endangerment. In *Stabilizing Indigenous Languages*, ed. Gina Cantoni, Pp. 16–21. Flagstaff: Center for Excellence in Education, Northern Arizona University.

Krauss, Michael (1998). The conditions of Native North American languages: The need for realistic assessment and action. *International Journal of the Sociology of Language*, no. 132:9–21.

Krauss, Michael, and Victor Golla (1981). Northern Athapaskan languages. In *Handbook of North American Indians*. Vol. 6, *Subarctic*, ed. June Helm, Pp. 67–85. Washington, DC: Smithsonian Institution.

Krech, Shepard (1980). Northern Athapaskan ethnology in the 1970s. *Annual Review of Anthropology* 9:83–100.

Kroskrity, Paul V. (1993). *Language, History and Identity: Ethnolinguistic Studies of the Arizona Tewa*. Tucson: University of Arizona Press.

Kroskrity, Paul V. (1998). Arizona Tewa Kiva Speech as a manifestation of a dominant language ideology. In *Language Ideologies* ed. Bambi Schieffelin, Kathryn A. Woolard, and Paul V. Kroskrity, Pp. 103–122. Oxford: Oxford University Press.

Kroskrity, Paul V., ed. (2000). *Regimes of Language.* Santa Fe, NM: School of American Research Press.

Kroskrity, Paul V. (2002). Language renewal and the technologies of literacy and postliteracy reflections from Western Mono. In *Making Dictionaries: Preserving Indigenous Languages of the Americas,* ed. William Frawley, Kenneth C. Hill, and Pamela Munro, Pp. 171–192. Berkeley and Los Angeles: University of California Press.

Kroskrity, Paul V., and Margaret C. Field, eds. (2009). *Native American Language Ideologies: Beliefs, Practices, and Struggles in Indian Country.* Tucson: University of Arizona Press.

Kroskrity, Paul V., and Jennifer Reynolds (2001). On using multimedia in language renewal: Observations from making the CD-ROM *Taitaduhaan.* In Hinton and Hale 2001, Pp. 317–330.

Kulick, Don (1992). *Language Shift and Cultural Reproduction: Socialization, Self, and Syncretism in a Papua New Guinean Village.* Cambridge: Cambridge University Press.

Kulick, Don (1993). Growing up monolingual in a multilingual community: How language socialization patterns are leading to language shift in Gapun (Papua New Guinea). In *Progression and Regression in Language: Sociocultural, Neuropsychological and Linguistic Perspectives,* ed. Kenneth Hyltenstam and Åke Viberg, Pp. 94–121. Cambridge: Cambridge University Press.

Latour, Bruno (1993). *We Have Never Been Modern.* Translated by Catherine Porter. Cambridge: Harvard University Press.

Leap, William (1981a). American Indian language maintenance. *Annual Review of Anthropology* 10:209–236.

Leap, William (1981b). Language maintenance and language revival. In *Anthropological Careers,* ed. Ruth H. Landman, Pp. 86–98. Washington, DC: Anthropological Society of Washington.

Leslie Gardner and Associates (1993). *Walking the Talk: Implementation Evaluation of the Canada–Yukon Funding Agreement on the Development and Enhancement of Aboriginal Languages, 1988/89–1992/93.* Whitehorse: Queen's Printer.

Leslie Gardner and Associates (1997). *We Are Our Language: An Evaluation of the Implementation and Impact of the Canada–Yukon Cooperation and Funding Agreement on the Development and Enhancement of Aboriginal Languages 1993–1998.* Whitehorse: Queen's Printer.

Lieberson, Stanley (1980). Procedures for improving sociolinguistic surveys of language maintenance and language shift. *International Journal of the Sociology of Language*, no. 25:11–27.

Littlefield, Alice (1993). Learning to labor: Native American education in the United States, 1880–1930. In *The Political Economy of North American Indians*, ed. John H. Moore, Pp. 45–59. Norman: University of Oklahoma Press.

Lo Bianco, Joseph, and Mari Rhydwen (2001). Is the extinction of Australia's indigenous languages inevitable? In *Can Threatened Languages Be Saved?* ed. Joshua Fishman, Pp. 391–422. Clevedon, UK: Multilingual Matters.

Lomawaima, K. Tsianina (1993). Domesticity in the federal Indian schools: The power of authority over mind and body. *American Ethnologist* 20(2):1–14.

Lomawaima, K. Tsianina (1994). *They Called It Prairie Light: The Story of Chilocco Indian School*. Lincoln: University of Nebraska Press.

Lomawaima, K. Tsianina, and Teresa L. McCarty (2006). *To Remain an Indian: Lessons in Democracy from a Century of Native American Education*. Multicultural Education Series, ed. James A. Banks. New York: Columbia University, Teachers College Press.

Maffi, Luisa, ed. (2001). *On Biocultural Diversity: Linking Language, Knowledge, and the Environment*. Washington, DC: Smithsonian Press.

Maguire, Gabrielle (1991). *Our Own Language: An Irish Initiative*. Clevedon, UK: Multilingual Matters.

Magun, Liza (1999). The first time we saw white people. In *Dene Gudeji*, ed. Patrick Moore, Pp. 429–443. Whitehorse: Kaska Tribal Council.

Mahon, Maureen (2000). The visible evidence of cultural producers. *Annual Review of Anthropology* 29:467–492.

Mannheim, Bruce (1998). A nation surrounded. In *Native Traditions in the Postconquest World*, ed. Elizabeth Hill Boone and Tom Cummins, Pp. 383–420. Washington, DC: Dumbarton Oaks.

Maurer, Bill (2003). Comment: Got language? Law, property, and the anthropological imagination. *American Anthropologist* 105(4):775–781.

McCarty, Teresa L. (1998). Schooling, resistance, and American Indian languages. *International Journal of the Sociology of Language*, no. 132:27–41.

McCarty, Teresa L. (2002). *A Place to Be Navajo: Rough Rock and the Struggle for Self-Determination in Indigenous Schooling*. Mahwah, NJ: Erlbaum.

McCarty, Teresa L., ed. (2005). *Language, Literacy, and Power in Schooling*. Mahwah, NJ: Erlbaum.

McCarty, Teresa L., Tamara Borgoiakova, Perry Gilmore, K. Tsianina Lomawaima, and Mary Eunice Romero (2005). Indigenous epistemologies and education—self-determination, anthropology and human rights. *Anthropology and Education Quarterly* 36(1):1–7.

McCarty, Teresa L., Mary E. Romero, and Ofelia Zepeda (2006). Reclaiming the gift: Indigenous youth counter-narratives on native language loss and revitalization. *American Indian Quarterly* 30(1–2):28–48.

McCarty, Teresa L., Lucille J. Watahomigie, and Akira Y. Yamamoto, eds. (2001). Reversing language shift in indigenous America: Collaborations and views from the field. *Practicing Anthropology* 21 (special issue).

McCarty, Teresa L., Lucille J. Watahomigie, Akira Y. Yamamoto, and Ofelia Zepeda (2001). Indigenous educators as change agents: Case studies of two language institutes. In Hinton and Hale 2001, Pp. 371–383.

McCarty, Teresa L., and Ofelia Zepeda, eds. (1998). Indigenous language use and change in the Americas. *International Journal of the Sociology of Language* 132 (special issue).

McClellan, Catharine (1975). *My Old People Say: An Ethnographic Survey of Southern Yukon Territory.* Ottawa: National Museums of Canada.

McKee, Cecile (1994). What you see isn't always what you get. In *Syntactic Theory and First Language Acquisition: Cross-Linguistic Perspectives.* Vol. 1, *Heads, Projections and Learnability,* ed. Barbara Lust, Margarita Suñer, and John Whitman, Pp. 201–212. Hillsdale, NJ: Erlbaum.

McLaughlin, Daniel (1992). *When Literacy Empowers.* Albuquerque: University of New Mexico Press.

Meek, Barbra (2001). Kaska language socialization, acquisition and shift. PhD diss., Tucson, University of Arizona.

Meek, Barbra (2002). Manufacturing Kaska, constructing linguistic authority. Paper presented at the American Anthropological Association Annual Meetings, New Orleans, November 20–24, 2002.

Meek, Barbra (2007). Respecting the language of elders: Ideological shift and linguistic discontinuity in a Northern Athapascan community. *Journal of Linguistic Anthropology* 17(1):23–43.

Meek, Barbra (2009). Language ideology and Aboriginal language revitalization in Yukon, Canada. In *Revealing Native American Language Ideologies: Beliefs, Feelings, Practices, Policies,* ed. Paul Kroskrity and Margaret Field, Pp. 151–171. Tucson: University of Arizona Press.

Meek, Barbra, and Jacqueline Messing (2007). Framing indigenous languages as secondary to matrix languages. *Anthropology and Education Quarterly* 38(2):99–118.

Mendoza-Denton, Norma (1999). Style. *Journal of Linguistic Anthropology* 9(1–2):238–240.

Mercier, Ann, and Jocelyn Wolftail (1994). *Kaska Language Lessons: Watson Lake Dialect.* Whitehorse: YNLC.

Mertz, Elizabeth (1996). Recontextualization as socialization: Text and pragmatics in the law school classroom. In *Natural Histories of Discourse*, ed. Michael Silverstein and Greg Urban, Pp. 229–249. Chicago: University of Chicago Press.

Mertz, Elizabeth (2007). *The Language of Law School: Learning to "Think like a Lawyer."* Oxford: Oxford University Press.

Milroy, James, and Lesley Milroy (1985). *Authority in Language*. London: Routledge.

Mithun, Marianne (1998). The significance of diversity in language endangerment and preservation. In *Endangered Languages*, ed. Lenore A. Grenoble and Lindsay J. Whaley, Pp. 163–191. Cambridge: Cambridge University Press.

Mithun, Marianne (1999). *The Languages of Native North America*. Cambridge: Cambridge University Press.

Miyashita, Mizuki, and Laura Moll (1999). Enhancing language material availability using computers. In *Revitalizing Indigenous Languages*, ed. Jon Reyhner, Pp. 113–116. Flagstaff: Center for Excellence in Education, Northern Arizona University.

Moore, Leslie C. (2004) Learning languages by heart: Second language socialization in a Fulbe community (Maroua, Cameroon). PhD diss., University of California, Los Angeles.

Moore, Patrick, ed. (1999). *Dene Gudeji: Kaska Narratives*. Whitehorse: Kaska Tribal Council.

Moore, Patrick (2002). Point of view in Kaska historical narratives. PhD diss., Indiana University, Bloomington.

Moore, Patrick, and Kate Hennessy (2006). New technologies and contested ideologies: The Tagish FirstVoices Project. *American Indian Quarterly* 30(1–2):119–137.

Moore, Robert (1988). Lexicalization versus lexical loss in Wasco-Wishram language obsolescence. *International Journal of American Linguistics* 54(4): 453–468.

Moore, Robert (1993). Performance form and the voices of characters in five versions of the Wasco coyote cycle. In *Reflexive Language: Reported Speech and Metapragmatics*, ed. John Lucy, Pp. 213–240. Cambridge: Cambridge University Press.

Moore, Robert (2000). "The People Are Here Now." The contemporary culture of an ancestral language: Studies in obsolescent Kiksht (Wasco-Wishram dialect of Upper Chinookan). PhD diss., University of Chicago.

Moore, Robert (2006). Disappearing, Inc.: Glimpsing the sublime in the politics of access to endangered languages. *Language and Communication* 26:296–315.

Morgan, Mindy J. (2005). Redefining the Ojibwe classroom: Indigenous language problems within large research universities. *Anthropology and Education Quarterly* 36(1):96–103.

Mufwene, Salikoko (2001). *The Ecology of Language Evolution.* Cambridge: Cambridge University Press.

Mufwene, Salikoko (2003) Language endangerment: What have pride and prestige got to do with it? In *When Languages Collide,* ed. Brian Joseph, Pp. 324–346. Columbus: Ohio State University Press.

Mufwene, Salikoko (2004). Language birth and death. *Annual Review of Anthropology* 33:201–223.

Mühlhäusler, Peter (1992). Preserving languages or language ecologies? A top-down approach to language survival. *Oceanic Linguistics* 31(2):163–180.

Mühlhäusler, Peter (1996). *Linguistic Ecology: Language Change and Linguistic Imperialism in the Pacific Region.* London: Routledge.

Mühlhäusler, Peter (2002). Why one cannot preserve languages (but can preserve language ecologies). In *Language Endangerment and Language Maintenance,* ed. David Bradley and Maya Bradley, Pp. 34–39. London: RoutledgeCurzon.

Munro, Pamela (2002). Entries for verbs in American Indian language dictionaries. In *Making Dictionaries: Preserving Indigenous Languages of the Americas,* ed. William Frawley, Kenneth C. Hill, and Pamela Munro, Pp. 86–107. Berkeley and Los Angeles: University of California Press.

Nadasdy, Paul (2003). *Hunters and Bureaucrats: Power, Knowledge, and Aboriginal-State Relations in the Southwest Yukon.* Vancouver: University of British Columbia Press.

Nettle, Daniel, and Suzanne Romaine (2000). *Vanishing Voices: The Extinction of the World's Languages.* Oxford: Oxford University Press.

Nevins, M. Eleanor (2004). Learning to listen: Confronting two meanings of language loss in the contemporary White Mountain Apache Speech community. *Journal of Linguistic Anthropology* 14(2):269–288.

Nichols, Johanna (1992). *Linguistic Diversity in Time and Space.* Chicago: University of Chicago Press.

Ochs, Elinor (1988). *Culture and Language Development: Language Acquisition and Language Socialization in a Samoan Village.* Cambridge: Cambridge University Press.

Ochs, Elinor, Emanuel A. Schegloff, and Sandra A. Thompson, eds. (1996). *Interaction and Grammar.* Cambridge: Cambridge University Press.

Ochs, Elinor, and Bambi Schieffelin (1979). *Developmental Pragmatics*. New York: Academic Press.

Ochs, Elinor, and Bambi Schieffelin (1984). Language Acquisition and Socialization: Three Developmental Stories. In *Culture Theory: Essays on Mind, Self, and Emotion*, ed. Richard A. Shweder and Robert A. LeVine, Pp. 276–320. Cambridge: Cambridge University Press.

Ochs, Elinor, and Bambi Schieffelin (1995). The impact of language socialization on grammatical development. In *Handbook on Child Language*, ed. P. Fletcher and Brian MacWhinney, Pp. 73–94. Oxford: Blackwell.

Osgood, Cornelius (1971). *The Han Indians: A Compilation of Ethnographic and Historical Data on the Alaska–Yukon Boundary Area*. Yale University Publications in Anthropology, no. 74. New Haven: Yale University Press.

Patrick, Donna (2003). *Language, Politics and Social Interaction in an Inuit Community*. Berlin: Walter de Gruyter.

Pecos, Regis, and Rebecca Blum-Martinez (2001). The key to cultural survival: Language planning and revitalization in the Pueblo de Cochiti. In Hinton and Hale 2001, Pp. 75–82.

Penikett, Tony (2006). *Reconciliation: First Nations Treaty Making in British Columbia*. Vancouver: Douglas and MacIntyre.

Peters, Ann M., and Stephen Boggs (1986). Interactional routines as cultural influences upon language acquisition. In *Language Socialization across Cultures*, ed. Schieffelin and Ochs, Pp. 80–96. Cambridge: Cambridge University Press.

Philips, Susan U. (1975). Teasing, punning, and putting people on. Working Papers in Sociolinguistics, 28. Austin: University of Texas.

Philips, Susan U. (1979). Participant structures and communicative competence: Warm Springs children in community and classroom. In *Functions of Language in the Classroom*, ed. Courtney Cazden, Vera John, and Dell Hymes, Pp. 370–394. Prospect Heights, IL: Waveland Press.

Philips, Susan U. (1983). *The Invisible Culture*. Prospect Heights, IL: Waveland Press.

Platero, Paul (2001). Navajo Head Start language study. In Hinton and Hale 2001, Pp. 87–97.

Poser, William J. (2005). Noun classification in Carrier. *Anthropological Linguistics* 47(2):143–168.

Powell, John Wesley ([1891] 1991). *Indian Linguistic Families of America, North of Mexico*. Lincoln: University of Nebraska Press.

Prochner, Larry (2000). A history of early education and child care in Canada, 1820–1966. In *Early Childhood Care and Education in Canada*, ed. Larry

Prochner and Nina Howe, Pp. 11–65. Vancouver: University of British Columbia Press.

Prochner, Larry (2004). Early childhood education programs for indigenous children in Canada, Australia and New Zealand: A historical review. *Australian Journal of Early Childhood* 29(4):7–16.

Pye, Clifton (1988). Towards an anthropology of language acquisition. *Language Sciences* 10(1):123–146.

Pye, Clifton (1992). Language loss among the Chilcotin. *International Journal of the Sociology of Language*, no. 93:75–86.

Rafael, Vicente L. (1992). *Contracting Colonialism: Translation and Christian Conversion in Tagalog Society under Early Spanish Rule*. Durham: Duke University Press.

Reyhner, Jon (1997). *Teaching Indigenous Languages*. Flagstaff: Center for Excellence in Education, Northern Arizona University.

Rice, Keren (1989). *A Grammar of Slave*. Berlin: Mouton de Gruyter.

Rice, Keren, and Leslie Saxon (2002). Issues of standardization and community in aboriginal language lexicography. In *Making Dictionaries: Preserving Indigenous Languages of the Americas*, ed. William Frawley, Kenneth C. Hill, and Pamela Munro, Pp. 125–154. Berkeley and Los Angeles: University of California Press.

Rice, Sally (1998). Giving and taking in Chipewyan: The semantics of THING-marking classficatory verbs. In *The Linguistics of Giving*, ed. John Newman, Pp. 97–134. Philadelphia: John Benjamins.

Rickford, John R. (1987). The haves and have nots: Sociolinguistic surveys and the assessment of speaker competence. *Language in Society* 16(2):149–178.

Robins, Robert H., and Eugenius M. Uhlenbeck, eds. (1991). *Endangered Languages*. Oxford: Berg.

Romaine, Suzanne (2002). The impact of language policy on endangered languages. *International Journal of Multicultural Societies* 4(2):1–28.

Royal Commission on Aboriginal Peoples (1996). *Report of the Royal Commission on Aboriginal Peoples*. Ottawa: Government of Canada.

Rushforth, Scott (1985). Some directive illocutionary acts among the Bear Lake Athapaskans. *Anthropological Linguistics* 27(4):387–411.

Rushforth, Scott (1991). Uses of Bearlake and Mescalero (Athapaskan) classificatory verbs. *International Journal of American Linguistics* 57(2):251–266.

Sacks, Harvey, Emanuel Schegloff, and Gail Jefferson (1974). A simplest systematics for the organization of turn-taking in conversation. *Language* 50(4):696–735.

Samuels, David W. (2001). Indeterminacy and history in Britton Goode's Western Apache placenames: Ambiguous identity on the San Carlos Apache Reservation. *American Ethnologist* 28(2):277–302.

Samuels, David W. (2004). *Putting a Song on Top of It: Expression and Identity on the San Carlos Apache Reservation*. Tucson: University of Arizona Press.

Schecter, Sandra R., and Robert Bayley (2002). *Language as Cultural Practice: Mexicanos en el Norte*. Mahwah, NJ: Erlbaum.

Schieffelin, Bambi (1990). *The Give and Take in Everyday Life: Language Socialization of Kaluli Children*. Cambridge: Cambridge University Press.

Schieffelin, Bambi, and Elinor Ochs, eds. (1986a). *Language Socialization across Cultures*. Cambridge: Cambridge University Press.

Schieffelin, Bambi, and Elinor Ochs (1986b). Language socialization. *Annual Review of Anthropology* 15:163–191.

Schieffelin, Bambi, Kathryn Woolard, and Paul Kroskrity, eds. (1998). *Language Ideologies: Practice and Theory*. New York: Oxford University Press.

Scollon, Ronald, and Suzanne Scollon (1979). *Linguistic Convergence: An Ethnography of Speaking at Fort Chipewyan, Alberta*. New York: Academic Press, Inc.

Scollon, Ronald, and Suzanne Scollon (1981). *Narrative, Literacy and Face in Interethnic Communication*. Norwood: Ablex.

Silverstein, Michael (1976). Shifters, linguistic categories, and cultural description. In *Meaning in Anthropology*, ed. Keith Basso and Henry Selby, Pp. 11–55. Albuquerque: University of New Mexico Press.

Silverstein, Michael (1979). Language structure and linguistic ideology. In *The Elements: A Parasession on Linguistic Units and Levels*, ed. Paul R. Clyne, William F. Hanks, and Carol L. Hofbauer, Pp. 193–247. Chicago: Chicago Linguistics Society.

Silverstein, Michael ([1981] 2001). The limits of awareness. In *Linguistic Anthropology: A Reader*, ed. Alessandro Duranti, Pp. 382–401. Oxford: Blackwell.

Silverstein, Michael (1996). Encountering language and languages of encounter in North American ethnohistory. *Journal of Linguistic Anthropology* 6(2):126–144.

Silverstein, Michael (1998). Contemporary transformations of local linguistic communities. *Annual Review of Anthropology* 27:401–26.

Silverstein, Michael (2003). Indexical order and the dialectics of sociolinguistic life. *Language and Communication* 23(3–4):193–229.

Silverstein, Michael (2005). Axes of evals: Token versus type interdiscursivity. *Journal of Linguistic Anthropology* 15(1):6–22.

Silverstein, Michael, and Greg Urban, eds. (1996). *Natural Histories of Discourse*. Chicago: University of Chicago Press.

Sims, Christine (1998). Community-based efforts to preserve native languages: A descriptive study of the Karuk Tribe of northern California. *International Journal of the Sociology of Language* 132(1):95–114.

Sims, Christine (2001). Native language planning: A pilot process in the Acoma Pueblo community. In Hinton and Hale 2001, Pp. 63–73.

Sims, Christine (2005). Tribal languages and the challenges of revitalization. *Anthropology and Education Quarterly* 36(1):104–106.

Skutnabb-Kangas, Tove, and Robert Phillipson, eds. (1994). *Linguistic Human Rights: Overcoming Linguistic Discrimination*. Berlin: Mouton de Gruyter.

Smalley, William A. (1994). *Linguistic Diversity and National Unity: Language Ecology in Thailand*. Chicago: University of Chicago Press.

Speas, Margaret (2009). Someone else's language: On the role of linguists in language revitalization. In *Indigenous Language Revitalization: Encouragement, Guidance, and Lessons Learned*, ed. Jon Reyhner and Louise Lockard, Pp. 23–36. Flagstaff: Northern Arizona University, College of Education.

Statistics Canada (1996). Census. http://www.statcan.gc.ca/c1996-r1996/list-liste-eng.htm#1996.

Strong, Pauline (2005). Recent ethnographic research on North American indigenous peoples. *Annual Review of Anthropology* 34:253–268.

Strong, Pauline, and Barrik Van Winkle (1993). Tribe and nation: American Indians and American nationalism. *Social Analysis* 33(1):9–26.

Strong, Pauline, and Barrik Van Winkle (1996). "Indian Blood": Reflections on the reckoning and refiguring of Native North American identity. *Cultural Anthropology* 11(4):547–576.

Sturm, Circe (2002). *Blood Politics: Race, Culture and Identity in the Cherokee Nation of Oklahoma*. Berkeley and Los Angeles: University of California Press.

Szasz, Margaret (1977). *Education and the American Indian: The Road to Self-Determination since 1928*. Albuquerque: University of New Mexico Press.

Szasz, Margaret (2005). "I knew how to be moderate. And I knew how to obey": The commonality of American Indian boarding school experiences, 1750s–1920s. *American Indian Culture and Research Journal* 29(4):75–94.

Tlen, Daniel L. (1986). *Speaking Out: Consultations and Survey of Yukon Native Languages Planning, Visibility, and Growth*. Whitehorse: YNLC.

Tsitsipis, Lukas D. (1998). *A Linguistic Anthropology of Praxis and Language Shift*. Oxford: Oxford University Press.

Tsunoda, Tasaku (2005). *Language Endangerment and Language Revitalization: An Introduction*. Berlin: Mouton de Gruyter.

Underwood, Frances, and Irma Honigmann (1947). A comparison of socialization and personality in two simple societies. *American Anthropologist* 49(4, pt. 1):557–577.

UNESCO Ad Hoc Expert Group on Endangered Languages (2003). Language vitality and endangerment. Paper submitted to the International

Expert Meeting on UNESCO Programme Safeguarding of Endangered Languages. Paris, March 10–12, 2003.

VanStone, James W. (1963). *The Snowdrift Chipewyan.* Ottawa: Northern Coordination and Research Centre, Department of Northern Affairs and National Resources.

VanStone, James W. (1974). *Athapaskan Adaptations: Hunters and Fishermen of the Subarctic Forests.* Chicago: Aldine.

Walsh, Michael (2005). Will indigenous languages survive? *Annual Review of Anthropology* 34:293–315.

Warner, Sam L. No'eau (2001). The movement to revitalize Hawaiian language and culture. In Hinton and Hale 2001, Pp. 133–146.

Watson-Gegeo, Karen Ann, and David W. Gegeo (1986). Calling-out and repeating routines in Kwara'ae children's language socialization. In *Language Socialization across Cultures,* ed. Bambi B. Schieffelin and Elinor Ochs, Pp. 17–50. Cambridge: Cambridge University Press.

Wheelock, Angela, and Patrick Moore (1997) *(Dene) Gédéni: Traditional Lifestyles of Kaska Women.* Ross River, YT: Ross River Dena Council.

Whiteley, Peter (2003). Do "language rights" serve indigenous interests? Some Hopi and other queries. *American Anthropologist* 105(4):712–722.

Wilce, James (2005). Traditional laments and postmodern regrets: The circulation of discourse in metacultural context. *Journal of Linguistic Anthropology* 15(1):60–71.

Willie, Mary A. (2000). Individual and stage level predication and the Navajo classificatory verbs. *MIT Working Papers on Endangered and Less Familiar Languages* 1:39–50.

Wilson, William H., and Kauanoe Kamanā (2001). "Mai loko mai o ka 'I'ini: Proceeding from a dream": The 'Aha Pūnana Leo connection in Hawaiian language revitalization. In Hinton and Hale 2001, Pp.147–177.

Witherspoon, Gary (1977). *Language and Art in the Navajo Universe.* Ann Arbor: University of Michigan Press.

Woolard, Kathryn, A. (1998). Language ideology as a field of inquiry. In *Language Ideologies: Practice and Theory,* ed. Bambi Schieffelin, Kathryn Woolard, and Paul Kroskrity, Pp. 3–47. Oxford: Oxford University Press.

Woolard, Kathryn, and Bambi B. Schieffelin (1994). Language ideology. *Annual Review of Anthropology* 23:55–82.

Wortham, Stanton, and Betsy Rymes, eds. (2003). Linguistic Anthropology of Education. Westport, CT: Praeger.

Wurm, Stephen A. (1991). Language death and disappearance: Causes and circumstances. In *Endangered Languages,* ed. Robins and Uhlenbeck, Pp. 1–18. Oxford: Berg.

Yerbury, J. C. (1986). *The Subarctic Indians and the Fur Trade, 1680–1860*. Vancouver: University of British Columbia Press.

Young, Robert, and William Morgan Sr. (1992). *The Analytical Lexicon of Navajo*. Albuquerque: University of New Mexico Press.

Yukon Native Language Centre. (n.d.a) About YNLC. Available at: http://www.ynlc.ca/ynlc/index.html; accessed February 8, 2010.

Yukon Native Language Centre. (n.d.b) Native Languages in the Yukon. Available at: http://www.ynlc.ca/languages/index.html; accessed February 8, 2010.

Yukon Native Language Centre. (n.d.c) Principles. Available at: http://www.ynlc.ca/yblc/principles/index.html; accessed February 8, 2010.

Yukon Territorial Government. (2005) News release #05-074, March 22. Available at http://www.gov.yk.ca/news/2005/files/05-074.pdf; accessed February 25, 2010.

Zentella, Ana Celia (1997). *Growing Up Bilingual: Puerto Rican Children in New York*. Malden, MA: Blackwell.

Zepeda, Ofelia (2005). More than just words: Stages of American Indian language revitalization. Martin Luther King Jr. Day lecture. Department of Linguistics, University of Michigan, Ann Arbor. January.

Zepeda, Ofelia (2008). Walking with language. In Zepeda, *Where Clouds Are Formed*, P. 64. Tucson: University of Arizona Press.

Zepeda, Ofelia, and Jane H. Hill (1991). The condition of Native American languages in the United States. *Diogenes* 39(153):45–65.

Index

About the Author

Barbra A. Meek is an associate professor of anthropology and linguistics at the University of Michigan. She received her PhD in linguistics and anthropology from the University of Arizona. Her research interests include, among other things, language documentation, representation, and the politics of language. In addition to this research she has co-organized Kaska language workshops and co-produced Kaska language materials, including a collaborative alphabet book entitled *Kaska Alphabet K'úgé'* (2002). Her current research focuses on the ways in which particular aspects of speech participate in the stabilization and destabilization of concepts and processes of value.